Books by Alonzo Rothschild

PUBLISHED BY

HOUGHTON MIFFLIN COMPANY

"HONEST ABE." A Study in Integrity based on the Early Life of Abraham Lincoln.

LINCOLN, MASTER OF MEN. Illustrated.

"HONEST ABE"

ABRAHAM LINCOLN

From a woodcut by T. Johnson after a daguerreotype owned by Mr. Robert T. Lincoln

"HONEST ABE"

A STUDY IN INTEGRITY
BASED ON THE EARLY LIFE OF
ABRAHAM LINCOLN

BY

ALONZO ROTHSCHILD

AUTHOR OF "LINCOLN, MASTER OF MEN"

BOSTON AND NEW YORK
HOUGHTON MIFFLIN COMPANY

Published September 1917

IN MEMORY
OF
"DEAREST"
KATHERINE ROTHSCHILD
TO WHOM THE AUTHOR
OWES NOT LESS THAN
LINCOLN OWED HIS
"ANGEL MOTHER"
THIS BOOK IS
AFFECTIONATELY
DEDICATED

CONTENTS

ILLUSTRATIONS

"HONEST ABE"

CHAPTER I

PINCHING TIMES

HE who seeks to understand the character and achievement of Abraham Lincoln must begin with a study of the man's honesty. At the base of his nature, in the tap-root and very fiber of his being, pulsed a fidelity to truth, whether of thought or of deed, peculiar to itself. So thoroughgoing was this characteristic that it seems to have begun in him where in other men it generally leaves off. Politicians without number have yielded a work-a-day obedience to the rules of honor, but there is record of no other public leader in recent times who, among the vicissitudes of a trying career, has endeavored to balance actions and principles with such painstaking nicety. To trace these efforts from Lincoln's early years is to pass with him, pace for pace, over part of the road that led to distinction. As we go we shall have to take account of happenings, little as well as big; for every man is the sum of all his parts, and in no other way may we hope to comprehend how the esteem that began with a few rustic neighbors grew until it filled the heart of a nation.

To what extent, if any, Lincoln inherited his uprightness of mind from remote ancestors will probably never be known. The bare lines of the genealogical chart afford no clues to the characters of the men and women whose names appear there. If any of the threads spun out of their several lives met and twined in the broad strand of blue that enriched his, there is no way of identifying the spinners. Less obscure, though perhaps of only passing interest, is what may be gleaned under this head about two of Lincoln's nearer relations. His father's brothers, Mordecai and Josiah, appear to have enjoyed general respect on account of their probity. "They were excellent men," said one who claimed to know them intimately, "plain, moderately educated, candid in their manners and intercourse, and looked upon as honorable as any men I have ever heard of." [1] Their younger brother Thomas, however, cannot be so readily portrayed. He has, like his illustrious son, been, in turn, depreciated and idealized to such a degree that the inquirer, who would reach safe conclusions in respect to him, must tread warily through a maze of contradictions.

Rejecting the praise as well as the blame of hearsay historians, and following the testimony of those only who knew the man, we learn from one that he was "honest"; from another that he "was regarded as a very honest man"; and still another found him "always truthful — conscientious." [2] To these tributes must be added what one who was doubly connected with Thomas Lincoln had to say about him: —

"I'm just tired of hearing Grandfather Lincoln abused," said Mrs. Dowling, the daughter of Dennis

Hanks and Matilda Johnson, speaking to an attentive listener, not many years ago. "Everybody runs him down."

Then, going on to free her mind woman-fashion, she continued: —

"Uncle Abe got his honesty, and his clear notions of living, and his kind heart from his father. Maybe the Hanks family was smarter, but some of them could n't hold a candle to Grandfather Lincoln when it came to morals. I've heard Grandfather Lincoln say, many a time, that he was kind and loving, and kept his word, and always paid his way, and never turned a dog from his door." [3]

These qualities, so admirable in Thomas, were not lacking, it should be mentioned, in that particular member of "the Hanks family," his cousin Nancy, with whom he mated.[4] She is said to have brought to the rude Kentucky cabin, in which they began their married life, a sweetness of spirit and a firmness of character that nicely supplemented his rugged integrity. Yet here again traditions are more plentiful than facts, and the repute of the little family, in those early days, so far as it affords a point of departure for the study of Abraham Lincoln's straightforwardness, rests, in a manner, on the word of one neighbor, — a man of standing, however, — according to whom "they were poor," but "they were true." [5]

The poverty of the frontier, it has been said, is no poverty; but the Lincolns were poor almost to a proverb. Their condition appears to have been extreme, even for the primitive Kentucky settlement at Elizabethtown where they made their first home. The young husband was a carpenter by trade, but his new neighbors, with the self-reliance of pioneers, managed to do for themselves most of the work wherewith he had hoped to support his family. Its needs grew with the birth of a little daughter, but not its resources, which he presently sought to eke out by farming. The hut in Elizabethtown was abandoned for another hut and a piece of tillable land that Thomas had bought, — presumably on credit, — about fourteen miles away, near the Big South Fork of Nolin Creek.[6] There, in the following winter, was born the boy who became known to fame as Abraham Lincoln. He must have felt at an early age the tooth of the "stinted living" in those "pinching times," to which, during later life, he once sadly referred; for his father did not prosper with the hoe, any more than he had with the hammer. After a few unfruitful years on Nolin Creek, Thomas relinquished the place for a better farm, in the Knob Creek region, about fifteen miles distant, acquired like its predecessor on easy terms. Yet the fortunes of the family did not mend. Its luckless head "was always lookin'," as Cousin Dennis said, "fur the land o' Canaan." To his pioneer's vision the There ever seemed fairer than the Here. So removal followed removal, — now in Kentucky, then into Indiana, and again into Illinois, — until, to borrow one of Abraham's little stories, the chickens, if there were any, might have lain on their backs and crossed their legs to be tied, whenever they saw the wagon sheets brought out.[7]

Thomas Lincoln's futile shifts need not be set forth at length here,[8] but certain aspects of his inability to get on in the world have a peculiar significance. He responded with ready good nature to calls upon his time or his hospitality; and though he appears to have understood many things, he never learned how to turn his dealings with the little world around him to his own account. The few business ventures, in which he is said to have engaged, reveal how woefully he was lacking in what has been called "money sense." A typical instance, related by his son many years after the event, may have suggested to the narrator that there were at least two members of the Lincoln family who had each a blind side in the direction of the almighty dollar. Here is the story substantially as Abraham related it: —

"Father often told me of the trick that was played upon him by a 'pair of sharpers.' It was the year before we moved from Kentucky to Indiana that father concluded to take a load of pork down to New Orleans. He had a considerable amount of his own, and he bargained with the relations and neighbors for their pork, so that altogether he had quite a load. He took the pork to the Ohio River on a clumsily constructed flat-boat of his own make. Almost as soon as he pushed out into the river a couple of sleek fellows bargained with him for his cargo, and promised to meet him in New Orleans where they arranged to pay him the price agreed upon. He eagerly accepted the offer, transferred the cargo to the strangers, and drifted down the river, his head filled with visions of wealth and delight. He thought that he was going to accomplish what he had set out to do, without labor or inconvenience. Father waited about New Orleans for several days, but failed to meet his whilom friends. At last it dawned upon him that he had been sold, and all that he could do was to come back home and face the music."[9]

Consoling himself after such mishaps with the indolent philosophy of "Luck is ag'in' me," and "Whom the Lord loveth he chasteneth," Thomas would return to his sporadic farming, or to what he liked better — his rod and his gun. For there is a tradition that this unthrifty fellow — honest and well-meaning though he was — had a distaste for manual labor. When work had to be done he did it, after a fashion, nor did he spare the boy who was growing up at his side; but further than that he apparently did not go. Indeed, it may be doubted whether the father ever found, along their limited horizon, the path which might have led either him or his son to business success. They certainly did not enter upon it. Yet if Thomas Lincoln failed to teach Abraham how to put money in their purse, let it be remembered, to his lasting credit, that he did show him how an empty sack might — despite a time-honored adage to the contrary — stand upright.

Noteworthy as was the father's influence on the boy's character, that of the mother appears to have been of deeper consequence. Lincoln's earliest recollections of her, as he recalled in later years, pictured his sister and himself seated at her feet eagerly listening to the books that she read or the tales that she told. The poor lady succumbed early to the hardships of the Indiana backwoods; and the few facts that are known concerning her brief life set forth but a meager story.[10] If "the world knows nothing of its greatest men," may this not be so, in a measure, because it knows nothing of their mothers? The deficiency, as far as Nancy Hanks is concerned, was supplied, for all time, in perhaps the most pithy yet comprehensive tribute that a distinguished son ever uttered to the memory of a parent. Looking down over his career from the last eminence, and tracing it all back again to the frail, sweet-faced woman whose life had flickered out before his wondering gaze, in the cabin home of his boyhood, Lincoln once said, with moist eyes: "All that I am, or hope to be, I owe to my angel mother."[11]

When she passed on, the lad, it is true, was not quite eleven years old; nevertheless her teachings, during that first plastic period, had evidently left their sterling impress in his nature.

Nor did the home influence for right living stop there. After an interval of about a year, Thomas sought another mate. Leaving the little ones to manage the household on Little Pigeon Creek as best they might, he retraced his steps to Elizabethtown and offered himself in marriage to Mrs. Sarah Bush Johnston. She is said to have refused him, in their younger days, for Daniel Johnston, who, by a coincidence, had left her a widow with as many children as waited for her visitor at home.[12] On this occasion the lady listened more favorably to his proposal, yet she pointed out an obstacle, saying: "Tommy Lincoln, I have no objection to marrying you, but I cannot do it right off, for I owe several little debts which must first be paid." To which he replied: "Give me a list of your debts."

They amounted to about twelve dollars — not so mean a sum in those days of small things as present standards might indicate. At any rate, within a few hours our suitor had paid them, and had married the fair debtor. The settlement of these little accounts was, in a way, the central incident of their short courtship.[13] It puts one in mind of the good repute enjoyed by the Lincolns, from the beginning, in Elizabethtown. If the neighbor, who declared Thomas and his first wife to have been poor but true, had seen him and his second wife set out for home in a four-horse wagon loaded with her wealth of household belongings, — to say nothing of the three blooming Johnston children, — there might have been some hesitation about repeating the word "poor"; but in the face of those receipted bills, there would probably have been no desire to modify the word "true."[14]

Sally Bush was a worthy successor to Nancy Hanks. A woman of strong personality and high ideals, this stepmother — to use a designation that she ennobled — is credited by not a few writers with exerting the larger influence in the moulding of Abraham Lincoln's character. They have gone so far, some of them, as to assert that Lincoln himself, recognizing this to be so, had her in mind and not her predecessor, when he uttered that grateful acknowledgment to his "angel mother." [15] This view is hardly sustained by the language of the tribute, or by the facts; yet Abraham apparently missed no opportunity for expressing in deeds, as well as in words, what — to use his own phrases — he owed the "noble woman" who had been "a good and kind mother" [16] to an orphaned boy.

Perhaps, after all, the controversy concerning the two women, if controversy it may be called, is fairly disposed of by what Mr. Lincoln told one of his acquaintances, Governor William Pickering, who some years later thus restated their conversation. "Once when Lincoln referred to the fact that he owed much to his mother, I asked, 'Which mother, Mr. Lincoln, your own or your stepmother?' To which Mr. Lincoln replied, — 'Don't ask me that question, for I mean both, as it was mother all my life, except that desolate period between the time mother died and father brought mother into the home again. Both were as one mother. Hence I simply say, mother.'" [17]

With one or the other of these conscientious women at his side, Abraham Lincoln reached maturity. Almost every good man has had a good mother. Here was one who had two. It is not surprising, therefore, that his sense of right and wrong, after a few minor lapses, became developed to uncommon acuteness at an early age, nor should it be accounted a miracle that from the unsightly stumpage of a frontier clearing, emerged this blossom which grew, with time, into the finest flower of nineteenth-century honor.

Lincoln was brought up on the breast of things. The rugged actualities of life in a new country, rather than the literature about life, entered into his training; and when we name those colleges to which the world's great lights have severally owed their education, this man must be credited to the most venerable, though perhaps least honored, among them all, — the academy of hard knocks. Let us not infer, however, that the back settlements in which he spent his youth were wholly beyond the field of letters. Attending "A B C schools by littles," as the autobiography expresses it, and learning betimes how to read, the lad lost no opportunity to borrow or acquire the few books within his reach. Under the stimulation of first one mother, then the other, every volume that he could lay hold of for fifty miles around was eagerly studied. What this shifting library comprised will doubtless never be fully known. It is said to have included — besides certain elementary school-books [18] — the Bible, Bunyan's "Pilgrim's Progress," Æsop's "Fables," the "Arabian Nights," Defoe's "Robinson Crusoe," Weems's "Life of Washington," Ramsay's "Life of Washington," a history of the United States, Weems's "Life of Marion," the "Speeches of Henry Clay," with which was probably incorporated a "Memoir" of the statesman, the "Life of Benjamin Franklin," Riley's "Narrative of the Loss of the Brig Commerce," a few of Cooper's "Leather Stocking Tales," and the Revised Laws of Indiana, with which were bound, besides other documents, the Declaration of Independence and the Constitution of the United States.[19] Some of these works, if not all of them, left an ethical glow in the boy's heart. Thoughtfully absorbing the light that streamed from their pages, he caught glimpses here and there of a kinship that linked the everyday doings in his commonplace world with the ideals in his books.

A mishap to one of the borrowed volumes put these budding ideas of rectitude to the test. While in Abraham's keeping, a "Life of Washington"[20] that belonged to a neighbor, Josiah Crawford by name, was badly soaked one night during a rainstorm, which beat through the chinks of the Little Pigeon Creek cabin. Carrying the damaged book back to its owner, the boy acknowledged himself answerable for its condition;—but how was he to pay the seventy-five cents which Crawford demanded in settlement? Money was as scarce as literature at that time with young Lincoln, so he agreed to work out the claim in the farmer's corn-field. "You see," said Abraham, relating the incident to a friend, "I am tall and long-armed, and I went to work in earnest. At the end of the two days there was not a corn-blade left on a stalk in the field. I wanted to pay full damage for all the wetting the book got, and I made a clean sweep."[21] This ample submission to the laws of mine and thine was not, however, so graceful as it might have been. Our "long-armed" boy appears to have been still far removed from sainthood in those days; and, after the manner of boys, he nursed a grudge against Crawford for his unneighborly, though perhaps rightful, treatment of the accident.

Having satisfied that thrifty person's demands with the Scriptural "good measure, pressed down, and shaken together, and running over," Abraham — so tradition has it — lampooned the man whenever occasion offered, — now in humorous prose, now in doggerel rhymes,—until Josiah's "blue nose," as well as certain other unlovely features, became the laughing-stock of the neighborhood. Indeed, the gibes ran their merry course — if we may believe one veracious chronicler — all the way to "the Wabash and the Ohio." [22]

This unseemly persecution of Crawford, on the heels of an honorable settlement with him, narrowly saved the youthful Lincoln from occupying a place in the world's gallery of premature worthies beside the copper-plate little Washington portrayed by Parson Weems. Nevertheless, that myth-maker's model boy, who could not tell a lie, had left a deep impression in the mind of this real boy. To Abe's uncritical faculties the biography rang true in every detail. For its reverend author, with all his faults, had the literary merit of apparent sincerity; and his string of "curious anecdotes," as the title-page called them, had not yet been worn threadbare, to the verge of the ridiculous, by derisive repetition. Weems's Washington, boy and man, became Lincoln's hero — a cherished ideal which he never consented to modify, even after he had outgrown the story of the cherry tree and that truthful little hatchet-swinger.

Emulating the great Virginian, Abe carried himself, now consciously, now unconsciously, as this paragon of his fancy might have done, even to the point of leaving a hatchet, or more accurately speaking, an axe anecdote for later generations to admire. During those toilsome Indiana days, — so runs our tale, — the youth was engaged in clearing a piece of woodland some distance from the house. Leaving home early, he made it a practice to carry some luncheon and stay away until nightfall. The picnic element in the expedition appealed to the taste of his frolicsome stepsister, Matilda, whose frequent appeals for permission to accompany him met with her mother's peremptory refusals. Eluding maternal vigilance one morning, the girl slyly followed Lincoln as he strode through the forest, humming a tune, with his axe on his shoulder. At a favorable moment she darted forward and, exerting cat-like agility, leaped squarely upon him. Grasping a shoulder with each hand, she braced her knee in the middle of his back, and brought the young woodsman dexterously to the ground. Lincoln, taken by surprise, went down like a log, carrying his assailant with him. As they fell the axe cut the girl's ankle, making a painful wound that bled freely. After an improvised bandage had stanched the blood, Abe, mindful of Mrs. Lincoln's oft-repeated orders, looked down at the sobbing culprit and asked: —

"'Tilda, what are you going to tell mother about getting hurt?"

"Tell her I did it with the axe," she answered. "That will be the truth, won't it?"

To which he responded: —

"Yes, that's the truth, but it's not all the truth.

Tell the whole truth, 'Tilda, and trust your good mother for the rest." [23]

Whether 'Tilda did tell "the whole truth," and whether Sally Bush gathered her or Abraham or both of them to her heart, after the manner of Augustine Washington in the Reverend Mr. Weems's tale, is not definitely known. Nevertheless, when the Plutarch that is to be runs his parallel between these two greatest of Americans, the legendary hatchet and the historic axe may become symbolic of how closely both these heroes did actually hew to the line, in their early fondness for the verities.

But if further youthful similarities shall be sought by that hypothetical biographer, he will not linger over the next episode in this chronicle of Lincoln's moral growth. Abe had passed his nineteenth birthday when "the great man" of the Little Pigeon Creek neighborhood, old James Gentry, picked him out for a signal mark of confidence. That gentleman's son, Allen, was to make a trading voyage in a Mississippi flat-boat laden with goods, and Lincoln was hired to share the adventure. They planned to do business along the river all the way, if necessary, to the Gulf. Drifting down the Ohio and thence on the broad waters of the Mississippi as far as New Orleans, the young men made a prosperous, though not entirely uneventful journey. Only one incident of the expedition concerns us here. At certain landings they were paid for their merchandise — as they discovered too late — in counterfeit money. Gentry, lamenting over the matter, feared his father's anger; whereupon Lincoln consoled him with the suggestion that their employer would not care how much bad money they took in, if they brought the correct amount of good money home. "Never mind, Allen," he continued; "it will accidentally slip out of our fingers before we get to New Orleans, and then old Jim can't quarrel at us." [24] This prophecy did, in fact, come true. The counterfeits, we are told, "all went off like hot cakes"; but to what extent the prophet helped to bring about so sweeping a fulfillment is nowhere recorded. When he and his associates, however, on their return, rendered an account of their stewardship in currency that was not hopelessly discredited, old Mr. Gentry is said to have pronounced on Lincoln what corresponded with the Scriptural commendation, — "Well done, good and faithful servant."

In this approval the candid historian cannot concur, yet he hesitates to condemn. The demoralized condition of our currency throughout the Mississippi Valley for over half a century, the bewildering variety of counterfeit bills, to say nothing of wildcat notes, in circulation, and the scarcity of good money, left people small choice but to accept at varying discounts — unless too obviously spurious — what they were offered, and pass it along again with as little loss as possible.[25] One aspect of the trouble was later humorously set forth by Lincoln himself, in his story of the steamboat captain who, running short of fuel on the river, steered to a wood-pile alongshore.

"Is that your wood?" he inquired of a man near by.

"Yes," was the answer.

"Do you want to sell it?"

"Certainly."

"Will you accept wildcat currency?"

"Certainly."

"How will you take it?"

"Cord for cord." [26]

The passing of depreciated or fraudulent currency, in the ordinary course of business, was evidently not regarded, during those days of loose financiering, with the severity of more recent times.[27] Indeed, after Lincoln had become a lawyer, though the clients that offered themselves were accepted or rejected with scrupulous discrimination, he on one occasion employed his wit and ability to secure the acquittal of a man charged, under suspicious circumstances, with passing counterfeit money. "There was a pretty clear case against the accused," said Adlai E. Stevenson, who attended the trial, "but when the chief witness for the people took the stand, he stated that his name was J. Parker Green, and Lincoln reverted to this the moment he rose to cross-examine: — Why J. Parker Green? — What did the J. stand for? — John? — Well, why did n't the witness call himself John P. Green? — That was his name, was n't it? — Well, what was the reason he did not wish to be known by his right name? — Did J. Parker Green have anything to conceal; and if not, why did J. Parker Green part his name in that way? — and so on. Of course the whole examination was farcical," Mr. Stevenson continued, "but there was something irresistibly funny in the varying tones and inflections of Mr. Lincoln's voice as he rang the changes upon the man's name; and at the recess the very boys in the street took it up as a slogan, and shouted, 'J. Parker Green!' all over the town. Moreover, there was something in Lincoln's way of intoning his questions which made me suspicious of the witness, and to this day I have never been able to rid my mind of the absurd impression that there was something not quite right about J. Parker Green. It was all nonsense, of course; but the jury must have been affected as I was, for Green was discredited, and the defendant went free." [28] Perhaps, too, some of the twelve good men and true, like the highly respected counsel for the defense, could have severally recalled times when the exigencies of trade had wafted into their hands worthless bank-bills that, somehow, did not remain there.

Be that as it may, much water, in the language of the old byword, was to flow down the Mississippi River before this clever attorney evolved from the gawky young bow-hand on Gentry's flat-boat. Another trading voyage to New Orleans in the spring of 1831, shortly after he had begun life on his own account, appears to have been as successful as the first one. The crew comprised Lincoln, his step-brother John D. Johnston, and his cousin John Hanks, who accompanied them, however, but part way, leaving the responsibility of the undertaking largely on Abraham's shoulders. Their employer, Denton Offutt, a breezy speculator, — free-handed, optimistic, and given to superlatives, — conceived a warm admiration for Abe. The young fellow certainly conducted himself well. His manly qualities, his muscular powers, his unfailing good humor, his resourcefulness on certain trying occasions, his fidelity to the trust reposed in him, above all, his integrity, made so strong an impression on Offutt that at the termination of the voyage he established a general store at New Salem,[29] and placed Lincoln in charge of it with the assertion that this model clerk had not his equal in the United States.

Offutt's extravagant praise was, it is perhaps needless to say, not wholly merited. A keener merchant might have hesitated to entrust the management of his business, and of the neighboring mill that was presently merged with the enterprise, to a young man of Lincoln's peculiar make-up. Abe had, it is true, learned something of storekeeping during the old Gentryville days, in the grocery of his friend William Jones; and a small stock of goods purchased there, when the Lincoln family moved from Indiana to Illinois, had been profitably peddled, on the way. Moreover, those trading trips to New Orleans had doubtless contributed somewhat to his commercial training; but no amount of experience could make a successful business man of one so lacking, as was Tom Lincoln's son, in aptitude for hiving the nimble sixpence. How not to do so appears, in a sense, to have concerned him more. Yet the scrupulous care with which he shut Offutt's till against the sixpences that did not belong there would, had it been combined with mercantile ability, probably in the end have made the young clerk's fortune. His honesty became a by-word.

Two typical instances of uprightness in small things especially impressed themselves on the memory of the neighborhood. It is said that once, having sold a woman a bill of goods, he found after her departure that she had paid six and a quarter cents more than the purchases amounted to. When the store was closed at night, so the story goes, he walked several miles into the country to give his customer the fourpenny piece which balanced her over-payment. Here again Lincoln's punctilious honesty recalls that of Washington. It is related that a ferryman on the General's estate, in making change for a moidore, took out one and a half pence too much. Discovering the over-charge when the accounts for the week were made up, Washington wrapped three halfpence in a piece of paper, and had them delivered to the traveler on his return.[30]

The other anecdote concerning Lincoln, that belongs in this group, tells how one night, just before closing time, he hastily weighed, as he thought, half a pound of tea for a belated customer. Looking at the scales on the following morning, he discovered that a weight of four ounces, instead of eight, had been used. To wrap up another quarter of a pound of tea, close the store again, and deliver his parcel at the end of a long walk before breakfast, was the only method of repairing the error that presented itself to this primitive conscience.

The young clerk's ethical creed during those New Salem days seems simple enough. It has been preserved by a friend, who thus restates what he gathered, under this head, in the course of conversation:

"Lincoln said he did not believe in total depravity, and, although it was not popular to believe it, it was easier to do right than wrong; that the first thought was: what was right? and the second: what was wrong? Therefore it was easier to do right than wrong, and easier to take care of, as it would take care of itself. It took an effort to do wrong, and a still greater effort to take care of it. But do right and it would take care of itself. Then you had nothing to do but to go ahead and do right and nothing to trouble you."[31]

Out of this philosophy developed — to borrow a cynical phrase — the acute attacks of chronic integrity that attracted particular attention to Lincoln, even in the midst of an honest, plain-dealing community. The rude people around him, for the most part, led upright lives, and they expected others to do likewise; yet his efforts to treat every man with fairness were so pronounced as to evoke frequent comment among them. Their talk crystallized, at last, in the sobriquet, "Honest Abe." This name, having been generally adopted throughout the New Salem vicinage, fitted Lincoln so nicely that it clung to him, with slight variations, in one form or another, until the end of his career.

Meanwhile Offutt did not prosper. He appears to have had too many irons in the fire, and one of them, as we know, was under the care of a man who had no particular talent for keeping irons, or anything else, at a money-making glow. Neither the honesty nor the popularity of this clerk — for the young fellow had gained the good-will of their customers — sufficed to save the store from the general ruin in which the owner's several ventures became involved. Failure overtook the new business before the end of its first year. As the place is sold out, Offutt disappears from historic view; while Lincoln steps nearer to the lime-light for a brief but bloodless essay at soldiering in the Black Hawk War. Returning to New Salem upon the conclusion of the campaign, he made an unsuccessful canvass, on a National Republican platform, for election to the State Legislature. Then "without means and out of business," as he himself expressed it, but "anxious to remain with his friends," Lincoln looked about him for something to do. Stalwart of frame, with well-knit muscles, he naturally came to the thought of again earning a living by manual labor. The blacksmith's trade, which several of his forbears had creditably followed, was, for a time, seriously considered. It had, in fact, almost been decided on, when two of those new-found friends, the Herndon brothers, familiarly known as "Row" and "Jim," offered their general store for sale. James sold his interest to William F. Berry, the son of a neighboring Presbyterian minister, and Rowan soon after disposed of his share to Lincoln, receiving in lieu of money "Honest Abe's" promise to pay. When "Row" was asked how he came to make such liberal terms with a penniless man whom he had known for so short a time, he answered: "I believed he was thoroughly honest, and that impression was so strong in me I accepted his note in payment of the whole. He had no money, but I would have advanced him still more had he asked for it." [32]

Herndon was not the only New Salemite who was willing to transfer his business, after this fashion, for a promissory note. Soon after the transaction, a neighboring storekeeper, Reuben Radford by name, incurred the displeasure of a local gang, "the Clary's Grove boys," to such an extent that they made a riotous night of it in his place. On the following morning, standing discouraged amid the débris of the establishment, Radford sold it to the first comer, William G. Greene, a youth who had been a sort of junior clerk in the Offutt store. As the purchaser could not pay in cash the four hundred dollars agreed upon, he gave his note. Then, growing nervous over the transaction, he turned for comfort to his former associate. Lincoln said: "Cheer up, Billy. It's a good thing. We'll take an inventory."

They found that the flotsam and jetsam which had survived the storm, amounted in value to $1200. Whereupon Berry and Lincoln offered Greene a substantial profit on his bargain. This the young man eagerly accepted, with the stipulation that the firm should assume his indebtedness to Radford. There was a little more shuffling of notes, and the goods passed into the hands of Berry and Lincoln.[33] They shortly afterwards, in presumably the same manner, absorbed a small business owned by James Rutledge. Combining these three stocks, — all acquired by a few strokes of the pen, — Lincoln and his partner now had what the junior member later ironically referred to as "*the* store" of New Salem.

Despite its virtual monopoly along certain lines, the new firm was ill-adapted to succeed. Berry soon developed habits of idleness and intemperance that would have been fatal to any business; [34] while Lincoln, though ambitious and sober to an exceptional degree, was hardly more effective. His keen interest in books, study, newspapers, politics, funny stories, horse-races, wrestling-matches, feats of strength, — anything, in short, but buying and selling, — left him far from alert to what is commonly called the main chance. When one remembers these pursuits, moreover, to have been the preoccupations of a man who combined rigid integrity with a kindly nature, it is not surprising to learn, as Cousin Dennis relates, that "he purty nigh always got the wust of a trade." [35] The rest is soon told. Berry and Lincoln did not thrive. Giving up the struggle after several ineffectual shifts, they sold out, early in 1834, to Alexander and William Trent. The purchasers had no money, but they willingly gave notes, which the sellers as willingly accepted. Before these obligations fell due, however, the Trent brothers had disappeared, their few remaining goods had been seized by creditors, and the business had come to an inglorious close.

Berry's death, soon after, left the surviving member of the firm to face, alone, the consequences of their ill-starred venture. Yet he could not bring himself to join in the censure which was heaped upon the young man's memory. With characteristic consideration for his partner's father, the Reverend John M. Berry, whom he held in affectionate regard,

Lincoln declared that William's dissipation was a result rather than a cause of their misfortunes; and took on his own shoulders the burden of liabilities bound up in those unpaid notes to Herndon, Radford, Greene, and Rutledge.

How serious the whole affair was may be gathered from this account of it, given by the hapless debtor to a friend [36] of later days: "That debt was the greatest obstacle I have ever met in life. I had no way of speculating, and could not earn money except by labor, and to earn by labor eleven hundred dollars, besides my living, seemed the work of a lifetime. There was, however, but one way. I went to the creditors and told them that if they would let me alone, I would give them all I could earn, over my living, as fast as I could earn it." [37]

During the next few months no surplus, it is perhaps needless to add, was available for this purpose. In fact, the situation reduced itself to a struggle for bread. Lincoln's earnings from the office of local postmaster, to which he had been appointed before the above "winked out," were of course meager in the extreme; but he contrived to pick up a living by doing odd jobs about the neighborhood. Helping his friends — now Hill, now Ellis — behind their counters, working in the field as a farm laborer, splitting rails, lending a hand at the mill, — briefly, making himself useful on all sides, in his big, good-natured way, he just "kept," to quote the autobiography, "soul and body together." [38]

Throughout this trying period, however, Lincoln did not lose sight of his self-respect, or of the respect due to him from others. He began to manifest that sensitive chastity of honor which recoils from doubt as from a blow. So, when a patron of the post-office, upon payment of certain arrears demanded an acknowledgment, "A. Lincoln, P.M.," responded: "I am somewhat surprised at your request. I will, however, comply with it. The law requires newspaper postage to be paid in advance, and now that I have waited a full year, you choose to wound my feelings by insinuating that unless you get a receipt I will probably make you pay it again." [39]

The reputation for honesty, which Lincoln so jealously guarded, had meanwhile opened to him another channel for occasional employment. This opportunity came through John Calhoun, the surveyor of Sangamon County, who, overburdened with business, was looking about for an assistant of intelligence and unquestioned integrity. The latter qualification appears to have been especially important at the time, owing to a mania for speculation in land that had possessed the people of the region to such a degree as almost to put a premium on jobbery. A man beyond the reach of corruption was, therefore, what Calhoun sought when he offered to make Abraham Lincoln one of his deputies. The honor must have been not less flattering to the young National Republican, because it came, as had the postmastership, from a Democratic source, and with the assurance that his acceptance carried with it no obligation of party service, nor restraint upon his freedom of political action. To Lincoln's declaration that he knew nothing whatever about surveying, Calhoun responded with an offer to aid him. Books and material having been procured, six weeks of earnest study ensued. For assistance in learning the theory of the subject, Lincoln turned to his friend, Mentor Graham, the local schoolmaster; for guidance in the practical application of the rules, he depended on the surveyor himself. When the period of preparation had reached its close, the new-fledged deputy is said to have made his pathetic little speech: "Calhoun, I am entirely unable to repay you for your generosity, at present. All that I have you see on me, except a quarter of a dollar, in my pocket." [40]

Such extreme poverty left Lincoln, of course, unable to pay cash for the saddle-horse that his new duties obliged him to buy. He agreed to take care of the bill by installments; he did so, but ran behind when only ten dollars remained unpaid. Whereupon his creditor, a horse-dealer named Thomas Watkins, who is described as "a high-strung man," lost his temper and sued for what was still due. Lincoln did not deny the debt. He hastily raised the required sum and settled the suit.

A still more unpleasant experience followed, for the young surveyor was destined to drain his cup of mortification to its dregs. One of the Berry-Lincoln notes had passed into the hands of a certain Van Bergen, who forthwith brought suit and obtained judgment. Levying on the horse, saddle, and surveying instruments, he offered them for sale in satisfaction of his claim. But Lincoln's loyal friends were not disposed to stand idly by while he was deprived of the means of earning a livelihood. They bought the effects that had been seized, restored them to their former owner, and took the place of the impatient Van Bergen among his creditors.[41] The loans, so handsomely made, were in time repaid by Lincoln, principal and interest, as were all the obligations left in the train of his unfortunate business ventures. Disdaining to take advantage of a recently enacted law for the relief of insolvent debtors, he set himself resolutely to the task of seeing to it that no man should lose a penny by reason of any note which contained his signature. Yet the prospect might have appalled a stouter heart. At times, when the seeming hopelessness of the undertaking was borne in upon him, he referred to what was still to be paid, with whimsical humor, as "the national debt." How long the process of liquidation did, in fact, take is not precisely known. Lincoln's occasional payments on account of these claims would doubtless have made a braver showing had the only other demands upon him been for his own simple wants; but, in addition to such outlays, the frequent aid extended to his parents, and the requirements, after his marriage, of a growing family, all had to come out of earnings that never, at their best, were munificent. Nevertheless, through good times and bad, the load of indebtedness became steadily lighter, until, after seventeen years or more of self-denial, the last note, with its heavy accumulations of interest, was paid.[42]

A less scrupulous man than Abraham Lincoln might have appreciably shortened this debt-bound period from the very beginning. As deputy surveyor under John Calhoun, and later, under that officer's successor, Thomas M. Neale, he doubtless had opportunities enough for employing his knowledge of what was going on, together with his still unimpaired credit, in profitable land speculations. But he could not bring himself to mingle the pursuit of private gain with public duties; and he scorned to use, on his own account, information derived from official sources.[43] The same conscientious spirit so manifestly entered into the doing of the work itself that he soon gained the confidence of those who employed him. They believed in the young surveyor's accuracy, as well as in his fairness, to such an extent that disputes concerning boundaries or corners were frequently submitted to him for arbitration; and, what is of greater moment, his findings, we are told, were invariably accepted by the conflicting parties as final. A quarrel of this nature, about a corner, took place in the northern part of the county. "After a good deal of disputing," relates one of the owners, "we agreed to send for Lincoln, and to abide by his decision. He came with compass, flagstaff, and chain. He stopped with me three or four days and surveyed the whole section. When in the neighborhood of the disputed corner by actual survey, he called for his staff and, driving it in the ground at a certain spot said, 'Gentlemen, here is the corner.' We dug down into the ground at the point indicated and lo! there we found about six or eight inches of the original stake sharpened at the end, and beneath which was the usual piece of charcoal placed there by Rector, the surveyor who laid the ground off for the Government many years before." So well had the work been done that in this instance, as in the others, differences were at an end, and all concerned "went away completely satisfied." [44]

There is another aspect of Lincoln's early life that should not be overlooked. He was apparently never too busy for the contests of strength and skill from which came some of his first sweet triumphs in leadership. That these were won, for the most part, with ease must have made defeat, when it did on rare occasions occur, peculiarly hard to bear; yet he carried himself, according to all accounts, — whether victor or vanquished, — as a man of honor should. In fact, save for a single untoward act which must be charged to the hobbledehoy exuberance of his youthful Indiana days,[45] Lincoln treated whatever happened at these sports with the same extreme candor and nicety of good faith that marked his business dealings. Perhaps the most notable instance is that of a certain wrestling-match which took place during the Black Hawk War. At the risk of telling a twice-told tale, the story is repeated here, — told anew rather than repeated, for the later researches of an Illinois historian have contributed not a few additional details.[46] They reveal Lincoln in the full flower of sportsmanlike honesty.

Having been elected Captain of the Volunteers from Sangamon County, he was ever ready to uphold the credit of his company in the rough pastimes whereby the soldiers sought to relieve the tedium of that peculiar campaign. Proud of their leader's exploits, especially as a wrestler, they boasted that no man in the army could throw him; and he, at the same time, owed much of his ascendancy over their undisciplined natures to the uniform success with which he downed all comers. But Antæus himself met his match at last.

One evening on the march, our phalanx from Sangamon happened upon a choice piece of camping-ground at about the time it was reached by a company from St. Clair County. In the altercations which ensued a disgraceful scuffle seemed imminent, when Lincoln proposed to William Moore, the opposing commander, that they might settle their dispute after the good old-fashioned method of single combat — captain against captain. This suggestion met with a modified approval. As the officer from St. Clair had no skill in wrestling, it was agreed that each company should be represented by its stoutest champion. Accordingly, Lincoln soon stood within a circle of excited men, facing a redoubtable athlete from southern Illinois, in the person of private Lorenzo Dow Thompson. Both combatants had won the confidence of their respective friends, who hastened to back their faith with bets, eagerly offered and as eagerly accepted. Nor were the gathering crowds of soldiers from other companies slow to gratify their sporting tastes. "Up went powder-horns, guns, watches, coats, horses, pay-rolls, and reputations until," — so runs the chronicle, — "there remained not one solitary article of property in possession or expectancy thereof, which had not been put into the pot on that match." The referee,

Captain Moore's brother Jonathan, announced, as he tossed up a coin for choice of "holts," that two falls in three would decide the match; and the men grappled.

It did not take Lincoln long to discover that his record was in danger. Calling to his friends, with characteristic frankness, he managed to say: "This is the most powerful man I ever had hold of. He will throw me and you will lose your all, unless I act on the defensive."

Yet Thompson was too quick for him. All of Lincoln's extraordinary strength did not avail against the St. Clair man's skill, and in a few moments the pride of New Salem measured his six feet four inches on the ground — fairly thrown. Their second round did not differ widely from the first. After attempting his favorite devices in vain, the tall captain again went to earth, this time, however, pulling his antagonist down on top of him.

"Dog fall!" shouted Lincoln's supporters, seizing on a pretext for dispute.

"Fair fall!" defiantly retorted the others.

A general fight — and a serious one at that — seemed inevitable, when Lincoln springing to his feet averted, for the second time in this affair, a scene of bloodshed.

"Boys," he cried, "give up your bets; if he has not thrown me fairly, he could." [47]

This frank admission put an end to all hopes of further resistance. The "boys" reluctantly obeyed, and Captain Moore's followers took possession of their captured bivouac, laden with the spoils of victory.[48]

But were they the only victors? Marshaling the several elements which went to make up this little drama, recalling what defeat meant to the Sangamon chief, and how easy it might have been for him to hide his discomfiture under cover of the mêlée which he had prevented, thoughtful readers will perhaps agree that the true hero of the episode — all things considered — did not rest that night in the camp of the St. Clair rangers.[49]

Virile men, rude and cultured alike, admire a winner; but how their hearts go out to him who can lose or win with equal grace! So it was in Lincoln's case. During what might be called his New Salem period, he became the central figure of those occasional little gatherings at which the settlers sought to amuse themselves. They made him preside over horse-races, wrestling-matches, athletic games, and what not. Indeed, even cock-fights seemed incomplete if he was missing from the judge's corner. Expert knowledge of these pastimes, applied with tact, good nature, and ready wit, went far to make his decisions acceptable, even had they not been pronounced by a muscular giant, who could always be relied on to enforce compliance. More noteworthy, however, than all other circumstances was the abiding faith of this entire community in the young man's squareness. Said one old resident, reviving precious memories: "In the spring or summer of 1832, I had a horse-race with George Warburton. I got Lincoln, who was at the race, to be a judge of the race, much against his will, and after hard persuasion. Lincoln decided correctly, and the other judge said, 'Lincoln is the fairest man I ever had to deal with. If Lincoln is in this county when I die, I want him to be my administrator, for he is the only man I ever met with that was wholly and unselfishly honest.'"[50]

As might have been expected, this talent for holding the scales with a steady hand brought more serious duties. When arrangements were made, from time to time, in approved frontier fashion, for the fist-fights whereby these backwoodsmen sought to adjust their irreconcilable differences, Lincoln, if not called upon to second one of the principals, was usually named by both as referee. Such functions are, in the nature of things, difficult to perform; yet he conducted himself, according to all accounts, with spirit, and with painstaking fidelity to the rules of fair play. It is said, moreover, that he officiated on these occasions reluctantly — in fact, only after failing to bring about settlements of the quarrels by peaceable means. For it was as arbitrator between man and man that his ripening intuitions of equity — tempered by kindly sympathies with both sides — had their largest scope. With such precision — to quote from an ancient judicial oath — "as the herring's backbone doth lie in the midst of the fish," did he draw the line between conflicting interests. Even those who were inclined to demur at his decisions usually came to see that a lean compromise was better than a fat lawsuit. So, in one way and another, to not a few people along the Sangamon, Abraham Lincoln became, after a fashion, the court of last resort.[51] It would seem as if, at this early date, he himself might have been found worthy of the eulogy pronounced by him, some years later, on a departed friend: "In his intercourse with his fellow-men, he possessed that rare uprightness of character, which was evidenced by his having no disputes or bickerings of his own, while he was ever the chosen arbiter to settle those of his neighbors."[52]

So far, indeed, did Lincoln carry his peacemaking activities that the local justice, with an eye to diminishing fees, complained of interference. If this functionary, as seems likely, was Squire Bowling Green, who had befriended our amateur judge in many ways, the situation must have been peculiarly unpleasant. But, be that as it may, Lincoln did not adjourn court. Taking the rebuke amiably, he explained how hard it was for him to see his neighbors spend money in unnecessary litigation and — what was more important still — how desirous he felt of saving them from perhaps lifelong enmities which might be prevented. That reply was far-reaching. It opened a window, so to say, in the speaker's heart, and threw a flood of light forward upon many things which he did, and many more which he refrained from doing, throughout the fruitful years that were to come.

What motives first directed Lincoln's attention to the legal profession as a career are not definitely known. Whether the bar took his fancy on account of that ideal justice to which lawyers theoretically, at least, dedicate themselves, or whether he was moved by more commonplace incentives, such as a taste for study, the desire to gain a livelihood by means of an honorable calling, aspirations to become a controlling factor in other men's affairs, and the like, can only be surmised. Perhaps each of these considerations carried due weight. They certainly all had time enough to make their presence felt. For, as far back as the youthful days at Gentryville, we find Abraham, in his insatiable craving for the printed page, poring over a copy of the Indiana Statutes.[53] This volume was supplemented presently by such books as he could borrow from Justice John Pitcher of Rockport, whose kindly interest in the lad grew out of his admiration for a little composition on the American government, which one of the young writer's friends had submitted to judicial criticism. "The world could n't beat it," was Pitcher's comment, and thenceforth Lincoln had the run of his office.[54] At about the same time came opportunities — or rather Abe made opportunities — for seeing the law administered. Whenever sessions of the circuit court for the adjoining county were held in Boonville, he would trudge over the road — a matter of fifteen miles — to attend. What took place there doubtless repaid him. Closely following every word and act in the rustic drama of justice, as it unfolded itself before his fascinated gaze, he seemed identified, so to say, with the proceedings. They took such hold upon his mind that he rehearsed them at home, reënacting the court-room scenes and holding mock-trials in which a certain gawky country boy defended imaginary prisoners against unjust charges, with uniform success. If he might only become a lawyer! But such a notion was out of the question. His parents, as he explained to Judge Pitcher, were so poor that they could not spare him long enough for study. And there the matter rested while the years passed on. In fact, it was not until after Lincoln had left home and had become a business man at New Salem that his youthful ambition, dormant though never wholly forgotten during the long intervening period, began to revive. While casting about for something to do, on his return from the Black Hawk War, he again thought of taking up this calling; but the idea was promptly dismissed because, to quote his own opinion, he "could not succeed at that without a better education." Nevertheless, before many months had elapsed, a chance occurrence during the ill-starred Berry partnership quickened into life, beyond any previous experience, Lincoln's desire to study law. How this came about he himself, chatting once with an acquaintance, in a reminiscent mood, thus related: —

"One day a man who was migrating to the West drove up in front of my store with a wagon which contained his family and household plunder. He asked me if I would buy an old barrel for which he had no room in his wagon, and which he said contained nothing of special value. I did not want it, but to oblige him I bought it, and paid him, I think, half a dollar for it. Without further examination, I put it away in the store, and forgot all about it. Some time after, in overhauling things, I came upon the barrel, and emptying it upon the floor to see what it contained, I found at the bottom of the rubbish a complete edition of Blackstone's Commentaries. I began to read those famous works, and I had plenty of time; for, during the long summer days, when the farmers were busy with their crops, my customers were few and far between. The more I read" — this he said with a sweeping gesture and a high pitch of enthusiasm in his voice — "the more intensely interested I became. Never in my whole life was my mind so thoroughly absorbed. I read until I devoured them." [55]

Lincoln's re-awakened appetite for legal lore was destined soon to be gratified. After the store had, like that barrel of rubbish, passed into the limbo of discarded things, he turned from his surveying during the summer of 1834 long enough to make a second, and this time successful, canvass for election to the State Legislature. While traveling over his district, the young politician saw much of a fellow candidate on the Whig ticket, Major John T. Stuart, with whom he had served two years before through the Black Hawk War. Stuart, an attorney in reputable practice at Springfield, conceived a high regard for Lincoln's character and ability. So that when Abraham confided to him his inclination for the study of law, he met not only with instant encouragement, but with equally prompt offers of assistance. Here, indeed, was the stuff out of which lawyers at their best are made. Rigid honesty, a judicial temperament, candor, and ambition, as well as the less salient qualities, — common sense, perseverance, knowledge of human nature, and keen sympathy with human affairs, — of all these the aspirant had given abundant evidence. Nor could he be considered lacking in what, according to Lord Eldon, constituted the prime requisite for a beginner who sought distinction at the bar,—he was "not worth a shilling."

This last attribute, however, hardly commended itself as an advantage to Lincoln's troubled mind. Poverty alone would probably not have stayed his steps, but poverty staggering under a burden labelled "the national debt,"— there was a prospect that gave him pause. What did he owe to his creditors, what to himself? Pondering over these questions, he carried them with him on a surveying expedition. All day long the pros and cons of the matter jostled one another in his perplexed brain, without result. Yet the time for a decision had come. On his way home, he swung a pair of tired long legs across an old rail fence, and sat down resolved to stay there until some conclusion should be reached. Lincoln's destiny truly trembled in the balance; but a controlling thought, decisive enough to make one side outweigh the other, still failed to present itself. In this dilemma he bethought himself of a way out,— a way as freely utilized at the time, along our western frontier, as it has been among the children of men from the beginning of recorded days— the appeal to chance. Resting his Jacob's-staff erect on the ground, he determined to be guided by the direction in which it might fall. If forward, he too would go forward into the new career that beckoned him so alluringly; if backward, he would remain a surveyor. The staff fell forward.[56]

Lincoln now began to study, if we may adopt his own phrase, "in good earnest." Availing himself of Major Stuart's offer, he borrowed the necessary textbooks, in their order, from that gentleman's little library at Springfield. This required an occasional journey of twenty miles or more, each way, which our eager student appears to have traveled, for the most part, on foot.[57] Days so spent, however, were not wholly lost. As he strode across country with the precious volumes, Abraham made frequent pauses for the reading of successive paragraphs, which he recited aloud as he went.

Nor were these studies pursued with less zeal at home, though, in truth, there seemed but few waking hours left for them. Between sessions of the Legislature, which customarily made heavy drafts upon its members' time, Lincoln, facing the problem of how to live, "still mixed in the surveying" — so runs his homely expression — "to pay board and clothing bills." Moreover, the postmastership with its occasional duties, as well as sundry bread-and-butter jobs of a less exalted character, all crowded their demands upon his attention. Yet some scraps of opportunity remained. Employing these diligently, by day and by night, he worked his way through Stuart's collection.[58] To such good purpose, in fact, did he study the Major's books that, before the list was exhausted, though "not lawyer enough to hurt" him, Lincoln had acquired skill enough to draw up bills of sale, contracts, deeds, mortgages, and the like, for his admiring neighbors. He even went so far as to represent them before the local justice, in sundry suits whereby his reputation was much enhanced, but not his income, for he made no charges whatever on accounts of these activities. This seemingly Quixotic practice of working without pay, at a time when poverty pressed sharply, was quite in keeping with the young man's kindly nature, and his biographer is tempted to make the obvious comment. But here again, the hand of fact rudely intervenes. Brushing away the gossamer web of romance, it points to "an act concerning attorneys and counselors at law" in the statutes of Illinois that expressly prohibited unlicensed persons from formally practicing at the bar or from receiving fees for legal services.[59] After a while, however, this disability, as far as it concerned the New Salem amateur, was, by the customary steps, removed. Before his second year of preparation had elapsed, — in the spring of 1836, — the necessary certificate of "good moral character" had been entered on the records of the Sangamon County Circuit Court. In the following autumn a license was issued, and later Abraham Lincoln's name was duly inscribed on the roll of attorneys.[60] So "Honest Abe," at the age of twenty-eight, became a full-fledged practitioner in that notable company of scholars that have furnished mankind with some of its noblest and, at the same time, with some of its most pernicious impulses. On which side this newcomer would exercise his talents, none doubted who had observed him in any of the makeshift occupations whereby he sustained himself while toiling up the circuitous path that led to the portals of the Supreme Court.

CHAPTER II

TRUTH IN LAW

EARLY one spring morning long ago,— to be precise, on the 15th day of April, 1837, — a solitary horseman might have been seen riding along the wagon road that ran from New Salem to Springfield. He was obviously not one of G. P. R. James's jaunty heroes, nor yet a new-world variation on the melancholy Don, but romance and allegory alike can furnish forth few figures more striking than that which skirted the Illinois prairies on this particular forenoon. The traveler, sad-eyed and gaunt, was our friend Lincoln. His mount, a pony borrowed from Bowling Green, barely stepped high enough to keep the rider's lank extremities from touching the ground. Nor did the picture that he presented gain in grace, as one's eye rested on the man's ill-fitting garments. Yet they were the best he had, for the bulging saddle-bags contained — as we now know — not clothing, but a few articles of underwear, packed in with that well-thumbed set of Blackstone's Commentaries, several volumes of statute law, and two other books. Add to this inventory a small amount of money in pocket, — "about seven dollars," according to one friend's estimate, — and the whole sum of Lincoln's own portable assets at the moment is told. To complete the balance-sheet, his liabilities, or, more accurately speaking, the evidences thereof, might be traced, line for line, in that pensive countenance. The shadow of "the national debt," still brooding over all, did in fact overlay his prospective earnings as well as his actual means and leave him worse than penniless. It was in the hope of mending these broken fortunes that he now turned his back on the cherished associations of New Salem and rode with his scanty belongings to Springfield.

The city had held out welcoming hands. Its leading citizens felt grateful to Lincoln for effective aid rendered to them during the recent session of the General Assembly, in which they had secured a vote whereby the seat of government was transferred from Vandalia to Springfield; and his faculty, withal, for engaging the affections of men had already gained him several stanch friends in the new capital.

One of these admirers, William Butler, relates how after the victory at Vandalia, as the Sangamon delegation were returning home, Lincoln had, in a moment of depression, spoken to him of his gloomy prospects. Without money, resources, or employment, he did not know, as he said, "where to earn even a week's board." [1] The listener's ready sympathy had inspired him to suggest that Lincoln would prosper in the practice of his profession at Springfield; and before they parted company, Butler had fortified the proposal with a tender of hospitality at his own table, until the promised success should be attained. In response to this generous offer, as well as to other invitations hardly less cordial, the member from New Salem, a few weeks thereafter, came to make his home in the bustling little town, just quickening with a sense of its recently acquired dignity.

Having hitched his pony to a rack in the public square, Lincoln, with the saddle-bags over his arm, entered the general store of Joshua F. Speed. After an exchange of greetings, — for the two men knew each other, — the newcomer said: "I just want to put my saddle-pockets down here till I put up my beast at Bill Butler's, then I want to see you."

Returning in a short time, he continued: "Well, Speed, I've been to Gorman's and got a single bedstead; now you figure out what it will cost for a tick, blankets, and the rest."

After a brief interval with slate and pencil, the required furnishings were found to reach, so the storekeeper announced, a total of seventeen dollars.

Lincoln's countenance fell, as he exclaimed: "I had no idea it would cost half of that! It is probably cheap enough," he went on, "but I want to say that, cheap as it is, I have not the money to pay. But if you will credit me until Christmas, and my experiment here as a lawyer is a success, I will pay you then. If I fail in that I will probably never be able to pay you at all."

There was a note of dejection in the speaker's voice and an air of gloom in his manner that deeply affected the man behind the counter. Recalling the scene, toward the latter end of his life, Mr. Speed declared, "As I looked up at him I thought then, and think now, that I never saw a sadder face."

On the impulse of the moment, he said to his prospective customer: —

"You seem to be so much pained at contracting so small a debt, I think I can suggest a plan by which you can avoid the debt and at the same time attain your end. I have a very large room, and a very large double bed in it, which you are perfectly welcome to share with me if you choose."

"Where is your room?" asked Lincoln.

"Upstairs," answered Speed, pointing to the winding steps which led from the shop to the story above.

Without another word his questioner took up the saddle-bags, mounted the stairs, and coming down again in a trice, announced with a happy, smiling face: "Well, Speed, I'm moved." [2]

Thus dependent on the bounty of two friends, — on the one for food, on the other for a bed, — Lincoln began his life in Springfield.

The anxious uncertainty which followed was of brief duration. Before a fortnight had elapsed, Major Stuart invited his old comrade-in-arms to become his partner. This offer, it is perhaps needless to say, was eagerly accepted; and the modest office above the county court-room, that had been occupied by the senior member of the firm, became the headquarters of Stuart and Lincoln.

After they were well under way occurred a little incident which nicely exemplified the junior partner's elemental probity, in all its quaintness. He had ceased to be postmaster at New Salem, upon the discontinuance of that office about a year before his departure from the place. But his accounts with the Government still remained unsettled, and he had probably forgotten about them, when an agent of the Post-Office Department arrived in Springfield, one day, with a draft for the unpaid balance. How much this amounted to is not definitely known. It has been variously reported at figures ranging all the way from "seventeen dollars and sixty cents" to "over one hundred and fifty dollars." Nor do the official records at Washington throw any light on the matter, for the books covering this period have been destroyed. The claim, whether large or small, however, doubtless called for a greater sum than Lincoln had seemingly brought with him to the city. His profound poverty and distress at that time might well lead one who knew these circumstances to wonder how the required funds could possibly be forthcoming. So the affair impressed his friend, Dr. A. G. Henry, who happened to be present when the collector came. "I did not believe he had the money on hand to meet the draft," said the doctor, relating what took place; "and I was about to call him aside and loan him the money, when he asked the agent to be seated a moment while he went over to his trunk at his boarding-house, and returned with an old blue sock with a quantity of silver and copper coin tied up in it. Untying the sock, he poured the contents on the table and proceeded to count the coin, which consisted of such silver and copper pieces as the country people were then in the habit of using in paying postage. On counting it up there was found the exact amount, to a cent, of the draft, and in the identical coin which had been received. As the agent departed, Lincoln remarked, in a matter-of-fact tone, that he never used any money but his own." [3]

This excellent rule was carried to an extreme which became, at times, almost childish. It seemed especially so in Lincoln's dealings with the three friends, — Kentuckians all, — Stuart, Logan, and Herndon, who succeeded one another as his partners.[4] Yet, if one may judge by what has been told concerning them, they entered readily enough into the spirit of his primitive honesty. Whenever he received a fee, an immediate division followed. If his associate happened to be present, that gentleman's part was handed over at once. But if a payment took place in the absence of the other from their office, or while Lincoln was on circuit, he wrapped his partner's share in a piece of paper marked, "Doe *v.* Roe — Stuart's half," or "Logan's half," or "Herndon's half," as the case might be; and at the first opportunity thereafter the identical money, as originally divided, was delivered to its rightful owner.

In the case of one uncommonly large fee, however, even this method apparently failed to satisfy his eagerness for prompt settlements. When he collected his bill of forty-eight hundred dollars, on a judgment against the Illinois Central Railroad Company, Lincoln telegraphed to Herndon that he wished him to remain at their office until the return train reached Springfield. It was night when he arrived, and found his partner awaiting him. Counting out Herndon's portion of the receipts, with a characteristic little jest, he had the gratification of placing the money where it belonged before they slept.

To infer from all this that Lincoln had any aversion for the keeping of accounts, or that there were no fee-books in which these transactions were recorded, is wide of the facts. He did keep books and properly, too.[5] It was in the handling of payments that he differed from many honorable men around him. He had simply set up a financial creed of his own, as it were, according to which the money of another was sacred from being used by him, even temporarily, — yes, sacred from any act which might cause it to lose, for a moment, its distinctive character as the property of that other.

A lawyer conscientious to such a degree toward his partners would hardly be less so in the treatment of his clients. And they, for their part, were quick to appreciate the fact. One old chronicler records with warm approval how Lincoln, at the very outset, gained the confidence of the business men.[6] As traffic in the Mississippi Valley was generally based on long-time credit, merchants often found it necessary to commit the collection of their overdue notes to local attorneys. Some of these gentlemen were so dilatory in making returns that their clients, not infrequently, had as much difficulty getting the money from them as from their customers. Lincoln set a different pace. As soon as such payments reached him they were, in every instance, turned over, without delay, to their rightful owners who, by the way, lost no opportunity of proclaiming their satisfaction.[7]

But it was in the handling of more important matters that Lincoln evinced how scrupulous could be an attorney's attention to the true interests of those who sought legal aid. His office became, as should every good lawyer's, a court of conciliation; and when people came to him with their troubles, he usually tried, in the beginning, to bring about amicable adjustments. These endeavors went beyond a merely perfunctory observance of the time-honored dictum that it is a lawyer's duty to prevent not to promote litigation.[8] Addressing himself, in the notes for a lecture, to beginners at the bar, he wrote, after perhaps fifteen years of legal experience: "Discourage litigation. Persuade your neighbors to compromise whenever you can. Point out to them how the nominal winner is often a real loser — in fees, expenses, and waste of time. As a peacemaker the lawyer has a superior opportunity of being a good man. There will still be business enough." [9]

How earnestly Lincoln labored to reck his own rede, judges, attorneys, and other officers of the law agreed in attesting. They declared, according to one who canvassed their views, that "more disputes were settled" by his advice "out of the courts than in them"; and, what is perhaps of greater importance, it was added that "as a rule, these settlements left the litigants friends." [10] Quarrels, ranging over the whole field of human differences, from an altercation about a line fence to the unhappy preliminaries of a divorce suit, were smoothed out — if one may credit the current anecdotes — under his soothing touch.[11]

But were the mediations of this peacemaker satisfactory in every instance? Did the contestants who had been brought to lay their claims before him uniformly submit to his decisions with good grace? As though to answer these questions one of his most brilliant contemporaries at the bar, Leonard Swett, once said: —

"There is something remarkable about these Lincoln settlements and arbitrations. The parties always submit. They seem to think they have to submit, which is very little short of the power he exercises over a jury, before which these arbitrated disputes would otherwise come. He is so positive and final with them as to make his judgment equivalent to a settlement in court. In all my observations of these cases, only one man objected seriously and threatened to take his case into court. It happened he was one of Lincoln's clients; but when the man objected to Lincoln's arbitration, and said, 'I will take the case into court,' Lincoln gave him one of his deep-searching looks, and said, 'Very well, Jim, I will take the case against you for nothing.' But that was unnecessary, for the penetrating look had settled Jim and his case." [12]

On other occasions, even when there were no arbitrations, Lincoln could not wholly divest himself of the judicial spirit. He required those who sought his aid to come — as to the judgment-seat — with clean hands. A client, favored at the outset by some improper advantage, could hope for his services only after the balance had been redeemed by some adequate concession. Perhaps the best case in point is that of a widow who retained Lincoln and Herndon for the purpose of looking into certain alleged tax liens on a valuable piece of land to which she held title. While making a search of the records the attorneys came upon a description in one of the deeds that appeared to require verification. Lincoln went to the place with the necessary instruments and surveyed the ground himself. He found a material discrepancy. It was evident that Charles Matheney, a former grantor, selling the tract at a certain price per acre, had, by an error in the description, conveyed more land than had been paid for. These facts were laid before the widow, with a carefully made calculation showing how much, in the opinion of her attorneys, was due to Matheney's estate by reason of this erroneous conveyance. Their suggestion, however, that she make this restitution met with strenuous objection. Only after they had declined to continue as her representatives, unless she did so, was the required sum reluctantly placed in the firm's hands. The senior member himself divided it into a number of smaller sums, which he distributed, in due form, among the Matheney heirs.[13]

All refractory litigants were of course not amenable to reason. At times when persuasion or threats failed, strategy came into play. One client who insisted on bringing an unseemly action was circumvented by Lincoln in an amusing manner. Here is the story as it was told by Gibson W. Harris, a clerk at the time in that now famous law-office: —

"A crack-brained attorney who lived in Springfield, supported mainly, as I understood, by the other lawyers of the place, became indebted, in the sum of two dollars and fifty cents, to a wealthy citizen of the county, a recent comer. The creditor failing, after repeated efforts, to collect the amount due him, came to Mr. Lincoln and asked him to bring suit. Mr. Lincoln explained the man's condition and circumstances, and advised his client to let the matter rest; but the creditor's temper was up, and he insisted on having suit brought. Again Mr. Lincoln urged him to let the matter drop, adding, 'You can make nothing out of him, and it will cost you a good deal more than the debt to bring suit.' The creditor was still determined to have his way, and threatened to seek some other attorney who would be more willing to take charge of the matter than Mr. Lincoln appeared to be. Mr. Lincoln then said, 'Well, if you are determined that suit shall be brought, I will bring it; but my charge will be ten dollars.' The money was paid him, and peremptory orders were given that the suit be brought that day. After the client's departure, Mr. Lincoln went out of the office, returning in about an hour with an amused look on his face. I asked what pleased him, and he replied, 'I brought suit against Blank, and then hunted him up, told him what I had done, handed him half of the ten dollars, and we went over to the squire's office. He confessed judgment and paid the bill.' Mr. Lincoln added that he did n't see any other way to make things satisfactory for his client as well as the rest of the parties."[14]

This aptitude for disposing of quarrels so as to satisfy all concerned became generally recognized at the bar. Lincoln's fellow attorneys, conceding the disinterested skill with which he harmonized the discordant elements of a matter in controversy, at times coöperated with him by persuading their clients to accept his good offices. A few of these colleagues even went further. When consulted concerning certain cases in which Lincoln had been retained on the other side, they emulated his self-denial, and before accepting any fees advised that the settlement of these affairs be left wholly in his hands.

A typical instance was related, several years ago, by Henry Rice, a prominent resident of New York. During his younger days, while in business at Jacksonville, Illinois, he was requested by some Cincinnati merchants to recommend a reputable lawyer, who might look after their interests in the matter of a Decatur house that had made what they regarded as a fraudulent failure. Mr. Rice promptly suggested Abraham Lincoln, and meeting a committee of the creditors by appointment in Springfield, he guided them to that attorney's office. The ensuing interview was brief. Hardly had the spokesman entered upon the purpose of their visit, when Lincoln, raising his long arm high in the air, interrupted him with the words: —

"Stop! Gentlemen, I am sorry to say that I cannot take your claims. Just before you entered I received a message engaging me to act for the Decatur concern."

When asked whom the creditors had better retain, he suggested one of his most active political opponents — that able lawyer and party leader, John A. McClernand. To him the committee went. He heard them attentively, and then said: —

"If that man has planned to go through bankruptcy without paying you any part of his debts, he has chosen the poorest lawyer in Illinois to do the job. I advise you to return to Mr. Lincoln, and state your whole case as frankly as you have stated it to me. He is just the man to settle this for you. Go back and put the whole matter into his hands."

They did so. Mr. Lincoln, after hearing their statement, assured them that no injustice would be done. More than that, he agreed to confer with his client and arrange an equitable settlement. In an uncommonly short time the creditors, to their joy, received seventy-five cents on the dollar; the heavy expense, as well as the delays usually involved in such failures, were averted, and the debtor was enabled to resume business, with a name free from the stain of bankruptcy.[15]

These compromises between opposing interests constituted — it is perhaps unnecessary to say — only a part of Lincoln's legal activities. Accepting as a matter of course many cases that could not be arbitrated or settled offhand, he conducted them, with varying fortunes, through their several stages in the courts. But now and then came proposals for litigation which, according to his code, admitted of neither suit nor compromise. They belonged to that class of causes once wittily characterized by

Erskine, in the famous opinion, — "This action will not lie, unless the witnesses do." Such matters received short shrift at Lincoln's hands. When a prospective client was in the wrong he bluntly told him so. Nor did he hesitate to treat old patrons and friends, painful as this must at times have been, with the same embarrassing frankness. "You have no case; better settle," was heard in his office, over and over again. Stripping a discreditable story of its sophistries, he pointed out the sharp practice or worse in which those who concerned themselves with the affair would inevitably become involved, refused the proffered retainer, and urged the litigant to withdraw from an untenable position.[16] This was Lincoln's course toward one of his early neighbors, Henry McHenry, when that person desired him to bring an action of doubtful propriety. Declining to touch the case on the ground that his client was not strictly in the right, our attorney said: "You can give the other party a great deal of trouble and perhaps beat him, but you had better let the suit alone."[17]

So, too, Lincoln was careful — as he himself expressed it — not to "stir up litigation,"[18] or to do anything that might encourage the vexatious and costly suits which often arise over the administration of estates.

"Who was your guardian?" he asked a young man after weighing his inconsistent complaint that a part of the property bequeathed to him had been wrongfully withheld.

"Enoch Kingsbury," was the answer.

"I know Mr. Kingsbury," said Lincoln, "and he is not the man to have cheated you out of a cent; I can't take the case, and I advise you to drop the subject."[19]

In the same conscientious spirit more important opportunities for employment, holding forth prospects of generous fees, were turned away from Lincoln's door. His associates at the bar have recorded a few instances. One of these is related by Judge Samuel C. Parks. He recalls that in a matter entitled "Harris and Jones *versus* Buckles," the plaintiffs, having employed him and Ward Hill Lamon as their attorneys, desired them to secure Lincoln's services also. His reply was characteristic: "Tell Harris it's no use to waste money on me in that case; he'll get beat."[20]

Among the retainers so declined, most notable, perhaps, was that of Governor Joel A. Matteson, who, after his retirement from office, stood accused of having defrauded the State of Illinois by reissuing redeemed canal scrip and applying the proceeds to his own use. The alleged thefts amounted, in the end, with interest, to about a quarter of a million dollars. Matteson's fortune, as well as his good repute, and perhaps his very liberty, were at stake. He sought to gather around him a formidable array of counsel. Having engaged the eminent lawyers Benjamin S. Edwards and Major John T. Stuart for his defense, he tried likewise to retain Abraham Lincoln and another of that gentleman's former partners, Judge Stephen T. Logan. Both these last-mentioned attorneys, however, after carefully considering the facts submitted to them, reached the conclusion that the distinguished defendant was guilty. They conceded his right to such protection as one reputable advocate might properly afford him, but neither of them was willing to join a powerful combination of legal experts that should have for its object the culprit's escape from punishment. So, without conferring on the subject, indeed without each other's knowledge, they respectively declined to be concerned in the matter. Their course, it should be added, was justified before many months had elapsed by Matteson's virtual confession and by a heavy judgment rendered against him in the Circuit Court.[21]

But Lincoln's refusals to engage his services in actions of which he did not approve went still further. A cause to enlist his interest had to be intrinsically right as well as technically so. He ran no subtlety shop. What has been termed "law honesty" fell far short, now and then, in his opinion, of being genuine honesty. Indeed, it may be doubted whether any leading practitioner of the Illinois bar felt more keenly than he, at times, that "strictest law is oft the highest wrong."

How far, on such occasions, the man in him got the better of the lawyer was illustrated by the closing words of an interview overheard one morning in his office. Mr. Lincoln, seated at the baize-covered table near the center of the room, had been listening attentively, for some time, to a person who addressed him earnestly and in a low tone of voice. Suddenly the attorney interrupted the speaker with these words that rang out through the place: —

"Yes, we can doubtless gain your case for you. We can set a whole neighborhood at loggerheads. We can distress a widowed mother and her six fatherless children, and thereby get for you six hundred dollars to which you seem to have a legal claim; but which rightfully belongs, it appears to me, as much to the woman and her children as it does to you. You must remember that some things legally right are not morally right. We shall not take your case, but will give you a little advice for which we will charge you nothing. You seem to be a sprightly, energetic man; we would advise you to try your hand at making six hundred dollars in some other way."[22]

On another occasion, as a student in the office recalls, Lincoln sat gazing at the ceiling while a client unfolded the shabby details of a proposed suit. When the narrative was finished, the listener swung around in his chair and exclaimed: —

"Well, you have a pretty good case in technical law, but a pretty bad one in equity and justice. You'll have to get some other fellow to win this case for you. I could n't do it. All the time while standing talking to that jury, I'd be thinking, 'Lincoln, you're a liar'; and I believe I should forget myself and say it out loud."[23]

This last avowal discloses a striking justification — if justification is needed — of "Honest Abe's" course in rejecting clients whom he believed to be in the wrong. Whatever claims they may, on general principles, have had to his services were probably not pressed after such an acknowledgment. Even our legal casuists, piling high the reasons why it is an attorney's duty to appear on either side of a cause, right or wrong, — and some of the arguments are convincing enough, — would doubtless hesitate to enforce their rule in the case of a lawyer who thus frankly admits that, when his pleadings happen to be at variance with his conscience, he finds himself unable to control his powers. The greater those powers, the greater would seem the danger to the side that had engaged them, if they should balk. For Pegasus unwillingly in the traces might well be expected to make more trouble than a whole team of refractory plough-horses. And Lincoln, keenly alive to his peculiar limitations, realized that unless he himself believed in the justice of a contention, his advocacy thereof — half-hearted, perhaps fatally ingenuous — would do the case more harm than good.

In short, he was too "perversely honest," as one old acquaintance phrased it, to be of any use to a client who was not honest. The man's whole make-up harbored no trace of that mercenary, free-lance spirit which can fight for hire under one banner, as valiantly as under another — in a base cause as well as in a righteous one. Nor did pride of intellect, exulting in uncommon forensic dexterity, betray him into that habit of mind which derives its keenest gratification from making "the worse appear the better reason." And all his skill would have failed him here had he tried to be otherwise. For if there was one quality more than another that Abraham Lincoln lacked, it must have been the kind of versatility of which Cardinal Duperron boasted, when he said, in response to a compliment by King Henry III, on the convincing eloquence with which the prelate had proved the existence of the Deity: "Sire, I can now turn about, if it pleases Your Majesty, and prove to you, with arguments equally irrefutable, that there is no God."

Lincoln's intellect was of a wholly different cast. It had been devoted to the truth, with single-minded fealty, from boyhood. At a time when children's thoughts usually run on play, his had begun to puzzle out the problems of life. Nothing but the facts would content him. And whether he acquired them by observation, dug them out of books, or picked them up from chance conversations, there was no rest until they had been brought well within the circle of his comprehension. Referring, at a maturer period, to this trait, he said: —

"Among my earliest recollections I remember how, when a mere child, I used to get irritated when anybody talked to me in a way I could not understand. I don't think I ever got angry at anything else in my life. But that always disturbed my temper, and has ever since. I can remember going to my little bedroom, after hearing the neighbors talk of an evening with my father, and spending no small part of the night walking up and down, and trying to make out what was the exact meaning of some of their, to me, dark sayings. I could not sleep, though I often tried to, when I got on such a hunt after an idea, until I caught it; and when I thought I had got it, I was not satisfied until I had repeated it over and over, — until I had put it in language plain enough, as I thought, for any boy I knew to comprehend. This was a kind of passion with me, and it has stuck by me; for I am never easy now, when I am handling a thought, till I have bounded it North, and bounded it South, and bounded it East, and bounded it West."[24]

This eagerness to see every side of a subject made trouble, at times, for the juvenile inquirer. His Cousin Dennis has illustrated this, in a characteristic little thumb-nail sketch. Chatting about those early days, in his old age, Mr. Hanks said: —

"Sometimes a preacher, 'r a circuit-ridin' jedge, 'r lyyer, 'r a stump-speakin' polytician, 'r a school-teacher 'd come along. When one o' them rode up, Tom'd go out an' say, — "Light, stranger,' like it was polite to do. Then Abe'd come lopin' out on his long legs, throw one over the top rail and begin firin' questions. Tom'd tell him to quit, but it did n't do no good, so Tom'd have to bang him on the side o' his head with his hat. Abe'd go off a spell an' fire sticks at the snow-birds, an' whistle like he did n't keer. 'Pap thinks it ain't polite to ask folks so many questions,' he'd say. 'I reckon I was n't born to be polite, Denny. Thar's so darned many things I want to know. An' how else am I goin' to git to know 'em?'"[25]

The habit of asking questions remained with Lincoln to the end of the chapter. Frankly declaring himself ignorant concerning many things, on many occasions, he laid his face low, as the Persians say, at the threshold of truth. Indeed, no forceful character in recent history was so free from pride of mentality, so willing to admit that he did not understand some important matter, or that, perchance, a trivial one had escaped his knowledge. Taking stock of himself, during middle-life, for an inquiring biographer, he summed up his intellectual attainments in two words, — "education defective." To a young friend who, at a still later period, pointed out an error of speech, he called himself "deplorably ignorant." When an opponent taunted him with having "carefully written" an address, he replied before his next audience: "I admit that it was. I am not a master of language. I have not a fine education."

And when he had composed a certain notable letter, he laid it before a learned neighbor, with the words: "I think it is all right, but grammar, you know, is not my stronghold; and as several persons will probably read that little thing, I wish you would look it over carefully, and see if it needs doctoring anywhere."

Perhaps we should add that the missive did need a touch of "doctoring," and that the writer submitted to the treatment with good grace. Nor was he less ingenuous on other occasions. One day in court a lawyer, quoting a Latin maxim, bowed to him and said: "That is so, is it not, Mr. Lincoln?"

To which he answered: "If that's Latin, you had better call another witness."

So, during a visit by a distinguished company, when one gentleman turned to another and repeated a quotation from the ancient classics, Lincoln leaned forward in his chair, looked inquiringly at them, and remarked, with a smile: "Which, I suppose you are both aware, *I* do not understand."

Equally free from false pretense concerning his work at the bar, he would turn the compliment of an admirer with some such phrase as, "Oh, I am only a mast-fed lawyer."

The same spirit of candid self-appraisal was strikingly manifested during the McCormick reaper suit, in which Lincoln, with other lawyers, had been retained for the defense. When the cause came to trial, he found himself elbowed, so to say, out of a leading part by Edwin M. Stanton. Yet while listening to the argument of the colleague who had thus displaced him, he forgot his disappointment, keen though it was, in his admiration of the great advocate's masterly plea. Indeed, Lincoln is said to have been so moved that he hardly repressed his enthusiasm in open court; and upon the conclusion of the address, he remarked to one of the clients who had retained him: "Emerson, it would have been a great mistake if I had spoken in this case. I did not fully understand it." [26]

These confessions, under all their varying circumstances, showed how honest the man could be. The simple words, "I do not know," are among the hardest to pronounce in the language. Still he must use them freely who would find the key to Pilate's age-worn riddle, and behold the fair vision of Truth, at last, face to face. So believed this conscientious lawyer, who realized, however, that here his duty began rather than ended. For it was not until all the questions in a legal tangle had been answered and all the perplexities straightened out, not until he had gone at the very heart of a problem, — to use his own expression, — "like a dog at a root," and laid the facts bare to the last fiber, that Lincoln's intellectual probity arose to its full stature. Then all concessions were at an end. His logical mind, a marvel of close and clear thinking, progressed through a subject, step for step, from premise to conclusion, with unerring precision. There was no retreat, no dodging, no attempt to evade or color the inevitable result. If that result stood in the way of his desires, so much the worse for those desires. He sought the truth for the truth's sake. Having followed a chain of reasoning from start to finish, with an utter disregard of personal interests, — his own, no less than those of others, — he was as loyal to the outcome as he had been to the mental process whereby it had been reached. Lincoln never apparently resorted to the meanest of pettifogging — that of a man at the bar of his own conscience. As he could not tolerate a fallacious premise, he could not argue to a false conclusion. Utterly unable to deceive himself, he was incapable of deceiving others; and once an essential truth had entered into his consciousness, there was not room enough in that whole gigantic frame, if he spoke at all, for its concealment.

How marked were these characteristics may be inferred from the fact that they evoked comment among lawyers and judges who are credited themselves with a high standard of professional honor. David Davis, who presided for nearly fourteen years over the Eighth Judicial Circuit of Illinois, in which Lincoln tried most of his cases, said concerning this upright advocate: "The framework of his mental and moral being was honesty, and a wrong cause was poorly defended by him. The ability, which some eminent lawyers possess, of explaining away the bad points of a cause by ingenious sophistry, was denied him. In order to bring into full activity his great powers, it was necessary that he should be convinced of the right and justice of the matter which he advocated." [27]

Similar comments have been made by the Judges of the Illinois Supreme Court, in which, for a period of twenty years, he had an unusual number of cases. What these experienced jurists thought concerning this aspect of Lincoln's nature was summed up, so to say, by Judge Caton, in the single sentence: "He seemed entirely ignorant of the art of deception or of dissimulation." [28]

To which should be added the observations made by Judge Thomas Drummond, from the bench of the United States Circuit Court, at Chicago: "Such was the transparent candor and integrity of his nature that he could not well or strongly argue a side or a cause that he thought wrong. Of course he felt it his duty to say what could be said, and to leave the decision to others; but there could be seen in such cases the inward struggle of his own mind." [29]

Lincoln's commendable weakness in this respect was equally patent to his associates at the bar. Few of them, if any, knew him so well as Leonard Swett, who touches on his friend's inability to be otherwise than intellectually honest, in these words: "If his own mind failed to be satisfied, he had little power to satisfy anybody else. He never made a sophistical argument in his life, and never could make one. I think he was of less real aid in trying a thoroughly bad case than any man I was ever associated with. If he could not grasp the whole case and believe in it, he was never inclined to touch it." [30]

In the same strain wrote Henry C. Whitney: "It was morally impossible for Lincoln to argue dishonestly. He could no more do it than he could steal. It was the same thing to him, in essence, to despoil a man of his property by larceny or by illogical or flagitious reasoning; and even to defeat a suitor by technicalities, or by merely arbitrary law, savored strongly of dishonesty to him. He tolerated it sometimes, but always with a grimace." [31]

A number of other fellow-attorneys have expressed similar opinions. To quote them all might lead to a veritable paroxysm of citation; and needlessly so, for enough has been said to show that in refusing unworthy cases Lincoln did simple justice by the rejected litigants, as well as by himself.

But it should not be inferred that he looked with misgivings on every retainer which was offered to him, or that he peered unduly about in search of reasons for turning patrons away. On the contrary, Lincoln welcomed the general run of business as any lawyer might. Like most men who are free from guile, he usually suspected none in others.

He certainly did not guard himself against deception, as did that fine, old-fashioned practitioner of the Colonial school, George Wythe, who, when there seemed reason to mistrust a client's initial statement, required it to be made under oath. On circuit, moreover, Lincoln generally found but scant opportunity for probing into his suits before they came to trial. Acting as counsel for local attorneys, he had to rely upon them for the proper preparation of their cases; and so it happened that he found himself at times in court supporting litigants whose contentions the evidence wholly failed to sustain.

When a mishap of this nature occurred, trouble ensued. The recently alert advocate — all enthusiasm, courage, and skill — lapsed into a dispirited pleader whose movements seemed almost mechanical. In fact, if we may credit the traditions of the circuit, his thoughts were engaged, from that moment, not on how to win the case, but on how to get out of it. Particularly was this so when, taken by surprise in the midst of a criminal trial, he became convinced — as happened on several occasions — of his client's guilt.

An instance in point has been related by Judge Parks, a prominent member, at the time, of the Illinois bar. He writes: "A man was indicted for larceny. Lincoln, Young, and myself defended him. Lincoln was satisfied by the evidence that he was guilty and ought to be convicted. He called Young and myself aside, and said, 'If you can say anything for the man, do it, — I can't. If I attempt, the jury will see that I think he is guilty, and convict him, of course.' The case was submitted by us to the jury without a word. The jury failed to agree, and before the next term the man died. Lincoln's honesty undoubtedly saved him from the penitentiary." [32]

A similar difficulty arose in the Patterson murder trial, a case of some celebrity that held the center of the judicial stage for some days in Champaign County. The prosecution was conducted by District Attorney Lamon; the defense, by Leonard Swett and his friend Abraham Lincoln. As the evidence against the prisoner developed, his counsel realized that they were defending a guilty man. The discovery appears to have unnerved Lincoln who, as the District Attorney expressed it, "felt himself morally paralyzed." Acknowledging this condition to his associate, he said: "Swett, the man is guilty. You defend him, — I can't."

There is reason to think that Lincoln urged his colleague privately before Judge Davis, the presiding magistrate, to join him in arranging for a plea of manslaughter, with the understanding that their client should receive the minimum sentence. This proposition Swett apparently brushed aside. He conducted the defense to its formal conclusion, made his argument to the jury, and — again quoting Lamon — "saved the guilty man from justice." A considerable fee was paid for that signal service, but Lincoln is said to have declined any share of the money.[33]

In civil actions, he disposed even more summarily of clients who had deceived him, or who persisted in litigating over matters that were found to lack merit. Recalling such instances, Mr. Herndon says: "His retention by a man to defend a lawsuit did not prevent him from throwing it up in its most critical stage if he believed he was espousing an unjust cause. This extreme conscientiousness and disregard of the alleged sacredness of the professional cloak robbed him of much so-called success at the bar. He once wrote to one of our clients, 'I do not think there is the least use of doing anything more with your lawsuit. I not only do not think you are sure to gain it, but I do think you are sure to lose it. Therefore the sooner it ends the better.'" [34]

Another anecdote of similar bearing is furnished by J. Henry Shaw, a lawyer in practice years ago at Beardstown, Illinois. This contributor writes: "Lincoln came into my office one day with the remark, 'I see you've been suing some of my clients, and I've come down to see about it.' He had reference to a suit I had brought to enforce the specific performance of a contract. I explained the case to him, and showed my proofs. He seemed surprised that I should deal so frankly with him, and said he would be as frank with me; that my client was justly entitled to a decree, and he should so represent it to the court; and that it was against his principles to contest a clear matter of right. So my client got a deed for a farm which, had another lawyer been in Mr. Lincoln's place, would have been consumed by the costs of litigation for years, with the result probably the same in the end." [35]

Still another civil suit was well under way before Lincoln discovered the defendant, whom he represented, to be in the wrong. This man, a live-stock breeder, had sold the plaintiff a number of sheep at a stipulated average price. When the animals were delivered, many of them, according to the purchaser's claim, proved to be so young that they did not fulfill the conditions of the contract, and he sued for damages. The evidence produced at the trial sustained the complaint. Several witnesses testified, moreover, that according to usage such of the animals as were under a certain age should be regarded as lambs, and of less value than full-grown sheep. No sooner had these facts been established than Mr. Lincoln changed his line of action. Ceasing to contest the case, he directed all his attention to the task of ascertaining exactly how many lambs had been delivered. This done, he briefly addressed the jury. They were obliged, he conceded, to bring in a verdict against his client; but he asked them to make sure of the exact damage sustained by the plaintiff, in order that both parties might have simple justice. And this was done.[36]

To these stories should be added the testimony of Judge Joseph Gillespie, a leading Illinois attorney: "Mr. Lincoln's love of justice and fair play was his predominating trait. I have often listened to him when I thought he would certainly state his case out of court. It was not in his nature to assume, or attempt to bolster up, a false position. He would abandon his case first. He did so in the case of Buckmaster for the use of Dedham *versus* Beems and Arthur, in our Supreme Court, in which I happened to be opposed to him. Another gentleman, less fastidious, took Mr. Lincoln's place and gained the case."[37]

But perhaps his most notable desertion of a client occurred once at Postville, before Circuit Judge Treat, in the midst of a Logan County trial. The suit of Hoblit against Farmer had come up on appeal from a decision given by some local justice of the peace. What the alleged circumstances were Lincoln did not know until he was retained, in the Circuit Court, to represent the plaintiff. That worthy went upon the witness stand to prove his claim. After testifying about the items of the account against Farmer, and after allowing all set-offs, he swore positively that the balance had not been paid. Yet when the defendant's attorney, Asahel Gridley, produced a receipt in full, given prior to the bringing of the action, the witness was obliged to admit that he had signed the paper. Whether or not it had been introduced at the original hearing is left in doubt, as the story goes; but there can be no question about the plaintiff's surprise. Taken off his guard, Hoblit turned to his counsel and exclaimed that he "supposed the cuss had lost it." Whereupon Lincoln arose, and left the court-room. Taking notice of his departure, Judge Treat sent the sheriff, Dr. John Deskins, in pursuit. When that officer found the missing lawyer, he was seated in the tavern across the court-house square, with his feet on the stove and his head among the clouds.

"Mr. Lincoln," said the sheriff, "the judge wants you."

"Oh, does he?" was the reply. "Well, you go back and tell the judge that I can't come. My hands are dirty and I came over to clean them."[38]

The message was duly delivered to the honorable court, and Lincoln's unprincipled client suffered a nonsuit.[39]

There is a pretty little sequel to this episode. Some time later, when Gridley discontinued practice for more lucrative pursuits, he manifested his confidence in Lincoln, as well as his esteem, by transferring his entire law business to him without compensation. This was somewhat after the manner in which Robert Carter Nicholas, a veteran member of the profession during a former generation, had turned over his clientage to Patrick Henry. But no such encounter appears to have taken place between the Virginians as has just been related concerning the Illinois men. Nor is it to be expected. That abandonment by Lincoln of a case in mid-career, so to say, without regard for the judge's wishes, is perhaps unique. It certainly is characteristic. There are instances of honorable counsel, who, finding themselves in the course of a trial grossly misled by their clients, have declined to serve them further, and have obtained leave from the court to withdraw. But if any other celebrated American pleader, at any time during his career, rushed from a courtroom in a passion of righteous indignation over such a deception, and refused to return upon the mandate of the presiding magistrate, that occurrence is not commonly known. Moreover, from a professional point of view, the propriety, generally speaking, of Lincoln's course in these matters has been gravely questioned. Some critics, conceding the misconduct of the clients whom he deserted, still appear to think that his treatment of them detracted somewhat from his character as a lawyer. And with reason, if an advocate's first duty, as has been repeatedly asserted, is fidelity to the cause in which his services are enlisted. Yet how far does that duty require him to go after he has lost confidence in the rectitude of his cause? Some barristers — and the number includes men of distinction — have frankly set no limits to their obligations. They hold that a lawyer, once he has accepted a client's retainer, is pledged to stand by him through thick and thin. The blacker the evidence develops against him, in a criminal action, or the less palpable become the merits of his case in a civil one, the more firmly they consider his counsel bound in honor to battle for a verdict. Should that verdict, if it is finally won, seem contrary to morality or justice, the fault, in their opinion, does not lie with the man to whose skill and eloquence it may be due. His attention, they believe, was properly fixed, to the exclusion of everything else, upon that part of the proceedings which had been committed to his care. If the same singleness of purpose, perhaps the same ability with which he discharged this function, had been exercised by the attorney on the other side, as well as by the judge and the jury, to say nothing of witnesses and lawmakers, the administration of justice would, according to their code, have been secure. It is as though they were priests in the temple of the blindfolded goddess, interceding for sinners no less persuasively than for saints; as though, serving every comer however unclean, they thought it no shame on their sacred office if they seized a chance, when the divinity should relax her vigilance, or the high-priest should nod, to jog the delicately poised balance in their suppliant's favor.

Such a theory of advocacy revolted Lincoln. Indeed, his whole career at the bar was a protest against the conception of a lawyer's duty that imposes upon him any fancied requirement to procure a judgment of which his conscience disapproves. He had little or no sympathy, therefore, with the loyalty-at-any-cost practitioners; and he would not join them, it goes without saying, on those slippery paths of sophistry, which wind too often through the ivory gates of falsehood. What criticism, if any, he made of their conduct is not definitely known. Yet we almost seem to hear him exclaim, as Carlyle did, "Can there be a more horrible object in existence than an eloquent man not speaking the truth?"

These reflections, be it said, apply all in all to some only of the counselors who stand by their colors, after they discover them to be tarnished; for many faithful members of the profession regard the advocate's mission in a different light. He is bound, they admit, to remain in a case after a trial has begun, especially if retained for the defense; and this, however distasteful or even reprehensible his client's side may prove to be. That client, according to their theory, must be represented, to the close of the action, by his legal adviser, or the whole judicial machinery, of which an attorney on each side is an essential part, breaks down. In this nicely adjusted mechanism, they claim, the functions of the advocate, and those of the judge as well as the jury, are exercised on widely different planes, so that under normal conditions their operations can never coalesce. Should counsel, therefore, in the midst of a trial, assume the judicial rôle, condemn his own cause before the hour of judgment, and deny his own client the protection which had impliedly been pledged, he would, in their eyes, commit a gross breach of professional propriety. Nay, more, his course would involve, they contend, a betrayal of both court and client, — a Quixotic freak, in which private and public interests would alike be sacrificed. So far, both classes of practitioners who will not abandon a cause, after they find it tainted, appear to move abreast; but at this point their ways part. While the one advocate leaves not a stone unturned, as the expression goes, to extricate his man — right or wrong — with a sweeping victory, the other, deeming himself under no obligation to strive for an obviously unjust verdict, remains to safeguard his client's legal rights, presents his case fairly on the evidence, and does in his behalf all that an honorable officer of the court may do, without lending himself to an evasion of the law or a perversion of justice.

This latter conception of what a lawyer owes at once to conscience and to society had doubtless impressed itself on Lincoln's good sense. For he tried hard enough, in several instances, to conduct forlorn hopes to their bitter conclusions. But here again the compelling honesty of the man's nature thwarted his efforts, until it would almost seem as if, by a singular paradox, he really evinced more loyalty when he deserted, than when he stood his ground to make a half-hearted fight.

Lincoln's ineptitude on the latter occasions vexed his colleagues not a little. They appear to have been embarrassed more by his halting coöperation than by an out-and-out withdrawal from a case. One of his local associates on the circuit, Henry C. Whitney, has related several unpleasant experiences of this nature; and from the warmth with which he writes, many years after the event, one may infer how acute must have been the narrator's irritation at the time. Perhaps one of these anecdotes, in Mr. Whitney's own language, will best illustrate the whole peculiar matter. He is telling about the trial of a man for a homicide committed at Sadorus, Illinois: —

"When the facts were brought out before the petit jury, it was very clearly developed that the indictment should have been for murder, instead of — what it was — for manslaughter, and Lincoln was evidently of that opinion. Mr. Lincoln, Leonard Swett, and myself were associated for the defense. The wife of the accused had wealthy and influential relations in Vermillion County, and no pains were spared to make a good defense. Swett and myself took the lawyer's view, and were anxious to acquit entirely. Lincoln sat in our counsels, but took little part in them. His opinion was fixed and could not be changed. He joined in the trial, but with no enthusiasm. His logically honest mind chilled his efforts.

"Lincoln was to make the last speech to the jury

on our side, and Swett the speech preceding. Swett was then, as he was long afterward, the most effective jury advocate in the State, except Lincoln. He occupied one evening on this occasion, and when he closed, I was full of faith that our client would be acquitted entirely. Lincoln followed on our side, the next morning, and while he made some good points, the honesty of his mental processes forced him into a line of argument and admission that was very damaging. We all felt that he had hurt our case.

"I recollect one incident that we regarded as especially atrocious. Swett had dwelt with deep pathos upon the condition of the family — there being several small children, and his wife then on the verge of confinement with another. Lincoln himself adverted to this, but only to disparage it as an argument, saying that the proper place for such appeals was to a legislature who framed laws, rather than to a jury who must decide upon evidence. Nor was this done on account of any dislike to Swett, for he was especially fond of Swett as an advocate and associate. In point of fact, our client was found guilty, and sent to the penitentiary for three years; and Lincoln, whose merciless logic drove him into the belief that the culprit was guilty of murder, had his humanity so wrought upon, that he induced the Governor to pardon him out after he had served one year." [40]

If Mr. Lincoln's course during that trial struck his fellow-practitioners as "atrocious," it might be interesting to know what epithet would have sufficed to express their feelings had they been concerned with him in his first matter before the Supreme Court of Illinois. Appearing on that occasion for the appellant, — according to Judge Treat, the commonly accepted authority for an extraordinary tale, — he said: "This is the first case I have ever had in this court, and I have therefore examined it with great care. As the court will perceive by looking at the abstract of the record, the only question in the case is one of authority. I have not been able to find any authority to sustain my side of the case, but I have found several cases directly in point, on the other side. I will now give these authorities to the court, and then submit the case." [41]

That speech is probably without parallel in the history of appeals from judicial decisions. An approach to the spirit which actuated it may be found in the career of William Pinkney, the renowned Maryland advocate. Having gained a verdict for a client from the Court of Chancery, he became convinced of its injustice when the claim was made, on appeal, that not all the parties in interest were before the court. The point impressed itself on his mind as well taken. He promptly so declared, and without any attempt at sustaining the decree, allowed it to be reversed.

Lawyers, whose fealty to the truth exercised such an overmastering influence upon their conduct, would have graced the bench. Yet neither of these illustrious men, it should be added, attained judicial honors; unless indeed we count Lincoln's irregular elevation to the judgment-seat by David Davis, who appointed him, from time to time, — without legal sanction, however, for so doing, — to preside over his court. The substitution appears to have been made for the convenience of all concerned, when the judge could not be present; and both sides are said, as a rule, to have consented gladly thereto.[42] Once a whole term for Champaign County was held, it is asserted, in this unauthorized way. But how successfully the pseudo-magistrate dispensed justice must, by reason of the meager details that have been preserved, be left largely to conjecture. Did Lincoln, some may ask, really possess the attributes of a great judge? The query will, perhaps, suggest itself to those who are fond of reconstructing history around events that failed to happen. If they take account of his faculty for seeing both sides of a question with crystal clearness, his mellow wisdom, his inflexible love of truth, and, above all, his militant sympathy with the right against the wrong, their fancy may well picture him, under altered circumstances, mounting to a place beside the leading jurists of Illinois. Breese, Caton, and their compeers, developing that admirable system of jurisprudence which distinguished the Prairie State, might, indeed, have profited by his collaboration.

CHAPTER III

PROFESSIONAL ETHICS

IF the judicial rather than the forensic temperament swayed Lincoln's conduct as a lawyer, it should be remembered that this was a drawback only when he found himself on the wrong side of a suit. When he stood on the right side, with time enough to exert all the faculties of his slow-moving mind, no advocate in the State was more skillful and effective. Indeed, those very qualities which impaired his usefulness for the winning of a bad cause made him especially strong in a good one. After he himself was convinced that his client ought to prevail, he rarely failed to imbue judge and jury with the same belief.[1] This should be attributed somewhat to Lincoln's reputation for avoiding unworthy cases. The commonly accepted idea that he would appear only in matters of which his conscience approved, gave him, from the very beginning of a trial, an advantage not to be despised. But what he did, or omitted to do, as the proceedings advanced, contributed still more, it may be needless to add, toward the gaining of a verdict. His methods make one wonder whether there may not be more than a stale gibe at the legal profession tucked away somewhere in the query of the lad who asked, — "Father, do lawyers tell the truth?" and the jesting answer, — "Yes, my son; lawyers will do anything to win a case." For Lincoln in court was truth in action. His simple adherence to facts made as vivid an impression on those who heard him as did his intellectual powers, which were, by the way, of no mean order. The man's interpretation of the law, his logic, his eloquence, his humor, his homely, common-sense view of things — all shone in the light of a never-failing candor. While he was trying a cause, strangers who happened to enter the court-room usually found themselves, after a few moments, — if contemporary accounts may be accepted, — on his side and wishing him success. Yet success, in the ordinary meaning of that term, did not, to all appearances, alone concern him. What engaged most of his attention, apparently, was how to present the affair in hand as it had actually happened, without regard to his client's interests. In fact, every step that he took, as the trial moved along, seemed intended, not so much to secure a victory as to sift out the truth and establish justice at any cost.

Reverting, unconsciously perhaps, to the time-honored though quite obsolete idea of a counselor's duties, he conducted himself more like the helpful friend or adviser of the court than like a modern advocate striving for a decision. As one of his most intimate colleagues, Leonard Swett, relates: "Where most lawyers would object he would say he 'reckoned' it would be fair to let this in, or that; and sometimes, when his adversary could not quite prove what Lincoln knew to be the truth, he 'reckoned' it would be fair to admit the truth to be so-and-so. When he did object to the court, and when he heard his objections answered, he would often say, 'Well, I reckon I must be wrong.'"[2]

This equable disposition extended in a marked degree to Lincoln's manner of conducting an examination. His own witnesses usually told their story in response to a few straightforward, kindly questions, and those who took the stand on the other side were treated by him with the same frank courtesy. He had a good-natured way of making these people feel at home amidst unaccustomed surroundings, while draining them adroitly of what they knew about the case on trial. It was so clearly his aim, moreover, to arrive at the facts, rather than to score winning points, that time after time hostile witnesses mellowed under the charm of his sincerity and, contrary to their original intentions, told the truth. Candor begets candor. The light which shines through an upright man's eyes often kindles a responsive gleam in the heart of a shuffler. And when, as in Lincoln's case, that upright man was a shrewd lawyer, controlling an unwilling witness with all the masterful tact of a seer to whom human nature must have read like an open book, we begin to understand how one usually self-restrained biographer — himself a member of the bar — came to believe the cross-examiner "endowed," at such moments, "with psychic qualities of extraordinary power."

Less occult gifts, however, suffice to explain some of these achievements. For here, as elsewhere in Lincoln's practice, notable results were reached by simple, open methods. How easily he extracted the facts, for instance, from one unfriendly witness has been told in a characteristic anecdote by the man himself. This was the Honorable James T. Hoblit, of Lincoln, Illinois. Recalling his discomfiture and the attorney who caused it, he once said: —

"I shall never forget my experience with him. I was subpœnaed in a case brought by one Paullin against my uncle, and I knew too much about the matter in dispute for my uncle's good. The case was not of vital importance, but it seemed very serious to me, for I was a mere boy at the time. Mr. Paullin had owned a bull which was continually raiding his neighbor's corn, and one day my uncle ordered his boys to drive the animal out of his fields, and not to use it too gently either. Well, the boys obeyed the orders only too literally, for one of them harpooned the bull with a pitchfork, injuring it permanently, and I saw enough of the occurrence to make me a dangerous witness. The result was that Paullin sued my uncle, the boys were indicted for malicious mischief, Mr. Lincoln was retained by the plaintiff, who was determined to make an example of somebody, and I was subpœnaed as a witness.

"My testimony was, of course, of the highest possible importance, because the plaintiff could n't make my cousins testify, and I had every reason to want to forget what I had seen, and though pretty frightened, I determined, when I took the stand, to say as little as possible. Well, as soon as I told Mr. Lincoln my full name he became very much interested, asking me if I was n't some relative of his old friend John Hoblit who kept the halfway house between Springfield and Bloomington; and when I answered that he was my grandfather, Mr. Lincoln grew very friendly, plying me with all sorts of questions about family matters; which put me completely at my ease, and before I knew what was happening, I had forgotten to be hostile and he had the whole story. After the trial he met me outside the court-room and stopped to tell me that he knew I had n't wanted to say anything against my people, but that though he sympathized with me, I had acted rightly and no one could criticize me for what I had done. The whole matter was afterward adjusted, but I never forgot his friendly and encouraging words at a time when I needed sympathy and consolation." [3]

Of course, all opposing witnesses were not so pliant. They failed frequently to give Lincoln the answers that he sought; yet his patience and courtesy lost nothing of their fine flavor, as long as the man on the stand appeared to be telling the truth. There were no efforts made to confuse him by artfully framed questions, or to entrap him into seeming contradictions. Above all, he was safe from brow-beating, because this level-headed advocate apparently never committed the fault of harassing an honest witness. Lincoln's spirit of fair play forbade any such behavior, even if the spirit of wisdom had not taught him, from the very beginning, what so many learned gentlemen at the bar fail, throughout their entire careers, to grasp, that the art of cross-examination rarely consists in examining crossly.

But there came a time, now and then, when this even-tempered giant, with his homely, magnetic smile, did become cross — how cross, only those who caught the direct impact of his anger fully realized. Let some scamp try to tell him a lie from the witness-chair, and the fellow's troubles began. He could hardly have brought his spurious wares to a less profitable market. For, slow as Lincoln generally was to doubt another's probity, so quick was he to detect false values when that probity fell under suspicion. And cunningly woven, indeed, must have been the web of perjury which his logical mind — once it set about the task — could not unravel. He had a disconcerting way of stripping unsound testimony, with one searching question after another, until the futile cheat lay exposed in all its nakedness. Then his contempt for the discredited witness knew no bounds. Kindness gave way to severity. Words that scorched came hot and fast. It was as if some sacred thing had been violated. And what happens after one arouses the fury of a patient man, received uncommonly vivid illustration.

He was once trying a railway case for the defense, when the plaintiff, testifying in his own behalf, flagrantly misstated certain facts. The perjurer's attorney, on addressing the jury, tried to excite prejudice against the defendant company by making the trite charge that on one side was "a flesh-and-blood man," with a soul such as the jurymen had, while on the other was a soulless corporation. To which Lincoln indignantly replied: "Counsel avers that his client has a soul. This is possible, of course, but from the way he has testified under oath in this case, to gain, or hoping to gain, a few paltry dollars, he would sell, nay, has already sold, his little soul very low. But our client is but a conventional name for thousands of widows and orphans whose husbands' and parents' hard earnings are represented by this defendant, and who possess souls which they would not swear away as the plaintiff has done for ten million times as much as is at stake here." [4]

It would be wrong to infer that Lincoln's scorn for untruthfulness on the stand was visited upon the heads of opposing witnesses only. His own witnesses, when they sulked under cross-examination or tried to mislead counsel on the other side, had a taste of his quality in this respect. He even went so far, at times, as to rebuke them in open court for their misbehavior.

An occurrence of this character — there are said to have been several — is related by a colleague of Lincoln, Anthony Thornton, who says: "On one occasion he and I were associate counsel in an important lawsuit, when he exhibited his love of right and fairness in a remarkable manner. John T. Stuart, of Springfield, was counsel for the opposite party. It was a trial by jury. I examined the witnesses and Mr. Lincoln attended to the legal questions involved. I had examined an intelligent witness whose testimony was clear and satisfactory, and readily given. When the cross-examination commenced, this witness hesitated, manifested reluctance to answer, and was evasive in his replies. Mr. Lincoln arose and addressed the court, and publicly and severely reprimanded the witness. It was a dangerous experiment which might have brought discredit on our most important witness. His object, however, was accomplished, and the witness answered promptly all questions on cross-examination." [5]

This act is perhaps unique in the annals of the American bar. At all events, its fellow — if there ever was one — has not become known to general literature. Nor is this surprising, for there have not been many Lincolns, and reputable lawyers of today hardly see fit to follow such an example. A pleader who would do so — in fact, one who generally speaking would employ that remarkable man's methods with success — must not only have faith in the merits of his cases, but he must be efficiently honest, too, to the backbone. For Lincoln's plan of conduct rested upon the single virtue which, in the nature of things, is least easily simulated. Had he failed at crucial points to be straightforward, without shuffling or reserve, had the delicate image of truth, which he sought to rear, leaned ever so little out of true, to the north or the south or the east or the west, that entire fair fabric would, at the first jolt, inevitably have fallen to the ground in ruins before the very eyes of the jury.

How well this advocate stood the test in doubtless many trying situations, judges and lawyers have admiringly recounted. Justice Breese spoke, as it were, for the bench when he said that Lincoln practiced "none of the chicanery of the profession to which he was devoted, nor any of those mean, and little, and shuffling, and dishonorable arts all do not avoid." [6] The judgment of the bar was as comprehensively summed up in these words of Mr. Whitney: "Unlike the average lawyer, he would not do anything mean, or which savored of dishonesty or sharp practice, or which required absolute sophistry or chicanery in order to succeed."

Turning up a leaf in his own early experiences, that same associate says: "When I was new to the bar, I was trying to keep some evidence out, and was getting along very well with the court, when Lincoln sung out, 'I reckon it would be fair to let that in.' It sounded treasonable, but I had to get used to this eccentricity." [7]

Perhaps the clearest conception of Lincoln's fidelity to his own high standards of practice, even when beset by almost compelling temptations, is derived from Mr. Herndon's account of an incident which occurred during their partnership. To do the story justice it should be told, without abridgment, in the narrator's own language.

"Messrs. Stuart and Edwards," he relates, "once brought a suit against a client of ours, which involved the title to considerable property. At that time we had only two or three terms of court, and the docket was somewhat crowded. The plaintiff's attorneys were pressing us for a trial, and we were equally as anxious to ward it off. What we wanted were time and a continuance to the next term. We dared not make an affidavit for continuance, founded on facts, because no such pertinent and material facts as the law contemplated existed. Our case for the time seemed hopeless. One morning, however, I accidentally overheard a remark from

Stuart indicating his fear lest a certain fact should happen to come into our possession. I felt some relief, and at once drew up a fictitious plea, averring as best I could the substance of the doubts I knew existed in Stuart's mind. The plea was as skillfully drawn as I knew how, and was framed as if we had the evidence to sustain it. The whole thing was a sham, but so constructed as to work the desired continuance, because I knew that Stuart and Edwards believed the facts were as I pleaded them. This was done in the absence and without the knowledge of Lincoln. The plea could not be demurred to, and the opposing counsel dared not take the issue on it. It perplexed them sorely.

"At length, before further steps were taken, Lincoln came into court. He looked carefully over all the papers in the case, as was his custom, and seeing my ingenious subterfuge, asked, 'Is this seventh plea a good one?' Proud of the exhibition of my skill, I answered that it was. 'But,' he inquired incredulously, 'is it founded on fact?' I was obliged to respond in the negative, at the same time following up my answer with an explanation of what I had overheard Stuart intimate, and of how these alleged facts could be called facts if a certain construction were put upon them. I insisted that our position was justifiable, and that our client must have time or be ruined. I could see at once it failed to strike Lincoln as just right. He scratched his head thoughtfully and asked, 'Had n't we better withdraw that plea? You know it's a sham, and a sham is very often but another name for a lie. Don't let it go on record. The cursed thing may come staring us in the face long after this suit has been forgotten.' The plea was withdrawn. By some agency — not our own — the case was continued and our client's interests were saved."

To which Mr. Herndon adds the significant comment: "I venture the assertion that he was the only member of the bar in Springfield who would have taken such a conscientious view of the matter." [8]

Apparently Lincoln differed from his brother lawyers in being equipped with a vizualizing sense of what has well been called "the moment after." Taking a firm stand, moreover, on the old moral dictum that nothing can need a lie, he avoided the quirks and quillets which have so often brought reproach upon the administration of the law. For Cicero's theory of a pleader's occasional duty "to maintain the plausible, though it may not be the truth," evidently found no favor in his eyes. Nor did he look more kindly upon false pleas to impede justice when they were made by his friends and colleagues. Some of them, hard-pressed for a valid defense, did so in the Chase case — an action brought before Lincoln as deputy judge, during one of those irregular sittings on the Circuit Court bench that he owed, as we have seen, to Davis's appointment. This particular trial, if such it may be called, is the only instance among his judicial experiences of which a detailed report has come down to us. The suit was instituted to collect a promissory note given by some citizens of Champaign County to one Chase, with the understanding that he would establish a newspaper. Failing to keep his agreement he had, nevertheless, transferred the note before maturity to an innocent holder, who now sued for the money. There was no good defense, yet several young lawyers had been retained by the makers of the note to do what they could toward warding off a decision. Whenever the plaintiff pressed for judgment, this whole array of budding legal talent ranged itself before the bench and, by resorting to every conceivable shift, succeeded in securing postponement after postponement. Seemingly the old legal maxim, "justice delayed is justice denied," would soon have one more literal illustration. So matters stood on the last day of the term. Court was about to close, and the plaintiff again demanded judgment, to which counsel for the defendants, as before, strenuously objected. Finally Lincoln announced that he would return at candlelight to dispose of that case. He came accordingly, took his seat at the clerk's desk, and called for the papers. Finding no proper defense on file, he began to write an order, when one of the young attorneys, his friend and associate in several matters, interposed saying that a demurrer had been entered. But Lincoln continued to write, merely changing the form and reading aloud, as he wrote: —

L. D. Chaddon
vs.
J. D. Beasley *et al.* } April term, 1856. *In Assumpsit.*

Ordered by the Court: Plea in abatement by B. Z. Greene, a defendant not served, filed Saturday,

April 24, (?) 1856, at 11 o'clock A.M., be stricken from the files by order of Court. Demurrer to declaration, if ever there was one, overruled. Defendants, who are served now, at 8 o'clock P.M. of the last day of the term, ask to plead to the merits, which is denied by the Court, on the ground that the offer comes too late, and therefore, as by *nil dicit*, judgment is rendered for plaintiff. Clerk assess damages."

"How can we get this up to the Supreme Court?" inquired the somewhat dazed young man who had spoken last.

In Lincoln's ready reply may be discerned the pent-up scorn of a whole session. "You all have been so smart about this case," said he, "that you can find out for yourselves how to carry it up." And court stood adjourned.[9]

A more serious affair was that of the youthful practitioner who disgraced himself at the Bloomington bar. While serving as a law student, he had improved the opportunity to make himself acquainted with certain important facts concerning a suit in which his preceptor represented the plaintiff. Disclosing this information some time thereafter to the defendant, whose counsel he became, the young man used it in behalf of the one client against the other. Proceedings for his disbarment were about to ensue when the offender threw himself upon the clemency of the court, with a promise to leave the country and sin no more. This impressed Judge Davis as the simplest way out of an unpleasant duty. He stipulated, however, that the culprit, before departing, should submit to a rebuke in open court, and selected Lincoln to administer the lesson.

There must have been more of sorrow than of anger in the little speech whereby this delicate office was discharged. The speaker, it is said, sketched in a few well-chosen words an attorney's obligations to his client, and pointed out how the man at the bar, by betraying those who trusted him, had forfeited public confidence. But most impressive of all was the sympathy of this highly esteemed lawyer for the young colleague in disgrace. "We bid you God-speed," he concluded, with a clasp of the hand, "in a work that will make you a better man." And a better man the other did indeed become. Seeking out a new field beyond the borders of the State, he eventually made a place for himself there as an honored member of the profession.[10]

To infer from either of these two episodes that Lincoln was disposed to lord it over his less experienced fellow barristers would be far from the fact. How fairly he treated them many a timid beginner at the bar, facing him as opposing counsel, had reason to remember. Not only did his unaffected kindness set the young men at their ease and encourage their efforts, but his frank concessions met them, as we have seen, more than halfway in establishing points which otherwise might have been hard to make. Nor were these generous little acts confined to our attorney's dealings with juniors. Any of the lawyers pitted against him might have had similar experiences. They certainly were favored, at times, beyond their legal rights, and that, too, on occasions remote from the publicity of the court-room. A typical instance may be seen in the letter from Lincoln to an associate that has recently come to light. It read, in part: "Herewith I return the notices which I will thank you to serve and return as before requested. This notice is not required by *law;* and I am giving it merely because I think *fairness* requires it." [11]

Concerning the writer's deportment in court, the judge before whom he tried probably more causes than before all other judges combined, tells us: "Mr. Lincoln was the fairest and most accommodating of practitioners, granting all favors which he could do consistently with his duty to his client, and rarely availing himself of an unwary oversight of his adversary." [12]

To what lengths he carried this equitable procedure evinced itself during the trial of a railroad suit, at which counsel on the other side were, so to say, caught napping. The case having gone in Lincoln's favor, a decision was about to be given for the amount claimed by his client, deducting a proved and allowed counter-claim, when the successful attorney became convinced that his opponents had not proved all the items justly due them as offsets. He promptly called attention to this omission. The judge, agreeing with him, noted an additional allowance against his client, and pronounced judgment accordingly.[13] Even-handed Justice herself could not have trimmed the balance truer. Here was "the square deal" incarnate. And its spirit, interesting to observe, animated Abraham Lincoln's work-a-day conduct, in this most trying of all professions, half a century or so before another distinguished American, holding an ideal aloft for the admiration of a nation, raised the expression itself to the dignity of a political watchword.

Lincoln's tendency to concede all that might reasonably be demanded of him during a trial manifested itself chiefly when he came to the closing argument. Here, neither the law nor the evidence could be noticed to suffer the slightest perversion at his hands. In fact, as has been frequently remarked, the statement with which he customarily began a summing-up covered the case for the other side more fully and more forcibly than did anything offered by his opponent. For this man's conscience ruled his intellect. In his make-up were happily blended that rare faculty which can see, with comprehending eyes, the reverse of a shield, and that still rarer courage which can expose the unfavorable aspect to view, without flinching. So every point scored against him was frankly acknowledged. Giving up advantage after advantage, — even volunteering admissions which seemed well-nigh fatal to his cause, — he moved steadily forward through the opening portion of such an argument, like a seasoned philosopher conducting some abstract inquiry. There was a savor, too, of passionless logic about what he said, that still more suggests the ancient scholar. Indeed, his whole bearing, at this stage, reminds one of the serene candor and the equally placid confidence in the ultimate triumph of truth, whereby Thomas Aquinas, greatest among schoolmen, has endeared himself, for all time, to those who love honest reasoning.

Nor was Lincoln's sincerity lost, in his day, upon those who were best qualified to appreciate it. The judges of the Illinois Supreme Court rated these habitual acts of fair play at their true value; and one of them, Justice Koerner, speaking for the whole bench, once said: "We always admired his extreme fairness in stating his adversary's case as well as his own." [14]

But how did the practice impress others? As if to answer this query, a well-known newspaper man has left some good copy, made many years after the event, concerning a certain trial that he reported at Chicago, in the autumn of 1857.

"It was a railroad case," says Colonel Hinton who tells the story; "and as I was reading law at the time, I soon became interested in the points involved. I remember thinking as I made my notes that the counsel opposing the corporation had a sure thing of it. But my attention was soon closely attracted to the counsel who rose to reply. 'The homeliest man I ever saw,' was the thought I had. When I heard a judge speak to him as 'Mr. Lincoln,' I recalled having heard the name before. A reporter present told me that he was from Springfield, and at once I remembered the Boston mention of him, and my interest became alert. The one impression I retain apart from the striking and quaint appearance he presented, was the fact that in his opening remarks he seemed to me to be 'giving his case away' by the remarkably lucid and vigorous manner in which by recapitulating the summary of the previous argument he presented the argument and law of his opponent. With the 'freshness' of a cocksure student, I at once concluded he was a beaten man." [15]

The colonel goes on to relate how "the homeliest man" was not "beaten," but that is another story. Sticking to our text, we find ourselves wondering what Lincoln's clients, generally speaking, thought of him, at about this stage in the proceedings. And it is not surprising to learn that sometimes they "trembled with apprehension" for the verdicts which his tactics seemingly endangered.[16] Nor was this feeling of alarm confined to clients. Some of his colleagues at the bar, when concerned with him in the trying of causes, could never quite accustom themselves to sit tranquilly by, while he bestowed important admissions on counsel for the other side. His liberality toward adverse evidence, that so disturbed Mr. Whitney, as the reader will remember, must have seemed even more reprehensible to such associates when it cropped out in the final argument.

A striking instance of this occurred during the famous Rock Island Bridge litigation which, despite certain differences in the telling, may have been the case that Colonel Hinton reported. The action was tried at Chicago, in September, 1857, before the United States Circuit Court, the honorable John McLean presiding. It had grown out of the clash between the boatmen on the Mississippi River and the railroad people who maintained a recently erected bridge across that stream, from Rock Island,

Illinois, to Davenport, Iowa. When the structure was planned, several years previous, efforts to place legal obstacles in the way of the project had been made without success. And upon the completion of the undertaking, this quarrel appears to have raged more fiercely than ever, until it had culminated in the destruction of a steamboat, the Effie Afton, which came to grief on piers of the bridge. Her owners had promptly brought suit for damages. The case was entitled, "Hurd *et al. vs.* The Railroad and Bridge Company," but these words meant more than met the eye. Behind the litigants themselves were arrayed powerful antagonists. The action might not incorrectly have been called, "River Traffic *versus* Railroads," or "The Mississippi Valley *versus* The Far West," or "St. Louis *versus* Chicago"; for it involved vital points, on which turned the future welfare of all these conflicting interests. Their struggle naturally focussed the attention of a vast region on the trial, and when proceedings began, men from all over the West crowded the Federal court-room.

The Chicago and Rock Island Railroad Company, through its attorney, Norman B. Judd, had retained Lincoln, among others, as counsel for the defense. There was some favorable comment on the skill with which he brought out the evidence; but when he discussed this evidence, in the closing argument, one of his associates, Joseph Knox, was not so pleased. In fact, that gentleman became alarmed to such a degree over what Lincoln conceded that when court adjourned for the day, before the speech was finished, he despaired of success. His indignation found vent in a talk with Judd.

"Lincoln has lost the case for us," he said. "The admissions he made in regard to the currents in the Mississippi at Rock Island and Moline will convince the court that a bridge at that point will always be a serious and constant detriment to navigation on the river."

"Wait until you hear the conclusion of his speech," replied Mr. Judd. "You will find his admission is a strong point instead of a weak one, and on it he will found a strong argument that will satisfy you."[17]

So indeed it proved to be. Before he closed, Lincoln did his own side ample justice, and demonstrated to a victorious conclusion that, currents or no currents, one man has as good a right to cross over a river as another has to sail up and down.[18]

Judd was not the only colleague who appraised this method at its full value. Leonard Swett, sharing with our straightforward advocate the leadership, as some thought, of the Eighth Circuit, and conducting many causes, now with him now against him, had learned, when on the opposing side, to be wary of gifts from Lincoln's hands.

"If his adversary," said Swett, "did n't understand him, he would wake up in a few moments, finding he had feared the Greeks too late, and wake up to find himself beaten. He was 'wise as a serpent' in the trial of a case, but I have got too many scars from his blows to certify that he was 'harmless as a dove.' When the whole thing is unraveled the adversary begins to see that what he was so blandly giving away, was simply what he could n't get and keep. By giving away six points and carrying the seventh, he carried his case; and, the whole case hanging on the seventh, he traded away everything which would give him the least aid in carrying that. Any one who took Lincoln for a simple-minded man would very soon wake up on his back, in a ditch." [19]

This rather cynical analysis of the situation is significant. It discloses the controlling factor upon which almost every case at bar turns as on a hinge. To discern with precision where that pivotal point lies may perhaps be deemed the prime requisite for a successful pleader. The converse is of almost equal importance. "Never plead what you need not," said Lincoln, "lest you oblige yourself to prove what you cannot." [20] And when, as in his practice, the vital issue is pressed home, only after all vulnerable positions have been squarely surrendered, the effect must seem at times well-nigh irresistible. Even courts cannot help yielding something to one who yields so much. And what he holds on to naturally prevails, with double force, by reason of what he has given away. Addressing himself, then, to hearers thus favorably disposed, Lincoln's final statement of his own side left little need for argument. In fact, they said of him, — as has from time to time been said of Lord Mansfield, Chief Justice Marshall, Daniel Webster, and less distinguished lawyers endowed with equal power, — his statement of a case was worth the argument of another man. For here again, the precision, clearness, and veracity of his mental operations came into play. He would disentangle a complicated matter step for step, until the truth, the whole truth, and nothing but the truth, stood revealed to all. It was as if each successive word were set in place, after the manner of Hugh Miller's master, the Cromarty mason, who "made conscience of every stone he laid."

Lincoln's conscience withal did double duty. His fealty to the cause of justice was not allowed to crowd out an ever-present sense of what he owed his client. In only rare instances and then, it is true, to that client's detriment, as we have seen, did these obligations clash. When they harmonized, the advocate did not spare himself. Nor did his theory concerning the essentials of a case betray him into omissions. Making an argument once before one of the higher courts, he gave an elaborate history of the law governing the matter in question. It was a masterly discourse, prepared with much care, but as his partner thought, wholly unnecessary. On their way home, Mr. Herndon, who tells the story, asked Mr. Lincoln why he "went so far back in the history of the law," adding a surmise that the court knew it all.

"That 's where you 're mistaken," was the instant reply. "I dared not trust the case on the presumption that the court knows everything. In fact, I argued it on the presumption that the court did n't know anything." [21]

There are, sooth to say, judicial decisions which almost seem to justify such precautions. And we find ourselves wondering whether the speaker knew that venerable anecdote of the counsel who, when interrupted by a wearied Supreme Court Justice with the remark, "You must give this court credit for knowing something," replied, "That's exactly the mistake I made in the court below."

Lincoln was himself, according to certain colleagues, occasionally stopped from the bench, but for quite a different reason. His mere statement of a matter sounded so clear and convincing that judges would, at times, interpose before he could go on to his argument, with some such words as: "If that is the case, Brother Lincoln, we will hear the other side." [22]

Nor was he less felicitous in putting a winning touch to the confidence of juries. When he faced them, at last, his lucid, even-handed methods produced their strongest effects. "If I can free this case," he was wont to say, "from technicalities and get it properly swung to the jury, I'll win it." [23] To that end, the essential facts were so cogently presented that they became almost self-evident. And the jurymen, following a train of thought which reduced simplicity to its lowest terms, easily fancied themselves in the speaker's place, as though they, not he, were making the statement. His anxiety to be right quickened their anxiety to do right. It was seemingly their trial, not his; and he conducted himself as if he were only assisting them to do their duty. Every one of the twelve "free and lawful men," even those who were least intelligent, appear to have felt this. Indeed, throughout what Lincoln said in addressing them, may be discerned a purpose, above all things, to impress the truth upon that most important of all the personages in a court, the dullest occupant of the jury-box. And how well he succeeded, on the whole, is a matter of common repute. Some contemporaries went to the extreme of saying — if we may credit one of them — that they could not "expect a favorable verdict in any case where Lincoln was opposing counsel, as his simple statements of the facts had more weight with the jury than those of the witnesses." [24]

Such a result did, it is true, come about in at least one instance — the trial of a tramp accused of murder. No one had seen the deed, but the evidence, which proved to be purely circumstantial, pointed strongly toward the prisoner. As the crime was of a brutal nature, feeling ran high against him. A friendless stranger, in the midst of popular clamor, his conviction appeared to be a foregone conclusion; and Lincoln, who was appointed to defend, seemingly made but little headway. He contented himself with eliciting from the witnesses full statements of what they saw or knew. Evading nothing, suppressing nothing, making no attempt to confuse those who testified or to present matters other than they were, he helped the prosecuting attorney to bring out all the facts. When his time came for addressing the jury, he called attention to the absence of direct evidence. Frankly reviewing all the circumstances, and weighing what seemed to prove the defendant's guilt with what made for his innocence, he concluded in about the following language: "I have looked this matter over fully, candidly; and while I concede that the testimony bears against my client, I am not sure that he is guilty. Are you?"

The prisoner was acquitted, and properly so, for some time thereafter the real criminal was brought to justice.

"How different would have been the conduct of many lawyers!" exclaimed the late Justice Brewer, of the United States Supreme Court, as he told his story. "Some would have striven to lead the judge into technical errors, with a view to an appeal to a higher court. Others would have become hoarse in denunciation of witnesses, decrying the lack of positive testimony and dwelling on the marvelous virtue of a reasonable doubt. The simple, straightforward way of Lincoln, backed by the confidence of the jury, won." [25]

That combination was hard to beat. Frequent repetitions of it gave Lincoln, in time, a reputation which seems almost unique. There have been advocates with more notable gifts of learning and eloquence, than he could command; but few among them, if any, moved through our courts with so large a measure of esteem. Yet it is going too far to say, as Judge Caton did, that "no one ever accused him of taking an underhanded or unfair advantage, in the whole course of his professional career." [26] True, he was a general favorite on the circuit. His fair, not to say generous, tactics made for good feeling; and to him, perhaps, least of all that eager company, could have been applied the ancient aspersion of the lawyer as a brawler for hire. Moreover, the "I am holier than thou" pose, whereby the honored counselor sometimes seeks to place less reputable opponents at a disadvantage, was wholly absent from his demeanor. No practitioners, however low or discredited, met here with discourtesy. Indeed, unless an adversary misbehaved in the particular case on trial, Lincoln never uttered a word of personal reproach which might unduly prejudice the jury. "Hence," we are told, "the meanest man at the bar always paid great deference and respect to him." [27] But he did not wholly escape the penalty of his successes. Some colleagues — and they should have known better — gave way to jealousy. Those who sit in the shadow of the prophet's mantle do not always see the prophet. A few opponents were even known to question Lincoln's sincerity. His candor was in their eyes a cloak for trickery, his unconventional manner a means of springing surprises on the unwary, and his apparent fair dealing a bait for luring unsuspecting adversaries to defeat. That an attorney smarting under a sense of failure might now and then have felt this way is not surprising. Fresh from the reading of Mr. Swett's graphic little sketch, which left the vanquished one floundering "on his back in a ditch," we can appreciate the full force of a statement made within recent years by Ezra Morton Prince, a Bloomington attorney. Referring to these scattering charges of unfairness, Mr. Prince, who attended many trials in the old circuit days, says: "The truth is that Mr. Lincoln had a genius for seeing the real point in a case at once, and aiming steadily at it from the beginning of a trial to the end. The issue in most cases lies in very narrow compass, and the really great lawyer disregards everything not directly tending to that issue.

The mediocre advocate is apt to miss the crucial point in his case and is easily diverted with minor matters, and when his eyes are opened he is usually angry and always surprised. Mr. Lincoln instinctively saw the kernel of every case at the outset, never lost sight of it, and never let it escape the jury. That was the only trick I ever saw him play." [28]

If anybody knew Abraham Lincoln to do a dishonorable act, during all these busy years in the courts, evidence to prove it has not been forthcoming. And there have been iconoclasts enough at work on his record to insure the telling of the story, had such an incident taken place.

One opponent did, it must be said, in the heat of a certain famous trial, accuse him of duplicity. The case was that of young Quinn Harrison, sometimes called "Peachy," arraigned for the murder of Greek Crafton, a student in Lincoln's office. While quarreling over some political question, they had come to blows, and Crafton, sustaining a knife-wound, had died within a few days. The young men, besides being close friends, had been connected by marriage. Their families were highly regarded. The prisoner's people especially enjoyed good repute, and that his grandfather was Dr. Peter Cartwright, the noted Methodist circuit-rider, added not a little to popular sympathy in his behalf. Notwithstanding all this, strenuous efforts were made to secure a conviction. The regular prosecuting attorney, Amzi McWilliams, was assisted by John M. Palmer and John A. McClernand. The defense had been entrusted to Abraham Lincoln, Stephen T. Logan, William H.

Herndon, and Shelby M. Cullom. Able as the defendant's counsel were, they achieved but slight progress, for a time, in overcoming the strong case made out against their client. It was only when Lincoln put Harrison's grandfather on the stand that the tide seemed to turn. Under his examiner's sympathetic guidance, the venerable preacher evinced how fondly he loved the unfortunate young man, and told the story of his own final interview with Crafton — a touching scene, in which the dying youth charged Cartwright to tell "Peachy" that he forgave him. This formed the basis of an appeal for mercy, in Lincoln's closing argument. So wrought up was the speaker by the pathos of the whole affair that he put aside his dislike of such attempts to play on the sympathies of juries, and made an eloquent plea for a verdict which should not set at naught the slain man's act of forgiveness. This speech made a profound impression. It had moved those who listened, in fact, to a degree which disquieted the prosecuting attorneys. One of them, as he arose to reply, was determined that the effect must be counteracted, at all hazards.

"Well, gentlemen," said he, "you have heard Mr. Lincoln — 'Honest Abe Lincoln,' they call him, I believe. And I suppose you think you have heard the honest truth — or at least that Mr. Lincoln honestly believes what he has told you to be the truth. I tell you, he believes no such thing. That frank, ingenuous face of his, as you are weak enough to suppose, those looks and tones of such unsophisticated simplicity, those appeals to your minds and consciences as sworn jurors, are all assumed for the occasion, gentlemen, — all a mask, gentlemen. You have been listening for the last hour to an actor, who knows well how to play the rôle of honest seeming, for effect."

At this moment, amidst breathless stillness, Lincoln stood up. He was deeply moved. It seemed as if every line of his gaunt features twitched with pain. Facing the speaker he said: "You have known me for years, and *you know* that not a word of that language can be truthfully applied to me."

The prosecutor changed color, hesitated a moment, and then, his better nature gaining the mastery, responded with much feeling: "Yes, Mr. Lincoln, I do know it, and I take it all back."

Many of those who were present could not resist the impulse to applaud, as the two men approached each other and shook hands. The trial then went on to its anticipated conclusion—Harrison's acquittal.[29]

On another occasion Lincoln took quite a different method of meeting an unfair attack. His opponent in a case, while selecting the jury, challenged a man because he was acquainted with counsel on the other side. Such an objection appears to have been regarded, in those days, as a reflection upon a lawyer's honor. So Judge Davis, who was presiding at the time, sharply overruled the challenge. Yet when Lincoln's turn came to examine the panel, he gravely followed the other's lead and asked them, one by one, whether they were acquainted with his adversary. After several had answered in the affirmative, however, the judge interrupted him.

"Now, Mr. Lincoln," he said severely, "you are wasting time. The mere fact that a juror knows your opponent does not disqualify him."

"No, Your Honor," retorted the advocate; "but I am afraid some of the gentlemen may *not* know him, which would place me at a disadvantage." [30]

In only one other notable instance, so far as the writer's knowledge goes, has Lincoln's integrity at the bar been directly questioned. Charges of fabricating certain important evidence to save his client grew out of a sensational episode in the camp-meeting murder trial. The case was that of William (Duffy) Armstrong indicted for the killing of James Preston Metzker, during a brawl near the Salt Creek camp-grounds, a few miles from Mason City, on the night of Saturday, August 29, 1857. "Duff" and "Pres," as the two young men were called, after drinking heavily with other wild companions of their kind, quarreled. In the fracas which ensued late that same night, Armstrong and a friend named James Henry Norris, who came to his assistance, had, it was alleged, inflicted injuries on Metzker that, several days later, proved to be fatal. A true bill for murder had been found against both men. And Norris, brought first to trial, at Havana in Mason County, had, upon a verdict of manslaughter, gone to prison for eight years. His comrade's case looked darker still. Public sentiment condemned "Duff" out of hand; and from all sides came demands that the law should be enforced against him in its utmost rigor. Then, as if to make matters worse, his father died. The widowed mother, struggling alone for her boy's life, managed to secure the services of Walker and Lacey, local lawyers at Havana; but they could hold forth only slender prospects of success. At this juncture news of the trouble reached Lincoln. Occupied though he was, by that time, over the affairs of an extensive practice and the demands of a growing political leadership, this tragedy claimed his attention. He appears to have been deeply moved by the father's death, as well as by the son's peril. For that father was the Jack Armstrong of Clary's Grove fame, with whom he had wrestled and chummed during the by-gone New Salem days; that mother was the Aunt Hannah, in whose kitchen he had many a time been made welcome; and her baby, which he had rocked to sleep while she cooked him a meal, was the prisoner who, now arrived at manhood's estate, lay in jail awaiting trial for a capital crime. In this, her hour of dire need, the poor woman had naturally turned to their old friend. Going to his office at Springfield, she told the whole distressing story, and received instant promise of help.

"Abe," said Hannah, as one of her sons relates, "I can't pay you much money or money of any account, but I can pay you a little."

To which he replied: "You do not need to pay me a cent, for my services are free to the family as long as I live." [31]

So it happened that when the trial, by a change of venue, opened the following spring before Justice James Harriott, at Beardstown, in the less prejudiced atmosphere of Cass County, Lincoln led for the defense. He came into court with faith in his client. According to "Duff's" version of the affair, Metzker had been the aggressor, and the fight, as far as these two were concerned, had been with their bare fists only. Yet how could the jury be convinced of this? Such evidence, indeed, as was presented against Armstrong at the outset did not appear to be very damaging; but when the prosecution called its principal witness, Charles Allen, a painter from Petersburg, matters became serious. He testified that he saw the defendant strike Metzker on the head with a slung-shot. Under cross-examination, Allen averred that the assault occurred at about eleven o'clock in the night. When asked to explain how, despite the lateness of the hour, he could so distinctly have seen what took place, the witness stated that there was a bright moon, nearly full, and "about in the same place that the sun would be at ten o'clock in the morning." This answer, to use the language of the day, apparently put the hangman's noose around Armstrong's neck. In the opinion of his alert counsel however, it was just what undid that ghastly cravat. For, profiting by the testimony given at previous hearings, Lincoln had prepared to meet that very situation. On the morning of the trial he had placed in the keeping of Sheriff James A. Dick an almanac—probably Goudy's—for the year of the homicide. This document was now produced by that officer, at the request of the defense, and put in evidençe. It proved, as Lincoln pointed out, that on the night in question the moon had but slightly passed the first quarter, that it gave practically no light at eleven o'clock, and that its computed time for setting was at about midnight.[32] The effect of this announcement seemed almost magical. At one stroke of the master hand, Allen's spurious moonshine had turned into a lightning flash, by which the weakness of the prosecution stood revealed. There was an immediate revulsion of feeling in the prisoner's favor. His counsel were as quick to seize upon the lucky turn. Closing for the defense, Mr. Lincoln addressed the jury in words of which his associate, Mr. Walker, afterwards said, "A more powerful and eloquent speech never, in my opinion, fell from the lips of man." The perjured testimony, as well as the discrepancies in the evidence, were dwelt upon by the speaker with telling effect. So moved was he, moreover, by his ancient gratitude to "Duff's" parents, and by his own manifest belief in the young man's innocence of willful murder, that the tears which blurred his eyes as he spoke, no less than the sympathetic earnestness of his appeal, touched responsive chords among the wrought-up jurymen. They did not deliberate long. When they came in with their verdict, the foreman said "not guilty," and this remarkable case was at an end.

The case, indeed, was at an end, but the talk about it was not. Lincoln's dramatic introduction of that almanac appears especially to have stimulated the gossip, which took many forms, until out of it all in some unaccountable way emerged a strange canard. According to this tale he had tricked prosecutors, court, and jury by palming off on them, as of the year when the homicide took place, a calendar of some previous year. The obvious reply to this charge is that there would have been no reason whatever for such a piece of rascality. An almanac dated 1857 bears out — as any one may satisfy himself at his leisure — Lincoln's contention to the letter, and he could not have bettered his case by fraudulently using one for another year. Of course, those who repeated the story did not take the trouble to consult calendars, but a moment's reflection might have warned them of its absurdity. They should have known that an experienced lawyer, whose adherence to the highest ideals of his profession had by this time passed into a by-word, would hardly have jeopardized a cherished reputation, to say nothing of his standing as a public man, by stooping to any device at once so dishonorable and so futile. For it is not to be credited that an exhibit of such importance could pass through the hands of shrewd opponents, as well as those of judge and jurymen, without the closest scrutiny. This scrutiny did, in fact, take place.

How thorough it was may be gathered from the recollections of Judge Abram Bergen, who happened to be present. Attending the trial shortly after his admission to practice, he sat within the bar behind both groups of counsel engaged in the case, and watched what took place with the acute attention of a young lawyer studying the tactics of distinguished elders. This apparently credible witness, touching on the accusation of fraud, said: —

"When Lincoln finally called for the almanac he

exhibited it to the opposing lawyers, read from it, and then caused it to be handed to members of the jury for their inspection. I heard two of the attorneys for the State, in whispered consultation, raise the question as to the correctness of the almanac, and they ended the conference by sending to the office of the clerk of the court for another. The messenger soon returned with the statement that there was no almanac of 1857 in the office. It will be remembered that the trial occurred in 1858 for a transaction in 1857. In the Presidential campaign soon following, it was even charged that Lincoln must have gone around and purloined all the almanacs in the court-house. However, I well remember that another almanac was procured from the office of Probate Judge Arenz, in the same building. It was brought to the prosecuting attorneys, who examined it, and compared it with the one introduced by Mr. Lincoln, and found that they substantially agreed, although it was at first intimated by the State's attorneys that they had found some slight difference.

"All this I personally saw and heard, and it is as distinct in my memory as if it had occurred but yesterday. No intimation was made, so far as I knew, that there was any fraud in the use of the almanac until two years afterwards, when Lincoln was the nominee of the Republican Party for the Presidency. In that year, 1860, while in the mountains of southern Oregon, I saw in a Democratic newspaper, published at St. Louis, an article personally abusive of Mr. Lincoln, stating that he was no statesman and only a third-rate lawyer; and to prove the deceptive and dishonest nature of the candidate, the same paper printed an indefinite affidavit of one of the jurors who had helped to acquit Armstrong, to the effect that Mr. Lincoln had made fraudulent use of the almanac on the trial. For some inexplicable reason he failed to call this pretended knowledge to the attention of the other jurors at the time of the trial; but very promptly joined in the verdict of acquittal, and waited two years before giving publicity to what would at the proper time have been a very important piece of information.

"Soon after this, I saw an affidavit made by Milton Logan, the foreman of the jury, that he personally examined the almanac when it was delivered to the jury, and particularly noticed that it was for the year 1857, the year of the homicide. I had a better opportunity than any of the jurors to see and hear all that was publicly and privately done and said by the attorneys on both sides, and know that the almanacs of 1857, now preserved in the historical and other public libraries, sustain and prove to the minute all that was claimed by Mr. Lincoln on that trial, as to the rising and setting of the moon; although my best recollection is that the hour of the crime was claimed to be about midnight, instead of eleven o'clock, as stated in many of the books. I do not know that this calumny was ever called to Mr. Lincoln's attention, or if it was that he ever took the trouble to contradict it. He might well have pursued his regular habit of ignoring such things. If his public and private conduct and his reputation as a citizen and lawyer were not sufficient to refute the charges, his personal denial would have been of little more avail." [33]

Judge Bergen may be right. Perhaps, in fact, no proofs — not even His Honor's own lucid statements, sustained by the almanac itself — have vigor enough to overtake all the current versions of this absurd tale and retire them from circulation. In the region of the old Eighth Judicial Circuit, they are still passed around with variations to suit each teller's fancy; the press of the country helps them along with a fresh start now and then; while at least one law book — a treatise, strange to say, on "Facts" — throws an air of seeming authenticity over the whole foolish business, in an indexed note which relates how Lincoln once "procured an acquittal by a fraud." [34] Slander they say can travel around the world before Denial has had time to draw on his boots. This particular offender has been overtaken, again and again; but the story, in some guise, goes merrily on. It evidently belongs among those popular myths that thrive on refutation. To disprove them is easy enough; to destroy them, as experience abundantly shows, is quite another matter. Yet "hope springs eternal in the human breast"; and one more lover of historic justice here tries what may be achieved by turning the searchlight of truth full upon the discrepant features of this hoary falsehood.[35]

So much for the few specific instances in which doubts have been publicly cast on Lincoln's high ideals of practice. As to the rest, those ideals apparently suffered but little let-down under all the press and stress of his busy years at the Illinois bar. Yet he was not immaculate. A thoroughly human man, loyal to his clients and fond of his friends, he may have swerved ever so slightly to the right or the left in their behalf, when no breach of truth or law was involved. As often happens, moreover, with men of this type he appears to have been in such cases his own severest censor. And when a student once asked him whether the legal profession could stand the test, all in all, of the golden rule, he winced. It happened while they were walking together one afternoon after a trying day in court. The young man, Ralph Emerson by name, was the son of a reverend instructor in Andover Theological Seminary, and some things that he had seen Western lawyers do disturbed the poise of his New England conscience. If such acts were necessary at the bar, this would, he feared, be no career for him. In his perplexity the youth determined to consult the eminent lawyer who walked by his side. Turning suddenly to him, Emerson said: —

"Mr. Lincoln, I want to ask you a question. Is it possible for a man to practice law and always do by others as he would be done by?"

Lincoln's head dropped upon his breast. He walked on in silence for a long time. Then came a heavy sigh, and when he did finally speak, it was about another matter.

"I had my answer," adds Mr. Emerson, recalling the incident. "That walk turned the course of my life." [36]

Precisely what this little scene signified is not easy to determine; but that it was of weighty import those who have progressed thus far with us in the study of Lincoln's character will hardly believe. Still, the episode, however vague and inconclusive, must not be omitted from any appraisement of the man's honesty. Perhaps one explanation of that profound sigh is to be sought among occasional victories, won by him on technicalities, rather than on their merits. And then, again, a too sensitive memory may, at the moment, have put Lincoln in mind of certain acts which, while they hardly measured up to the standard set by the Golden Rule, were not by any means dishonorable. They had their origin, to some extent, in his distaste for trivial litigation, but still more, in his disapproval of those "contentious suits which," a great Lord Chancellor long ago declared, "ought to be spewed out, as the surfeit of courts." How Lincoln dissuaded his own clients from bringing actions of this kind has already been set forth. It may be needless to add that when situations were reversed, and they were the objects of such prosecutions by others, he willingly appeared in their behalf. Then woe to the plaintiffs if the facts afforded but the slightest scope for the play of his peculiar humor! Under his droll treatment, a petty cause, though not without merit, might become so ridiculous as to leave the claimant in a plight, from which nothing but an appeal to that same beneficent rule of ethical conduct could have saved him. Indeed, by these very tactics, Lincoln is said to have laughed more jury cases out of court than any other attorney on the circuit. How he went about it was well illustrated in a trial recalled by Judge Scott, who tells this story concerning the affair:

"A young lawyer had brought an action in trespass to recover damages done to his client's growing crops by defendant's hogs. The right of action, under the law of Illinois, as it was then, depended on the fact whether plaintiff's fence was sufficient to turn ordinary stock. There was some little conflict in the evidence on that question, but the weight of the testimony was decidedly in favor of plaintiff and sustained beyond all doubt his cause of action. Mr. Lincoln appeared for defendant. There was no controversy as to the damage done by defendant's stock. The only thing in the case that could possibly admit of any discussion was the condition of plaintiff's fence; and as the testimony on that question seemed to be in favor of plaintiff, and as the sum involved was little in amount, Mr. Lincoln did not deem it necessary to argue the case seriously. But by way of saying something in behalf of his client, he told a little story about a fence that was so crooked that when a hog went through an opening in it, invariably it came out on the same side from whence it started. His description of the confused look of the hog after several times going through the fence and still finding itself on the side from which it had started, was a humorous specimen of the best story-telling. The effect was to make plaintiff's case appear ridiculous. And while Mr. Lincoln did not attempt to apply the story to the case, the jury seemed to think it had some kind of application to the fence in controversy, — otherwise he would not have told it, — and shortly returned a verdict for the defendant." [37]

There are other accounts of similar achievements. Perhaps the most commonly known instance was that which Lincoln himself took pleasure in relating. According to one version, — for there are several, — this is how he told it: —

"I was retained in the defense of a man charged before a justice of the peace with assault and battery. It was in the country, and when I got to the place of trial I found the whole neighborhood excited, and the feeling was strong against my client. I saw the only way was to get up a laugh and get the people in a good humor. It turned out that the prosecuting witness was talkative. He described the fight at great length, — how they fought over a field, now by the barn, again down to the creek, and over it, and so on. I asked him, on cross-examination, how large that field was. He said it was ten acres. He knew it was, for he and some one else had stepped it off with a pole. 'Well, then,' I inquired, 'was not that the smallest *crap* of a fight you have ever seen raised off of ten acres?' The hit took. The laughter was uproarious, and in half an hour the prosecuting witness was retreating amid the jeers of the crowd." [38]

There is no more effectual way to dispose of a trifling suit, and Lincoln's ready wit was apparently equal to all such demands. Yet his sallies, telling as they were, left no stings rankling in the memory of unfortunate victims. Those who emerged beaten from these encounters were conscious of a certain quaint good humor in the man's demeanor that disarmed resentment.

He was, however, not so genial when it came to another type of litigants — the dishonest ones. They met, in fact, with a very different kind of treatment. For Lincoln saw nothing amusing in their devices, and as they could not be laughed out of court, his efforts were directed toward shaming them out. An occurrence of this nature took place at Tremont, in 1847, during the spring term of the Tazewell County Court. It appears that an old farmer named Case had sold what was called a "prairie team," comprising several yoke of oxen and a plough, to two young men known as the Snow boys. They had given their joint note in settlement, but when it became due they had refused to pay. The account was placed in Lincoln's hands for collection, and he promptly brought suit. When the case came to trial, this note, as well as the purchase of a team, was not denied by the lawyer who appeared for the defendants. He set up the plea of infancy, however, and offered to prove that both brothers were under twenty-one years of age at the time they signed the note. This fact, it was furthermore claimed, the plaintiff knew when the transaction took place. To all of which Lincoln quietly said: "Yes, I guess that is true, and we will admit it."

Things looked bad for farmer Case. "What!" thought a by-stander, — the teller of the story, — "is this good old man, who confided in these boys, to be wronged in this way, and even his counsel, Mr. Lincoln, to submit in silence!"

After the principle of law that a minor may avoid his contracts had been duly cited, Judge Treat who presided, inquired: —

"Is there a count in the declaration for oxen and plow, sold and delivered?"

"Yes," answered Lincoln, "and I have only two or three questions to ask the witness."

Addressing the men who had been called to prove the ages of the defendants, he asked: —

"Where is that prairie team now?"

"On the farm of the Snow boys," was his answer.

"Have you seen any one breaking prairie with it, lately?"

"Yes, the Snow boys were breaking up with it, last week."

"How old are the boys now?"

"One is a little over twenty-one, and the other near twenty-three."

"That is all," said Lincoln.

Arising slowly, when the time came for his closing argument, and standing in an awkward, half-erect attitude, he began: —

"Gentlemen of the jury, are you willing to allow these boys to begin life with this shame and disgrace attached to their character? If you are, I am not. The best judge of human character that ever wrote, has left these immortal words for all of us to ponder:

"'Good name in man and woman, dear my lord,
Is the immediate jewel of their souls.
Who steals my purse steals trash; 't is something, nothing;
'T was mine, 't is his, and has been slave to thousands;
But he that filches from me my good name,
Robs me of that which not enriches him,
And makes me poor indeed.'"

Then drawing himself up to his full height, and looking down upon the defendants as if with the compassion of an older brother, while his long right arm was extended toward their attorney, he continued: —

"Gentlemen, these boys never would have tried to cheat old farmer Case out of these oxen and that plow, but for the advice of counsel. It was bad advice — bad in morals and bad in law. The law never sanctions cheating, and a lawyer must be very smart indeed to twist it so that it will seem to do so. The judge will tell you, what your own sense of justice has already told you, that these Snow boys, if they were mean enough to plead the baby act, when they came to be men should have taken the oxen and plow back. They cannot go back on their contract, and also keep what the note was given for."

When Lincoln concluded with the words, "And now, gentlemen, you have it in your power to set these boys right before the world," — he almost seemed to be pleading for the misguided young men rather than for his own client. So it impressed the Snows themselves. Whatever their technical rights may have been, they agreed with his view, as well as with the reputed opinion of the jury, that the account ought to be paid. And paid it was.[39]

Whether all the circumstances attending this affair warranted Mr. Lincoln's severe arraignment of the defendants' counsel raises a nice point in professional ethics. Debts, as we know, may sometimes be barred by the law of infancy, still oftener by statutes of limitation. The debtors in such cases have been provided with legal defenses behind which honorable men, however, disdain, as a rule, to seek refuge. They realize that though these barriers shut creditors off from recovering on certain kinds of claims, the debts themselves remain unpaid; and that acts which are intrinsically wrong cannot be made right, however they may be sanctioned by law or custom. Still, if clients insist on availing themselves of such advantages, their attorneys are bound, in the judgment of not a few high-minded lawyers, to interpose the required pleas. So punctilious a practitioner as Horace Binney, the distinguished Philadelphian, whose conceptions of duty have already served us with some exalted standards, took this view. He once conducted the defense, it is said, in the trial of a certain action on a promissory note. His attempt to prove a set-off having failed, he arose and said, with an expression of intense scorn: "My client commands me to plead the statute of limitations."

This implied rebuke was not lost on the defendant. He quickly withdrew his plea, and paid, as did those abashed brothers, the contested note.[40] It is interesting to observe that here again the Western lawyer measured up to the lofty principles of his refined Eastern brother, and might, if confronted by a similar demand, have gone even a step beyond him.[41]

Where injustice was to be headed off, Lincoln never stopped halfway. His honesty became militant. "He hated wrong and oppression everywhere," as Judge Davis declared; "and many a man whose fraudulent conduct was undergoing review in a court of justice has writhed under his terrific indignation and rebukes." [42] These onslaughts appear to have been especially severe when the strong had robbed the weak or taken advantage of the unfortunate. One typical instance was that of a pension agent named Wright, against whom Lincoln brought suit to recover money wrongfully withheld from the widow of a Revolutionary soldier. The claim as collected amounted to about four hundred dollars, of which the go-between had retained one half. This was, of course, an exorbitant fee; but the friendless pensioner, bent and crippled with age, seemed to be at the fellow's mercy. He certainly expected no resistance from the old lady. Finding her way, however, one day into the office of Lincoln and Herndon, she told the whole sordid story. It aroused the instant sympathy of the senior partner. He called, without loss of time, on the agent to demand a fair settlement; and when this was refused, he as promptly began an action. What ensued is best told in his associate's own words.

"The day before the trial," writes Mr. Herndon, "I hunted up for Lincoln, at his request, a history of the Revolutionary War, of which he read a good portion. He told me to remain during the trial until I had heard his address to the jury. 'For,' said he, 'I am going to skin Wright, and get that money back.' The only witness we introduced was the old lady, who through her tears told her story. In his speech to the jury, Lincoln recounted the causes leading to the outbreak of the Revolutionary struggle, and then drew a vivid picture of the hardships of

Valley Forge, describing with minuteness the men, barefooted and with bleeding feet, creeping over the ice.[43] As he reached that point in his speech wherein he narrated the hardened action of the defendant in fleecing the old woman of her pension, his eyes flashed, and throwing aside his handkerchief, which he held in his right hand, he fairly launched into him. His speech for the next five or ten minutes justified the declaration of Davis, that he was 'hurtful in denunciation and merciless in castigation.'

"There was no rule of court to restrain him in his argument, and I never, either on the stump or on other occasions in court, saw him so wrought. Before he closed, he drew an ideal picture of the plaintiff's husband, the deceased soldier, parting with his wife at the threshold of their home, and kissing their little babe in the cradle, as he started for the war. 'Time rolls by,' he said, in conclusion. 'The heroes of '76 have passed away, and are encamped on the other shore. The soldier has gone to rest, and now, crippled, blinded, and broken, his widow comes to you and to me, gentlemen of the jury, to right her wrongs. She was not always thus. She was once a beautiful young woman. Her step was as elastic, her face as fair, and her voice as sweet as any that rang in the mountains of old Virginia. But now she is poor and defenseless. Out here on the prairies of Illinois, many hundreds of miles away from the scenes of her childhood, she appeals to us, who enjoy the privileges achieved for us by the patriots of the Revolution, for our sympathetic aid and manly protection. All I ask is, shall we befriend her?'

"The speech made the desired impression on the jury. Half of them were in tears, while the defendant sat in the court-room, drawn up and writhing under the fire of Lincoln's fierce invective. The jury returned a verdict in our favor for every cent we demanded. Lincoln was so much interested in the old lady that he became her surety for costs, paid her way home, and her hotel bill while she was in Springfield. When the judgment was paid we remitted the proceeds to her and made no charge for our services." [44]

Some of the finest traditions known to the legal profession had been observed in this case. St. Ives himself, "Advocate of the Poor" and patron of lawyers, might have held such a brief. We can fancy him, standing at the bar of the Springfield court, scroll in hand as he is sometimes pictured, speaking for the poor widow; but whether that scroll would have contained notes like those that Lincoln jotted down for the argument may perhaps be questioned. They read: "No contract. — Not professional services. — Unreasonable charge. — Money retained by Def't not given by Pl'ff. — Revolutionary War. — Describe Valley Forge privations. — Ice. — Soldiers' bleeding feet. — Pl'ff's husband. — Soldier leaving home for army. — *Skin Def't.* — Close."

And yet how could any true champion — inspired saint or just plain lawyer — have kept his hands off that defendant! Nothing but a flaying appears to meet the needs of the occasion. Even your gentle, courteous, sympathetic soul like Lincoln's, alert to the conflict between right and wrong, is stirred by such meanness to its very depths. Love of justice then flames into hatred of injustice. The patient pleader becomes the masterful prosecutor. In fact, the better the man, the fiercer grows his rage. Wielding a scourge of whipcord and striking home, he drives the object of his contempt in hot anger before him. Nor is he at that moment a respecter of persons. Certainly Lincoln was not. The wrath with which he bore down from time to time, as we have seen, on unprincipled litigants, witnesses, and attorneys did not stop there. Misconduct on the bench incensed him still more. If the judge before whom he was trying a cause persistently attempted to be unfair, serious friction ensued; and the deference with which even adverse rulings were customarily received, gave way at last to an outburst of indignation. "In such cases," writes Mr. Herndon of his associate, "he was the most fearless man I ever knew."

Describing a remarkable encounter which occurred during the Harrison murder trial, between Mr. Lincoln and Judge E. J. Rice, our junior partner relates how the presiding magistrate repeatedly ruled against counsel for the defense in such a way as to convince them that he was prejudiced.

"Finally," the narrator goes on to say, "a very material question — in fact, one around which the entire case seemed to revolve — came up, and again the court ruled adversely. The prosecution was jubilant, and Lincoln, seeing defeat certain unless he recovered his ground, grew very despondent. The notion crept into his head that the court's rulings, which were absurd and almost spiteful, were aimed at him, and this angered him beyond reason. He told me of his feelings at dinner, and said, 'I have determined to crowd the court to the wall and regain my position before night.' From that time forward it was interesting to watch him. At the reassembling of court he arose to read a few authorities in support of his position. In his comments he kept within the bounds of propriety just far enough to avoid a reprimand for contempt of court. He characterized the continued rulings against him as not only unjust but foolish; and, figuratively speaking, he peeled the court from head to foot. I shall never forget the scene. Lincoln had the crowd, a portion of the bar, and the jury with him. He knew that fact, and it, together with the belief that injustice had been done him, nerved him to a feeling of desperation. He was wrought up to the point of madness. When a man of large heart and head is wrought up and mad, as the old adage runs, 'he's mad all over.' Lincoln had studied up the points involved, but knowing full well the calibre of the judge, relied mostly on the moral effect of his personal bearing and influence. He was alternately furious and eloquent, pursuing the court with broad facts and pointed inquiries, in marked and rapid succession. . . . The prosecution endeavored to break him down or even 'head him off,' but all to no purpose. His masterly arraignment of law and facts had so effectually badgered the judge that, strange as it may seem, he pretended to see the error in his former position, and finally reversed his decision in Lincoln's favor. The latter saw his triumph, and surveyed a situation of which he was the master. His client was acquitted, and he had swept the field." [45]

This appears to have been one of the great advocate's last important victories at the bar. It forms, in certain respects, a fitting climax to his legal career. For the admirable honesty of word and act with which he started out would hardly have carried him far, had they not been reinforced betimes by the wisdom that comes to the sincere truth-seeker alone, and by the courage that is born of truth's fairest offspring — an abiding love of justice. Looking back over the scenes of his labors, we become aware, despite their commonplace settings, of something akin to chivalry. They recall, as it were, those epic days when disinterested zeal inspired, or was thought to inspire, chevalier and barrister alike. No counselor of old, who took on himself a knightly obligation to plead the cause of the defenseless, could have acquitted himself, all in all, more nobly. Faithful to his ideals through many temptations, yet free from self-complacency; chivalrous to his adversaries, yet striking hard blows for the cause in which he was enlisted; afraid to make a false plea, yet not afraid of a false judge, — homely, unassuming Abraham Lincoln rode over the circuit in much the same spirit as quickened the knight errant on his ancient journeyings. No paladin of the law, at least in his day, bore himself more gallantly. None seemed to do more toward conferring a practical, latter-day meaning on Bayard's motto, "Without fear and without reproach."

CHAPTER IV

DOLLARS AND CENTS

THE love of money never twined its sinister roots around the heart of Abraham Lincoln. He was wholly free of any desire to amass riches, nor could he understand why others should be eager to do so. The mere piling up of possessions seemed to him unworthy of an able man's ambition, and the benevolence which manifests itself in grinding the faces of many fellow-beings, so as to acquire a fortune for a few public benefactions, hardly appealed to one whose humanity took the form of honest, kindly abnegation toward all those with whom he came in contact. Pecuniary rewards, therefore, occupied a minor place among his incentives to action. In fact, when there was an end to be achieved, he became so engrossed over the work which should bring it about that not much attention was given to the pay. Although his faculties usually worked in striking harmony with one another, the harmony of thrift, whereby a man can perform a good action and, as the phrase goes, make a good thing out of it at the same time, was foreign to his nature. He appears to have been utterly lacking in the rather commonplace talent for transmuting people's necessities into comfortable revenues. His whimsical humor once defined wealth to be "simply a superfluity of what we don't need"; and his frankness, at another time, led him to say: "I don't know anything about money. I never had enough of my own to fret me."

How this condition came about, we have already, in a measure, seen. What Lincoln learned of business, at the outset, from his luckless father, from the ill-regulated Offut, and the dissipated Berry, did not carry him far on the road to fortune. Indeed, he can hardly be said to have made a fair start toward that delectable goal. To all appearances, the stuff which passes, as Mowgli says, "from hand to hand and never grows warmer," was slow in coming his way; and what little did reach him rarely remained long enough to allow a test for heat or cold. Where money is concerned, some men are sponges, some are sieves.

One of this man's first large coins that he earned for himself, by a single piece of work, passed through his fingers with ominous celerity. It happened in this way. While engaged on a voyage, during the youthful river days, — he was about eighteen years old at the time, — Lincoln stood near the water's edge as a steamboat came in sight. Relating what followed to some friends many years later, he explained that there were usually no wharves for large boats along the shores of the Western rivers, and that it was customary for passengers to board the vessels, as best they could, in mid-stream.

"I was contemplating my new flatboat," the speaker continued, "and wondering whether I could make it stronger or improve it in any particular, when two men came down to the shore in carriages with trunks, and looking at the different boats singled out mine, and asked, 'Who owns this?' I answered, somewhat modestly, 'I do.' 'Will you,' said one of them, 'take us and our trunks out to the steamer?' 'Certainly,' said I. I was very glad to have the chance of earning something. I supposed that each of them would give me two or three bits. The trunks were put on my flatboat, the passengers seated themselves on the trunks, and I sculled them out to the steamboat. They got on board, and I lifted up their heavy trunks, and put them on deck. The steamer was about to put on steam again, when I called out that they had forgotten to pay me. Each of them took from his pocket a silver half-dollar, and threw it on the floor of my boat. I could scarcely believe my eyes as I picked up the money. Gentlemen, you may think it was a very little thing, and in these days it seems to me a trifle; but it was a most important incident in my life. I could scarcely credit that I, a poor boy, had earned a dollar in less than a day — that by honest work I had earned a dollar. The world seemed wider and fairer before me. I was a more hopeful and confident being from that time." [1]

But the sequel, as Lincoln told it on another occasion, sounds less inspiring. For while playing with the coins after the steamboat had departed, he dropped one of the pieces overboard. "I can see the quivering and shining of that half-dollar yet," the narrator thoughtfully added, "as in the quick current it went down the stream, and sank from my sight forever." [2]

This incident was typical of the brief but inglorious business career which followed. In a certain sense Lincoln's commercial life may be said to have begun with the fiasco of the lost fare, and to have closed about seven years thereafter, even more disastrously, as the reader will remember, under the cloud of "the national debt." During that period he experienced, from all accounts, few if any of the joys found by the smug trader in the give-and-take of barter.

Nor did he, while pursuing his next occupation as a surveyor, evince any livelier appreciation of the opportunities for speculation which presented themselves on every side. Promising town-sites or fertile quarter-sections interested him only so far as they afforded the employment whereby he earned his daily bread. For greed of land, like greed of money, had no place in the man's make-up. He regarded with kindly toleration, however, the struggles of investors who scrambled after title-deeds. Yet if their activities took a dishonest turn, his contempt for the offenders was keener than that which Christian is said to have visited upon the pupils of Mr. Gripeman. In the ancient allegory those worthies were dismissed with a reprimand; but their successors, in this latter-day narrative, did not, on certain occasions at least, escape so easily.

"Land-sharks," or "land-grabbers," as they have been variously called, should be rated among Lincoln's pet aversions. From the time of his admission to the bar, he lost no opportunity of exposing their rascalities and of protecting their victims. Many a poor settler, struggling to save the homestead from blackmailers, who too often infested the government land-offices, would have fared badly if it had not been for this man's sympathetic help. What he managed to do for the pioneers when so beset, took well-nigh as many forms as did the various kinds of dangers which threatened them. These services, in fact, ranged all the way from the giving of legal aid to the lending of a horse.

It is related that one spring morning, as some of the lawyers on the Eighth Judicial Circuit were riding leisurely toward Springfield, from the West, they were overtaken by a traveler who was hurrying in the same direction. His desperate efforts to quicken the pace of the stumbling, mud-flecked animal which he bestrode, and the appearance in the distance of another horseman, evidently in pursuit, told their own story. Such a scene was not unfamiliar to the little cavalcade of attorneys. They recognized in the first rider a home-maker, racing against time, with perhaps his final payment, to the land-office; and in the second, a home-wrecker pushing forward, no less eagerly, to take advantage of a possible default. For if by a certain hour the settler should fail to reach his goal, the property on which he had spent much toil as well as money would be forfeited, the claim would be reopened, and his pursuer, or any one else, might become the owner. All this passed, like a flash, through the mind of at least one lawyer in the little company that sat their horses, curiously observing the race.

As the first rider came up with them, Lincoln

called out: "John, is this the day of your final entry, and have you the money?"

There was a look of despair in the man's haggard face. Reining up his spent beast, and gazing anxiously down the muddy road that still lay before him, he answered: "Yes, I've got the money; but my horse can't make it."

"Mine can," said Lincoln. "Take him, and save your land. Take the right-hand road a mile ahead of this, and get on the south road into town. By this you will save a mile. Take care of the horse as well as you can, but be sure to get there in time to save your land."

This exchange having been rapidly effected, the settler pushed on, and did reach Springfield in time to win the day. He had not been at the land-office long when his benefactor appeared on the scene, for the purpose of still further aiding him as an attorney. The proffered services were gladly accepted, John's title was perfected, and one more homestead rested secure from the malevolence of the "sharks." How many of these scurvy creatures were gaffed by Lincoln is of course not known. He was, as one friend expressed it, "a terror" to the whole breed; and common report credited him with being more active in thwarting their devices than any other lawyer throughout the State. Always on the side of the settlers, he could not, it is said, be hired to take any of the public-land cases against them. They appear to have been people of little or no means, yet his ability, influence, and untiring perseverance were at their command, without reserve. Homes trembled in the balance; that was enough for him. And whether these pioneers paid small fees or none at all, their cause never failed to enlist the stalwart championship of Abraham Lincoln.[3]

Nor was it among these unfortunates alone that we find the numerous instances of those who enjoyed his protection free of charge. For looking upon the law as a profession, not a trade, as a factor in the administration of justice, not a mere money-getting business, he could not bring himself to the point of increasing any poor client's embarrassments by demanding fees. In fact, as has been the case with many a truly great lawyer, his skill was ever at the service of the indigent and oppressed, without regard to compensation. Their plights, not their depleted purses, concerned him. Taking such clients into his affections, with all the sympathy of an older brother who had himself trodden the stony path over which he was helping them, Lincoln found a pleasure in the relationship that money could not buy. If the question of pay were raised by some grateful but impoverished litigant, Portia's answer might readily have served: —

> "He is well paid that is well satisfied;
> And I, delivering you, am satisfied,
> And therein do account myself well paid."

This was Lincoln's attitude of mind when he refused to make a charge for saving Hannah Armstrong's graceless son from the gallows. But his liberality on that occasion should perhaps be credited to gratitude rather than to humanity. Not so, however, his generous treatment of the Revolutionary soldier's widow. What he did for that chance client, in winning her suit without pay and defraying all costs besides, must be set down to pure benevolence. It reminds one of the spirit which prompted Theophilus Parsons, with his fine scorn for money, in the presence of distress, to decline fees from widows. How much further than that Lincoln went along unmercenary lines has been variously related. A few of the typical stories may be pertinent here.

Some time during 1843, Isaac Cogdal, the Rock Creek quarryman, was in financial difficulties. He employed Mr. Lincoln to do the necessary legal work and settled therefor with a promissory note. Not long after this, the luckless client, while making a blast, had an accident whereby he lost one of his arms. Meeting Lincoln some time after, on the steps of the State House at Springfield, he stopped in response to the lawyer's kindly greeting. Cogdal's sad face told its own tale, and a sympathetic question as to how he was getting along, elicited the reply: "Badly enough, I am both broken up in business, and crippled." Then he added, "I have been thinking about that note of yours." "Well, you need n't think any more about it," rejoined the attorney, laughing, as he took out his wallet and handed him the paper. Much moved, Cogdal protested, but Lincoln, with the remark, "If you had the money, I would not take it," hurried away.[4]

Labors of a more serious character were at times hardly more profitable. For instance, during the summer of 1841 Lincoln, together with his partner, Stephen T. Logan, and Edward D. Baker, conducted the defense of three brothers who were charged with murder. Two of the accused men, William Trailor, from Warren County, and Henry Trailor, from Clary's Grove, accompanied by their friend Archibald Fisher, had come to visit the third brother, Archibald Trailor, in Springfield. Shortly after their arrival, Fisher mysteriously disappeared. A hue and cry ensued. The missing man was known to have had money; the Trailors were known to be in debt. While search-parties went in various directions to find Fisher's dead body, the brothers were placed under arrest. Then certain police officers so played upon the fears of Henry, who was weak-minded, that he made what purported to be a confession. His story set forth in great detail how William and Archibald, after killing their friend, had thrown the corpse into Spring Creek; but no sign of the remains could be discovered by the eager investigators who dragged that stream. At the examining trial, before two magistrates, many witnesses were introduced by the prosecution. Henry Trailor repeated his narrative under oath, and the prospect looked black, indeed, for his two brothers, when their counsel showed by reputable evidence that Fisher, afflicted with occasional aberration of mind, had in several previous instances wandered away. This led to more intelligent inquiry, and Fisher was traced to Warren, whither he had indeed walked in a demented condition. The Trailors were, of course, promptly discharged. As William and "Arch" rushed into each other's arms, weeping like children, the court is said to have become "like Bedlam."

An outline of this remarkable case was sketched by Lincoln, in a letter still extant, to his absent friend, Joshua F. Speed. It is from another source, however, that we learn our most significant fact. An admiring account of the affair has been preserved by a student in the Springfield law-office. He relates that Lincoln — whatever the other attorneys may have done — not only gave his services to these harassed men without charge, but that he even defrayed some of their expenses from his own pocket.[5]

How much of this generosity was due to the old Clary's Grove associations may not now be determined. Certain it is that Lincoln found difficulty in bringing himself to the point of making out bills against those early neighbors. "He was always kind to his friends," said one of them, William McNeely, "and attended to some law business for me — frequently gave me advice, — and I do not recollect of his ever charging me anything for it." [6]

Another of these favored associates, Harvey L. Ross, appears to have had a similar experience. Carrying the mails in pioneer days for his father, Ossian M. Ross, who was postmaster at Havana, Illinois, he had become well acquainted with the tall, good-natured young incumbent of the post-office at New Salem. Lincoln took a fancy to this youthful messenger, and they became good friends. So later, upon Ossian's death, when Harvey needed legal help, he called upon his former associate, in practice by that time at Springfield. Young Ross had inherited from his father's estate a quarter-section of land with a defective title. This could be made good only by the evidence of a man named Hagerty. Bringing him to Lincoln's office, one summer day, Harvey showed the papers and told his story. After listening attentively, the attorney said: "I am sorry to have to tell you that you are a little too late, for the court has adjourned, and will not meet again for six months, and Judge Thomas has gone home. He lives on a farm a mile east of town, but we will go and see him, and see if he can do anything for you."

Mindful of the warm August weather, Ross wished to hire a carriage; but Lincoln answered, "No, I can walk if you can." So after shedding his coat, off he strode with a bandana handkerchief, which did frequent duty, in one hand, the papers in the other. Client and witness followed as best they could. Arriving at the judge's residence, the party was directed to a distant field, in which they found him busily engaged, with his men, on a new corncrib. He stopped to hear Lincoln's tactful statement of their errand, sent for writing materials, examined Hagerty, and signed the desired papers. The magistrate, like the attorney, — to say nothing of the other participants in this little scene, — was coatless, which led Lincoln to remark that they had been holding "a kind of a shirt-sleeve court." "Yes," replied His Honor, "a shirt-sleeve court in a cornfield." The hint was not lost on our amiable counselor. Upon his motion, all hands, including bench and bar, united their strength to raise the heaviest logs — a service which Judge Thomas gratefully accepted in lieu of fees. Court then stood adjourned, and the visitors departed.

When they had returned to the office in Springfield, Ross, taking out his pocket-book, said: "Now, Mr. Lincoln, how much shall I pay you for this long walk through the hot sun and dust?"

As the lawyer applied the big handkerchief to his perspiring face, he answered: "I guess I will not charge anything for that. I will let it go on the old score."

Recalling the many kindnesses already credited from this source to "the old score," Harvey — so runs the tale — could not control himself, and the tears came into his eyes.[7]

The lawyers among Lincoln's friends were, at times, not more successful in obtaining bills from him for services rendered. "You must not think of offering me pay for this," he wrote after submitting a legal opinion which one of them had requested him to prepare.[8] Somewhat similar in tone was his response to General Usher F. Linder, when that colleague at the bar, and occasional political opponent, appealed for assistance during a period of dire distress. The general's son Dan had, in the heat of a quarrel, shot a young man named Benjamin Boyle. When he was placed under arrest, the assailant seemed, for the moment, without even the customary legal supports, as his father, seriously ill with inflammatory rheumatism, could hardly move hand or foot. The affair had happened "in a quarter of the country where," as General Ewing relates, Lincoln "was a tower of strength; where his name raised up friends; where his arguments at law had more power than the instructions of the court." But these triumphs, be it said, left the potent advocate unspoilt. For they had not perceptibly increased the size of his head, nor decreased the size of his heart. In a sympathetic reply to Linder's agonized cry for help, Lincoln promised that no business, however important, should be allowed to keep him from being present and aiding in the trial. He felt deeply moved over the general's trouble, yet what appears to have disturbed him almost as much was an offer of fees. This called forth a spirited but gentle protest, declining pay of any kind. No act of his, he asserted, justified the supposition that Abraham Lincoln would take money from a friend for assisting in the defense of an imperiled son.[9] But no trial took place; for, as Boyle recovered, Dan was finally released. He went South, entered the Confederate army during the Civil War, and became, when taken prisoner, the recipient of still further kindnesses from the hand of that same attorney engaged, at the time, in trying the great cause entitled, Union *versus* Disunion.[10]

What Lincoln did on occasions for those who were not of his party, he did as cheerfully, it is perhaps needless to say, for the faithful. His political associates always found him ready and willing to render proper legal services, but they never found him keen about setting a price upon the work when completed. This was especially so with regard to matters of a public nature. One case in point, which may be regarded as typical, has been related by Henry B.

Blackwell. Recalling some of his own early experiences, he said, a few years ago: —

"In 1857, in behalf of New York publishers, I went from Chicago to Springfield with Mr. Powell, the state superintendent of public instruction, to consult Mr. Lincoln as to the details of a proposed contract for the introduction of district school libraries. We met him as he was coming out of the court-house with his green bag in his hand. Greeting us cordially, he took up our affair, giving us the advice we sought; but with characteristic unselfishness, he declined to accept compensation for his legal services on a question of public interest." [11]

More numerous still were the instances of valuable counsel given by Lincoln, without price, to the clients whom he dissuaded from bringing contemplated suits. Some of these cases, as we have seen, involved unprincipled demands, but others rested upon honestly mistaken convictions. To this latter class, apparently, belonged the real-estate claim which a lady once placed in his hands for prosecution. She told him her story, wrote out a check by way of retainer, and left some papers for the attorney's examination. At their next interview Mr. Lincoln reported frankly that a careful reading of the documents had disclosed "not a peg" to hang the claim upon. He felt obliged, therefore, to advise against bringing an action. The lady, evidently satisfied that she had no case, thanked him, took her papers, and arose to go.

"Wait a moment," said he. "Here is the check you gave me."

"But," she replied, "Mr. Lincoln, I think you have earned that."

"No, no," he rejoined, handing it back to her; "that would not be right."

A few words more of the same tenor followed. Then the surprised client departed, richer by the rejected fee and an expert opinion for which she had paid nothing.[12]

In similar fashion many a matter that had reached a more advanced stage was settled by Lincoln, as the reader will remember, out of court and usually without charge. He appears to have been governed, on such occasions, by the rule which led Sir Matthew Hale to refuse fees for his services as an arbitrator. "In these cases," said the great English jurist, "I am made a judge, and a judge ought to take no money." The American peacemaker, however, explained his moderation, whether as attorney or referee, on less lofty grounds. To a young associate, who suggested that he should render bills in such instances, Lincoln laughingly replied: "They would n't want to pay me. They don't think I have earned a fee unless I take the case into court and make a speech or two." [13]

There are always suitable reasons enough as to why a man should work without recompense, if he looks for them in anything like Lincoln's mood of lovable self-forgetfulness. How far this was sometimes carried by him may be inferred from his treatment of certain wealthy clients at the close of his legal career. He had been retained for the stockholders of the Atlantic Railroad Company, in a suit brought against them by some creditors of that corporation. Their case was in charge of former Lieutenant-Governor Gustave Koerner, at whose request the great lawyer's services had been enlisted. Many important consultations between the associated counsel had taken place, and their carefully prepared answer for the defense had been put in, when Mr. Lincoln received his nomination to the Presidency. He asked to be relieved, at once, from further attendance on the case, a request which was of course complied with. His clients, moreover, appreciative of the work that had already been done by him, arranged for the payment of a handsome fee. To their surprise it was declined. "He utterly refused," relates Koerner, "to take anything, although they almost pressed the money on him." [14] And so, to the very end of the chapter, this remarkable man evinced more agility, at times, in dodging payments than most men expend in reaching for them.

But there is one instance, at least, of Lincoln finding himself paid against his will. The circumstances have not been made entirely clear, yet one cannot scan the meager details of the affair without an uncomfortable feeling that something about it was discreditable — whether to Lincoln or to others remains equally vague. The episode presents peculiar interest, however, as an illustration of the extreme to which he went in dealing with a fee that had been forced upon him. His partner, Mr. Herndon, relating what happened to a magazine writer shortly after the war, said: —

"One morning a gentleman came here and asked

him to use his legal influence in a certain quarter, where Lincoln again and again assured him he had no power. I heard him refuse the five hundred dollars offered, over and over again. I went out and left them together. I suppose Lincoln got tired of refusing, for he finally took the money; but he never offered any of it to me; and it was noticeable that, whenever he took money in that way, he never seemed to consider it his own or mine. In this case, he gave the money to the Germans in the town, who wanted to buy themselves a press. A few days after, he said to me in the coolest way, 'Herndon, I gave the Germans two hundred and fifty dollars of yours the other day.' 'I am glad you did, Mr. Lincoln,' I answered. Of course I could not say I was glad he took it." [15]

Some years after this recital, when Mr. Herndon wrote the life of his illustrious associate, he made no reference to the incident. As that biography, whatever else can be said concerning its merits, manifestly aimed to set forth the real Lincoln, without undue eulogy on the one hand or the suppression of unfavorable facts on the other, this omission is significant. It indicates that the retainer at which he balked may not, after all, have required any considerable departure from his customary high standards. Perhaps, indeed, as he had anticipated, nothing was done to earn the fee. That alone would suffice to explain why Lincoln did not consider the money his, and why he cast it into the first conscience fund which offered itself.

Next to retaining payments for which no equivalents in services have been rendered ranks the dishonesty of charging too much for work that has actually been done. So thought Lincoln. He wished to avoid the one fault as much as the other. And his anxiety to make fair prices led him, at times, into the opposite error, that of asking fees which fell absurdly short of what they should have been. Money, it is true, was far from plentiful in Illinois during those days of small things. Such limited sums as people possessed had to supply many wants; and legal services, like other kinds of labor, seemed relatively cheap. Yet when Lincoln came to the making out of bills, his charges were not infrequently so light as to fall sheer below even these moderate standards. How far in this direction he sometimes went may be gathered from a multitude of anecdotes concerning him that still pass current throughout the region comprised within the old Eighth Judicial Circuit. Every one of these tales, however trivial, opens a window into the man's soul; and it is only by having regard to many, if not all of them, that we can reach the various angles at which he should be scrutinized.

In depicting a great personage, the historian may rest content with broad generalizations; the biographer may stop at a few specific illustrations of prominent features in his subject's make-up; but the student of character, recognizing the value of cumulative instances, must go further and, at the risk of seeming prolix, — perhaps unskilled, — must marshal enough kindred happenings in line to demonstrate the presence or absence of significant traits.

Lincoln's proneness to underrate his services,

when he tried to express them in terms of dollars and cents, occasionally took a striking form. One instance is related by Abraham Brokaw, of Bloomington, Illinois. He had brought an action against a neighbor who owed him considerable money. The debt was collected by the sheriff, but that officer, becoming insolvent, had failed to make proper return of the proceeds. Whereupon Brokaw retained Lincoln's great political rival, Stephen A. Douglas, to sue the sureties on the official bond. This resulted in prompt payment of the claim. But the "Little Giant," engrossed in one of his strenuous campaigns for Congress, proved to be no improvement over the delinquent sheriff, so far as that waiting creditor was concerned. King Log had been exchanged for King Stork. Douglas, with characteristic heedlessness, let the money slip somehow through his fingers, and returned to Washington without having made a settlement. Then Brokaw's overstrained patience snapped. Neither the man's ardent Democracy nor his admiration for the party's dashing young leader was proof against such a succession of disappointments. He engaged Lincoln to obtain an immediate accounting, and that gentleman, nothing loath, sent Douglas, who was still at the capital, a rather sharp letter demanding prompt payment. This deeply incensed the recipient. Writing an indignant reply to Brokaw direct, he protested against the outrage of placing any such weapon in the hands of a political opponent. So delicate a matter, urged the complaint, might at least have been entrusted to a Democrat. The letter was remailed to Lincoln, who entered briskly enough into the humor of the situation. Taking Douglas at his word, he forwarded the claim to "Long John" Wentworth, a Democratic member of Congress from Chicago. Then the "Little Giant" capitulated, and Brokaw at last received his money.

"What do you suppose Lincoln charged me?" queried the successful claimant, telling the story. "He charged me exactly three dollars and fifty cents for collecting nearly six hundred dollars."

When asked his reason for retaining so small a fee, the attorney is said to have replied: "I had no trouble with it. I sent it to my friend in Washington, and was only out the postage." [16]

This naïve explanation deserves a place side by side with that of the hospitable hostess, who, setting an elaborate luncheon before her guests, brushed away their protests by assuring them of its cheapness. "Why," said she, "the whole affair cost almost nothing. I had everything in the house but ten cents' worth of cinnamon."

The Brokaw episode, moreover, recalls another instance of how liberally Lincoln discounted the value of his services when a friendly colleague had helped him out. It has been related by Isaac Hawley, a citizen of Springfield. He was sued in an action of ejectment from a piece of land on the so-called "military tract" of Brown County. The suit had been brought in the United States Court, so Hawley employed Mr. Lincoln to look after the case, whenever it should come up for trial at Chicago. After giving the matter considerable attention through several terms of court, the attorney arranged with a local lawyer to watch the case in his absence. The man on guard did this work so well that when the case was called he had it dismissed. Delighted at the outcome, Mr. Hawley asked for a bill, expecting, as he afterward explained, to pay not less than fifty dollars. But great was his astonishment when Lincoln said: "Well, Isaac, I think I will charge you about ten dollars. I think that would be about right." [17]

Another Lincoln client, George W. Nance by name, who settled at even a larger ratio of difference between what he thought was due and what he actually paid, writes: "I engaged his services in a lawsuit, and on asking his charge, to my surprise he only asked me two dollars and fifty cents. I had no idea of paying less then ten dollars." [18]

Still another friend and client, John W. Bunn, of Springfield, bears testimony to the same general effect. He tells how George Smith & Company, a firm of Chicago bankers, requested him to retain an attorney who should look after their defense in a local attachment suit which involved several thousand dollars. Mr. Bunn entrusted the case to Lincoln. That skillful advocate won a verdict at the trial, and charged twenty-five dollars for his victory. When the bill reached them, the Chicago men wrote to their correspondent: "We asked you to get the best lawyer in Springfield, and it certainly looks as if you had secured one of the cheapest." [19]

No less an authority than Daniel Webster was similarly impressed with Lincoln's moderation. The

"Great Expounder" employed him to transact some legal business concerning a certain speculation in land, at the place where Rock River flows into the Mississippi. An embryo city, laid out there by the promoters, had not been a success, and most of the property, on which but one payment had been made, reverted finally to the original owners. For such services as he could render Mr. Lincoln charged ten dollars, a fee so far from adequate, in Mr. Webster's estimation, that he frequently referred to its smallness and declared himself still his attorney's debtor.

An English barrister, quite as eminent, perhaps, as our "Godlike Daniel," once facetiously defined the lawyer to be "a learned gentleman who rescues your estate from your enemies and keeps it himself." Such a view of the profession has, from time to time, been held in sober earnest by not a few citizens of both countries. Certainly the Illinois matron, whom her son quotes in the following characteristic little anecdote, appears to have been of this opinion. But it is interesting to notice how, on one occasion, at least, she had to modify the gibe in favor of Abraham Lincoln.

"My father," relates Henry Rickel, "had a claim against a man of the name of Townsend, to the amount of fifteen hundred dollars or more; and he learned one day that he was about to leave the country, and had a drove of cattle, and was on the way to Oregon. My father went to Mr. Lincoln, secured an attachment, Mr. Lincoln furnishing the bond, and there was a vigorous contest over the matter. I remember the evening after the trial my father came home, and my mother asked him how he came out. His reply was: 'I came out ahead, of course, because I had Abe for my lawyer.'

"My mother seemed to have a pretty poor opinion of lawyers in general, and she said: 'I suppose the lawyers will take most of it.'

"And father replied: 'Why, mother, what do you suppose Abe charged me?'

"She mentioned a very large sum. My father said: 'You are greatly mistaken. He said to me, "Mr. Rickel, I will only charge you twenty-five dollars, and if you think that is too much, I will make it less."'" [20]

As surprisingly small a fee — the same sum, in fact — contented Lincoln after another verdict of even more importance. This had been reached in what was called the Dungee slander suit. That it involved far heavier labors on his part, and that it may be classed among those triumphs in which a good round charge is peculiarly appropriate, appears to have made no difference. He had carried all before him through a hotly contested trial; but in the supreme hour, when nothing remained save to gather the fruits of victory, his hand fell limp at his side. It makes rather a long story, yet to appreciate fully what happened one must know the salient details.

To begin, this action was brought before Judge Davis, at Clinton, during the spring of 1856, after Lincoln had attained prominence as a lawyer. It grew out of a quarrel between two brothers-in-law, Jack Dungee and Joe Spencer. The former, a dark-complexioned Portuguese, had married the latter's sister. How their broil originated is not now definitely known. When it was at its height, however, Spencer called Dungee a "nigger," and followed this up, as they said, by adding "a nigger married to a white woman." The words were slanderous because, under Illinois law, such a union constituted a crime. Laying his damages at several thousand dollars, the aggrieved man employed Mr. Lincoln to bring suit, whereupon the defendant enlisted the services of Clifton H. Moore and Lawrence Weldon. When the matter came up, these two able lawyers demurred to the complaint, on technical grounds; and their motion, to Lincoln's great chagrin, was sustained by the court. It touched his professional pride to have a case thrown out, in that manner, because of faulty papers, as indeed it would any practitioner. Gathering himself together, he leaned across the trial table, and shaking a long bony finger toward his opponents, he exclaimed: "Now, by Jing, I'll beat you boys!"

To make good that threat Lincoln appeared at the next term of court with amended pleadings. He threw himself into the trial with a mastery which gave evidence of painstaking preparation; while the logic, wit, and eloquence that marked his argument to the jury compelled the admiration of even his adversaries. After a hard-fought battle extending over two days, the case terminated in a heavy judgment for the plaintiff.

His counsel had said that Dungee sought vindication, not money; accordingly the defendant's lawyers came and said: "Mr. Lincoln, you have beaten us, as you said you would. We want now to ground the weapons of our unequal warfare, and as you said your client did not want to make money out of the suit, we thought you might get him to remit some of the judgment. We know Spencer has acted the fool, but this judgment will break him up."

"Well," replied Lincoln, "I will cheerfully advise my client to remit on the most favorable terms. The defendant is a fool. But he has one virtue. He is industrious and has worked hard for what he has, so I am not disposed to hold him responsible. If every fool was to be dealt with by being held responsible in money for his folly, the poorhouses of the country would have to be enlarged very much beyond their present capacity."

Guided by this benevolent spirit, Dungee consented to forego the whole judgment on condition that Spencer would defray all costs, and pay Mr. Lincoln's bill. When the proposition had been eagerly accepted, a question arose as to what the bill should be. Lincoln referred this to Moore and Weldon, but they both insisted that he, not they, ought to fix the amount of his fee.

"Well, gentlemen," came the response, after a few moments' thought, "don't you think I have honestly earned twenty-five dollars?"

What the gentlemen thought was thus expressed by Judge Weldon, in after life, when he told the story: "We were astonished, and had he said one hundred dollars it would have been what we expected. The judgment was a large one for those days. He had attended the case at two terms of court, had been engaged for two days in a hotly contested suit, and his client's adversary was going to pay the bill. The simplicity of Mr. Lincoln's character in money matters is well illustrated by the fact that for all this he charged twenty-five dollars." [21]

An equally striking undervaluation was remarked in another slander suit, — one of wide repute, — which took place at about the same period. This case is known as the Chiniquy affair. It was brought in the Circuit Court of Kankakee County, by Peter Spink, a prominent citizen of L'Erable, against Father Charles Chiniquy, the famous priest of St. Anne. That reverend gentleman had, in the course of a sermon, charged the plaintiff, one of his parishioners, with having committed perjury; and the object of this attack had lost no time in seeking reparation. His attorneys were Messrs. Starr, Norton & McRoberts. Chiniquy was represented by John W. Paddock and Uri Osgood. According to the defendant's own overcharged, not to say hysterical, narrative, this prosecution had been set on foot at the instigation of his superior, Bishop O'Regan, with whom he then already waged the unequal warfare which later attracted so much attention. The merits of his polemic do not concern us here. Certain members of the church may, as the priest states in his book, have conspired to ruin him, and that particular diocese may, at the time, have harbored those shameful abuses which he decries; but what Chiniquy says about Spink's suit should be received with caution, for it departs materially, at important points, from the official court records.

When the case came up in Kankakee, during the autumn of 1855, counsel for the plaintiff secured a change of venue to Champaign County. This greatly troubled Father Chiniquy. The heavy expense — far beyond his means — of bringing witnesses and lawyers to a distant tribunal, as well as the perils of a trial among strangers appalled him. He was leaving the court-room cast down by these prospects, when an unknown well-wisher, hurrying up with eager words of sympathy, urged that Abraham Lincoln be retained to take part in the defense.

"But," queried the priest, "who is that Abraham Lincoln? I never heard of that man before."

To which the other responded: "Abraham Lincoln is the best lawyer and the most honest man we have in Illinois."

Returning to where his counsel were still in consultation, Chiniquy asked their opinion of the suggestion. They warmly approved, so he accompanied this new-found friend to the telegraph office. In a brief exchange of messages over the Springfield wire, Lincoln promised his aid. Then the stranger, still preserving his incognito, paid the operator, gave the priest a few further words of encouragement, and hastened away. He had not been gone long before Spink entered the office, for the purpose of retaining that same attorney, but it was too late.

At the May term of the following year, when the trial opened in Urbana, Mr. Lincoln, according to agreement, appeared for the defense. He aroused the admiration of his client by the skill with which he both met the evidence of the prosecution and marshaled the witnesses on their own side. As most of the persons concerned were French Canadians, the testimony had to be taken chiefly through an interpreter. This drew the proceedings out to tedious lengths, and increased the labors of counsel not a little. The trial was, however, slowly approaching its close when one of the jurymen appeared to be in great distress.

"What is that juror crying about?" asked Judge Davis, who presided.

"My child is dying," was the sobbing answer.

A neighbor, coming into court had, unperceived by any one, whispered these tidings to the unfortunate father. His grief so moved the judge that, after a few questions addressed to the newcomer, he said to the juryman: 'You're discharged,—go at once."

Then, turning to the counsel in the case, His Honor inquired: "Gentlemen, will you proceed with the eleven jurymen?"

After both sides had consulted, Lincoln responded, "We will"; but Norton replied, "We decline." So the jury had to be discharged, and the case was continued to the October term.

Another trial appears to have been well under way in the following autumn when Lincoln exerted his powers as peacemaker and brought about a compromise. He probably framed the agreement under which the suit was dismissed, for the final order still stands on the court records in his handwriting. By its terms Chiniquy's charges against Spink were withdrawn, and each party consented to pay his own costs. The reverend Father's expenses must have borne heavily upon him. If his own statement is to be credited, Messrs. Paddock and Osgood asked him for a thousand dollars each. Commenting on the size of the fee, he adds, "I had not thought that too much."

So, when it came to settling with Mr. Lincoln, the third counsel, whose services in Chiniquy's estimation were more than again as valuable, the poor priest asked for a bill with some trepidation. To his bewilderment, as he relates, the lawyer replied: "You owe me nothing; for I suppose you are quite ruined. The expenses of such a suit, I know, must be enormous. Your enemies want to ruin you. Will I help them to finish your ruin, when I hope I have the right to be put among the most sincere and devoted of your friends?"

But Father Chiniquy would not let the matter rest there. He urged that Mr. Lincoln should at least charge his hotel bills and traveling expenses. Whereupon the attorney wrote on a scrap of paper:

URBANA, *May* 23, 1856.

Due A. Lincoln fifty dollars, for value received.

"Can you sign that?" he asked. And the overwrought client, breaking into sobs, affixed his signature.[22]

So large a disparity in size between Lincoln's fees and those of other lawyers engaged on the same case, as occurred in the Chiniquy matter, was probably not common. There were differences enough, however, to provoke comment; and one of them, at least, led to an amusing situation. On that occasion he gained a verdict for an aged German who was in danger of losing his farm. The suit had been a trying one, but after years of litigation from court to court, it resulted in their favor. Then Lincoln charged two hundred dollars, which the old man, secure of his property, willingly paid. Yet the attorney's conscience was not quite at ease in the matter. His reflections were disturbed by a fear that the bill might have been excessive, and the more he thought about it the stronger became his feeling. So, seeking out the lawyer on the other side, who happened to be his brother-in-law, Ninian W. Edwards, Lincoln asked him what he — the losing advocate — had charged his client.

"Two hundred and fifty dollars," was the reply.

It touched the questioner's ever-ready sense of humor. He laughed, and decided to keep his fee without further parley.

But there are instances in which fees, or rather such portions of them as appeared exorbitant, were not kept. One of these episodes has, within recent years, been related by Mr. George P. Floyd. Having rented the Quincy House at Quincy, Illinois, from the owner, Mrs. Enos, who lived in Springfield, he employed Mr. Lincoln to draw up a lease and have it executed. When the document reached Mr. Floyd, no bill for services accompanied it. A proper charge would, in his estimation, have been twenty-five dollars. So he sent the attorney that amount. Within a few days, to his astonishment, came this reply: —

SPRINGFIELD, ILL., *February* 21, 1856.

MR. GEORGE P. FLOYD,
Quincy, Ill.

DEAR SIR: — I have just received yours of 16th, with check on Flagg & Savage for twenty-five dollars. You must think I am a high-priced man. You are too liberal with your money. Fifteen dollars is enough for the job. I send you a receipt for fifteen dollars, and return to you a ten-dollar bill.

Yours truly,
A. LINCOLN.[23]

On another occasion the writer of this singular missive went further. He not only returned part of his own fee, but he also insisted that his associate should do likewise. The associate himself — it was Ward Hill Lamon, one of Lincoln's local partners on circuit — tells the story. He had been retained in a case of some importance by a client named Scott. The man was acting as conservator for a demented sister, who possessed property that amounted to ten thousand dollars, mostly in cash. This ready money — a neat sum for those days — had excited the cupidity of a certain adventurer who sought to marry the unfortunate girl, and as an essential preliminary to that step a motion had been made for the removal of her conservator. It was to oppose this action that Scott retained Lamon, insisting, however, at the time, upon having the amount of his fee determined in advance. The attorney advised him to wait, as the matter might not give much trouble, in which event a comparatively small charge would be sufficient. But the suggestion met with no favor, so Lamon named two hundred and fifty dollars. This sum, Scott, anticipating a prolonged contest, eagerly agreed to pay. When the case came on, however, Lincoln, who appeared for him, won a complete victory inside of twenty minutes. And as they stood within the bar, Scott, much elated, paid Lamon the stipulated fee. Mr. Lincoln, who had been looking on while the money was counted out, said to his colleague, after their client's departure: "What did you charge that man?"

When the amount was stated, he exclaimed: "Lamon, that is all wrong. The service was not worth that sum. Give him back at least half of it."

But the other protested that the figure had been agreed on in advance, and that Scott expressed himself as perfectly satisfied. To which Lincoln, sorely displeased, rejoined: "That may be, but I am not satisfied. This is positively wrong. Go, call him back, and return half the money at least, or I will not receive one cent of it for my share."

There was naturally only one course open to the embarrassed junior. He hastened after Scott and, to that gentleman's astonishment, restored half the fee.

This little colloquy had attracted the attention of both bench and bar. It appears to have especially interested the presiding judge, David Davis, who, calling the fault-finding attorney to him, said in a poorly controlled whisper, which could be heard throughout the court-room: "Lincoln, I have been watching you and Lamon. You are impoverishing this bar by your picayune charges of fees, and the lawyers have reason to complain of you. You are now almost as poor as Lazarus, and if you don't make people pay you more for your services, you will die as poor as Job's turkey."

The rebuke was warmly applauded, but it made no impression on the man against whom it had been directed.

"That money," said he, "comes out of the pocket of a poor, demented girl, and I would rather starve than swindle her in this manner." [24]

The matter was not allowed, however, to rest there. In the evening of that same day, Lincoln found himself arraigned for his offense before the "orgmathorial court." This was a sort of mock-tribunal maintained by Davis, on circuit, to try lawyers who might be charged with breaches of decorum. No member of the jocund company, it is safe to say, had ever before been placed in the dock for the heinous crime of undervaluing his services. Yet complaints against this particular respondent, as the judge implied, had been frequent enough. Lamon was not the only attorney who had suffered, in mind and pocket, because of his Quixotic acts. Partner Herndon, himself a kindly man, is said to have expostulated repeatedly without effect; and so far as the bar at large was concerned, some of its pillars doubtless felt the jolt at times of Lincoln's absurdly low standards. He had, moreover, been caught red-handed in the Scott case, so that the plea of a certain famous British barrister, similarly on trial before the circuit mess for disgracing his profession by accepting too small a fee, would hardly have answered. This earlier offender, Sergeant William Davy, is said to have made the since oft-quoted defense: "I took silver because I could not get gold. But I took every farthing the fellow had in the world, and I hope you don't call that disgracing the profession."[25]

Davy was nevertheless found guilty and fined. So was Lincoln. His fellow anglers in the turbid waters of the law had no sympathy with the rare sportsmanship which had prompted him to throw back half his catch. He proved to be a true sport, however, in more ways than one. The fine was paid, we are told, with great good humor; and then the culprit told stories that kept the court in an uproar of laughter until after midnight.

There is another — a serious — side to this question. It was succinctly stated by Mr. Hoffman in this passage from one of his resolutions: "As a general rule I will carefully avoid what is called the 'taking of half fees.' And though no one can be so competent as myself to judge what may be a just compensation for my services, yet when the *quiddam honorarium* has been established by usage or law, I shall regard as eminently dishonorable all underbidding of my professional brethren."

But Lincoln could not see it so. Strong as was his sympathy with these colleagues at the bar, they were forgotten when he sat down to write a bill. His own modest estimate of himself, his compassion for clients in distress, and above all his ever-present fear of taking a dishonest advantage, proved to be the controlling factors. Influenced by such habits of mind, to the very end, he declared, as Lamon states, that their firm should never, with his consent, deserve the reputation enjoyed by those shining lights of the profession — "Catchem and Cheatem."

To infer from all these things that Lincoln was wholly shiftless in monetary matters, or that he did not, at times, gladly receive the fees which had, according to his own rigid standards, been fairly earned, would be wide of the mark. He welcomed, for the most part, in fact, the gleanings of ordinary practice from clients who could afford to pay. Such small sums as the circuit yielded, and they usually were small, meant much to him; how much, may be seen in the little side-light thrown on the subject by another one of his local partners. Henry C. Whitney, recalling the end of a session, in the summer of 1856, at Urbana, says: "He had collected twenty-five or thirty dollars for that term's business thus far, and one of our clients owed him ten dollars, which he felt disappointed at not being able to collect. So I gave him a check for that amount, and went with him to the bank to collect it. The cashier, T. S. Hubbard, who paid it, is still living in Urbana, and will probably remember it. I do not remember to have seen him happier than when he had got his little earnings together, being less than forty dollars, as I now recollect it, and had his carpet-bag packed, ready to start home." [26]

There is something almost pathetic in this scene, when one stops to think that the central figure was at the time a leader of the Illinois bar, and the very man whose persistent tenderness of his clients' purses had made him an object of censure from the bench. Lincoln himself still further illuminates the topic. Early in his practice, while associated with the thriftiest of his Springfield partners, he wrote to one James S. Irwin: "Judge Logan and myself are willing to attend to any business in the Supreme Court you may send us. As to fees, it is impossible to establish a rule that will apply in all, or even a great many cases. We believe we are never accused of being unreasonable in this particular, and we would always be easily satisfied, provided we could see the money; but whatever fees we earn at a distance, if not paid before, we have noticed, we never hear of after the work is done. We, therefore, are growing a little sensitive on that point." [27]

Under this same head, one of the younger lawyers has recollected a piece of "fatherly" advice given to him by Lincoln, while they were engaged in court. Addressing the fledgling as the jury went out, and referring to his client, a shifty fellow who sat near by, the older lawyer whispered: "You had better try and get your money now. If the jury comes in with a verdict for him, you won't get anything." [28]

So much for what the speaker once termed a "mere question of bread and butter." As to the rest, when clients did not pay, Lincoln was averse to suing them. His high ideals of professional ethics, no less than a certain personal fealty toward those who had honored him with their confidence, stood in the way of such prosecutions. And when any associates did, on rare occasions, carry the collection of unpaid bills for legal services into court, it was done contrary to his wishes.

An instance of what would then be likely to happen has been related by Mr. Herndon. "I remember," says he, "once a man who had been indicted for forgery or fraud employed us to defend him. The illness of the prosecuting attorney caused some delay in the case, and our client, becoming dissatisfied at our conduct of the case, hired some one else, who superseded us most effectually. The defendant declining to pay us the fee demanded, on the ground that we had not represented him at the trial of the cause, I brought suit against him in Lincoln's absence, and obtained judgment for our fee. After Lincoln's return from the circuit, the fellow hunted him up and, by means of a carefully constructed tale, prevailed on him to release the judgment without receiving a cent of pay. The man's unkind treatment of us deserved no such mark of generosity from Lincoln, and yet he could not resist the appeal of any one in poverty and want."[29]

A notable exception to the rule against suing for fees was made in the case of one wealthy client — the Illinois Central Railroad Company. That corporation, through its attorneys, Mason, Brayman, and James F. Joy, sent Mr. Lincoln, during the year 1853, a retainer of two hundred dollars in an important action. Suit had been brought by the corporation against McLean County to enjoin the collection of taxes assessed on railroad lands. The question at issue involved the interpretation of the charter whereby the corporation had been granted exemption from local taxation, on condition that it paid annually a certain percentage of its gross earnings into the State Treasury. Such immunity the Legislature, according to some county officers, had no right to confer; and the McLean authorities insisted upon taxing so much of the railroad property as lay within their jurisdiction. This course had brought about the case at bar by which it was planned to test the constitutionality of that law. When the suit came to trial, Lincoln, facing Stuart and Logan, is said to have conducted the plaintiff's side "with rare skill"; but the verdict, despite all his exertions, went against him. An appeal was promptly taken, however, to the Supreme Court, where, after twice arguing the case, and after two years of laborious litigation, all told, he succeeded in reversing the decision of the Circuit Court.

This victory meant much to the Illinois Central Railroad Company. Although a comparatively small sum was involved in the suit itself, an adverse result would have brought down upon the company a mass of claims, which, as some thought, might have led to bankruptcy. The road owned nearly two million acres of land and ran through twenty-six counties. Had all these several jurisdictions succeeded in laying their annual burdens upon the company, half a million dollars at interest would hardly have defrayed the tax. In view of all these facts, Lincoln considered two thousand dollars a moderate compensation, and presented a bill for that amount. What was his chagrin, however, to have Mr. Joy disallow the account, because it impressed him as an exorbitant charge from a "common country lawyer." The modesty of a Socrates or a Cato might have succumbed before such a rebuff. Lincoln withdrew the bill, and started for home. On the way, he stopped at Bloomington, where the affair became known to some of his colleagues on the circuit. In their indignation over the company's shabby conduct, they persuaded him to make the charge five thousand dollars, and to set forth the increased demand by means of the following unique document:—

The Illinois Central Railroad Company,
To A. Lincoln *Dr.*

To professional services in the case of the Illinois Central Railroad Company against the County of McLean, argued in the Supreme Court of the State of Illinois at December term, 1855, ... $5000.00

We, the undersigned members of the Illinois Bar, understanding that the above entitled cause was twice argued in the Supreme Court, and that the judgment therein decided the question of the claim of counties and other minor municipal corporations to the property of said railroad company, and settled said question against said claim and in favor of said railroad company, are of opinion the sum above charged as a fee is not unreasonable.

Grant Goodrich. N. H. Purple.
N. B. Judd. O. H. Browning.
Archibald Williams. R. S. Blackwell.

These signatures were probably not all appended at Bloomington, nor were these signers the only lawyers whom Lincoln consulted. Anxious to deal fairly with the company beyond the shadow of a doubt, he appealed to several other prominent attorneys for their opinions. One of these, Mr. Koerner, who had enjoyed peculiar opportunities for reaching a judgment in the matter, says: "He wrote me a letter stating that as I knew all about the case, and had been present when it was argued, he would be obliged to me to give him my opinion whether his demand was unreasonable or not. He also stated that he had written to some other members of the bar, and he would be guided by our opinion. I advised him that his charge was very unreasonable, and that he ought to have charged at least ten thousand dollars. I presume he received about the same answer from the other gentlemen."

At all events, Lincoln's bill, as revised, was sent in. The company still refused payment, and there seemed but one course open to him. So he promptly brought suit, in McLean County Circuit Court, for the amount of his strangely amended reckoning, with costs.

When the cause was reached for trial, before Judge Davis, on the morning of June 18, 1857, "the defendants," as the ancient judicial formula expresses it, "came not." A jury having been empaneled, Mr. Lincoln briefly presented his case, and upon its verdict was awarded a judgment in full. By afternoon one of the company's general solicitors, John M. Douglas, who had been delayed, arrived from Chicago, too late, of course, for the trial. Greatly disturbed by the embarrassing position in which the default placed him, he sought out Lincoln and begged to have the case reopened so that the corporation might have its day in court. This was readily consented to, the judgment was set aside, and a few days later the issue was again tried. On that occasion, Mr. Douglas called attention to the two hundred dollars paid four years previously as a retainer. It had been forgotten by Lincoln, who at once reduced his claim accordingly. So when the new jury brought in a second verdict, the figure stood at four thousand eight hundred dollars, and that amount, with costs, the defendant promptly paid.[30]

In justice to the Illinois Central Railroad Company its own statement of this affair should not be overlooked. From an elaborately printed monograph, illustrated by reproductions of the documents in the case, and published within recent years, we quote what is offered as an official explanation: "The then general counsel of the road advised Mr. Lincoln that while he recognized the value of his services, still, the payment of so large a fee to a Western country lawyer without protest would embarrass the general counsel with the board of directors in New York, who would not understand, as would a lawyer, the importance of the case and the consequent value of Mr. Lincoln's services. It was intimated to Mr. Lincoln, however, that if he would bring suit for his bill in some court of competent jurisdiction, and judgment were rendered in his favor, the judgment would be paid without appeal."

This version of the affair seems hardly convincing. The verdict of the trial court was, it is true, accepted as final by the railroad officials; but they have left slender evidence on which to base the latter-day inference that the suit was a mere formality, framed up between friends to guard against the censure of non-resident directors. The company's own exhibits, examined in the light of statements made by certain contemporary lawyers, lead one — with all candor be it said — to a contrary conclusion. Even the claim that amicable relations continued uninterrupted, and that Lincoln acted as counsel for the railroad in several important matters thereafter, loses its force when one remembers his peculiar sweetness of character. He might well have conducted the suit, in serious earnest, without losing his temper or his client.[31] Indeed, it is difficult for us, after studying the man thus far, to conceive of him as really quarreling over a sum of money — large or small. And if, when enforcing the collection of perhaps his biggest fee, he managed to take a somewhat arrogant patron into court without snapping delicate professional ties, the feat should be explained, not by the fanciful surmise that there was no cause of irritation between them, but rather by the fact that he was — Lincoln.[32]

This man, of all men, bringing suit to collect a disputed bill for his services, presents a spectacle which should be classed among the caprices of history. It would have seemed more natural, by far, had the plaintiff's rôle in that action been filled by any one of the colleagues who certified to the fairness of the claim. Though hardly a mercenary bar, the lawyers of the Eighth Judicial Circuit were largely, as the phrase goes, alive to the main chance. Not a few of them at this period laid up competencies; while here and there an able practitioner managed to grow rich. The presiding judge himself, David Davis, — he who had lectured Lincoln on his "picayune charges," — possessed the true Midas touch. Yet the ample fortune which was eventually credited to him, as indeed much of the wealth amassed by the others, may be traced back to activities and speculations outside the law. Such modes of money-getting held no attractions for Lincoln. His early misadventures in business had cured him of mercantile ambitions, and when friends presented alluring opportunities for profitable investments they were invariably declined. He might truly have replied as did Webster once, under similar circumstances: "Gentlemen, if you have any projects for money-making, I pray you keep me out of them. My singular destiny mars everything of that sort, and would be sure to overwhelm your own better fortunes."

In Lincoln's case, however, this unwillingness to seek revenues beyond the pale of the profession lay deeper than any mere question concerning profit or loss. The old-fashioned ideals, which debarred an advocate from pursuing any outside occupation of a gainful nature, had taken firm hold upon his convictions. Indeed, he carried to its extreme this aversion for hampering himself with whatever smacked of trade, going so far as to reject even the mint, anise, and cummin of related business that many able attorneys about him were glad to cull from adjacent fields. Accordingly, when some Springfield property had been levied upon, in a suit brought by Logan and Lincoln, for certain wholesale merchants at Louisville, the junior partner thus curtly dismissed a request of their clients that they collect the rents which might accrue: "As to the real estate, we cannot attend to it as agents, and we therefore recommend that you give the charge of it to Mr. Isaac S. Britton, a trustworthy man, and one whom the Lord made on purpose for such business." [33]

Yet the man who wrote those lines was in debt. His situation, generally speaking, must have been far from prosperous. At about this very period, we find him frankly giving poverty as the reason for declining an invitation to visit Joshua F. Speed, whom he very much desired to see again. That dear friend, happily married and domiciled in the South, had been sending insistent messages to which Lincoln finally replied: "I do not think I can come to Kentucky this season. I am so poor, and make so little headway in the world, that I drop back in a month of idleness as much as I gain in a year's sowing." [34]

The writer — gaunt and grimly humorous — might well-nigh have gone as far as once did another threadbare limb of the law, who declared, "I am so poor, I do not make a shadow when the sun shines." Indeed, to complete the traditional picture of a needy barrister, Lincoln apparently lacked but one thing — a family. And so he married. Within a few months after the writing of that lugubrious message,

Mary Todd, a high-spirited, well-nurtured Kentucky lady, who was living with relatives in Springfield, became his wife. Their marriage ceremony, conducted by the Reverend Charles Dresser according to the ritual of the Episcopal Church, appears to have been somewhat of a novelty in Springfield at that time. Certainly one of the guests was taken off his guard when he heard it. For as the bridegroom repeated after the rector, in an impressive manner, the formula, "With this ring I thee endow with all my goods and chattels, lands and tenements," Judge Thomas C. Browne, the Falstaff of the bench, standing close to the high contracting parties, exclaimed: "Good gracious, Lincoln, the statute fixes all that!"

This sage interruption was too much for the good minister's sense of humor, and some moments elapsed before he could proceed.[35] One wonders whether, on the under side of his merriment, there may not have frolicked a suspicion that, had rite or statute been invoked, then and there, in the bride's behalf, she would have carried away but a slim endowment of worldly goods. On her part, moreover, the lady was apparently quite as poor as the man she married. For like many other wives whose mates have attained professional eminence, Mary Todd brought her husband no fortune to paralyze his industry.

The young couple would gladly have made a honeymoon journey to their native State and availed themselves of Speed's now repeatedly offered hospitality; but again, poverty stood in the way. They were fain, therefore, to content themselves with a room at Mrs. Beck's Globe Tavern, where the munificent sum of four dollars paid their whole bill, each week, for board and lodging. This frugal arrangement lasted somewhat more than a year, after which the birth of their first child necessitated a change.[36] So they bought from the Reverend Mr. Dresser his frame cottage, on the corner of Eighth and Jackson Streets, that was to serve them as a residence for the rest of their days in Springfield. It appears to have been a modest home among modest surroundings. Here the little family took root, here the problems of the growing household were worked out, and here Abraham Lincoln lived the simple life of an honest gentleman.[37] His personal wants were few, — so few, in fact, as to make him almost seem rich. He had no expensive habits and one looks in vain for what cynics sometimes term redeeming vices. A man whose parents were, to quote one old settler, "torn-down poor," does not enter upon life handicapped by a love of luxury. In Lincoln's case the privations of earlier days had left him largely indifferent even to such creature comforts as the refinements of later times brought within reach. And though he rarely then referred to those trying backwoods experiences, the primitive ways instilled by them never quite got out of his system. Always in some degree a son of the soil, he consciously bore himself as belonging to "the plain people." It was the plain mode of living, therefore, that appealed to him, not only because the more elegant customs were distasteful, but also because he felt keenly aware of how incongruous they would have been with his real self. Nor does the closest scrutiny reveal in all this any trace of affectation. The ostentatious display of poverty, on the one hand, and on the other, the vulgar mannerisms whereby our so-called self-made men sometimes make capital out of their lowly origins, were alike foreign to his nature. He was true here as elsewhere. In fact, when all is said, the man's simplicity of life must be counted but one more expression of his inherent honesty.

Lincoln made it a practice to serve himself. He really disliked to have others wait upon his wants. Self-reliant in the extreme, to go for a thing came easier with him than to send for it; to do what was required seemed simpler than to order it done. He would walk to the house from the office for a document, though willing clerks were on hand eager to act as his messengers. If the open fire, at home or elsewhere, needed a fresh supply of fuel that did not happen to be promptly forthcoming, he took up the axe, shed his coat, and went vigorously to work over the woodpile. When a small stick was once wanted for some special purpose by a visitor at the Springfield residence, the master of the house fetched it after a brief session with his saw in the rear shed; and when a surprised comment ensued, Lincoln laughingly replied: "We're not much used to servants about this place. Besides, you know, I have always been my own wood-sawyer." [38]

The speaker was so little used to servants, in fact, that even when latterly they were at hand, he often opened the front door for visitors himself. This habit keenly annoyed Mrs. Lincoln, particularly as his attire on these occasions appears not always to have conformed with the conventional requirements laid down by authorities on etiquette.

But once, when she was lamenting over certain social breaches of that kind, a member of her family said: "Mary, if I had a husband with a mind such as yours has, I would n't care what he did."

To which the lady, much mollified, replied: "It is very foolish. It is a small thing to complain of."

And what might one have expected of a man, who was not only his "own wood-sawyer," but his own stable-boy as well? For when at home, Mr. Lincoln usually, during that period, milked the cow, fed the horse, and looked after their several wants, in a rudely constructed little barn which stood behind the house.[39] This same democratic simplicity and absence of all pretentions to elegance were observed about the untidy little offices in which he successively practiced his profession. Nor was it otherwise on circuit. The sorry nag that he sometimes bestrode and the shabby buggy in which the animal at other times pulled him from town to town looked consistent with the rest. When accommodations, moreover, at the local hotels were poor, — as they frequently appear to have been, — his easy-going temper remained unruffled. "He never complained of the food, bed, or lodgings," said Judge Davis. "If every other fellow grumbled at the bill-of-fare, which greeted us at many of the dingy taverns, Lincoln said nothing." [40] To which Joseph Gillespie, another friend of the old circuit days, adds: "He had a realizing sense that he was generally set down by city snobs as a country Jake, and would accept, in a public-house, any place assigned to him, whether in the basement or the attic, and he seldom called at the table for anything, but helped himself to what was within reach. Indeed, he never knew what he did eat. He said to me once that he never felt his own utter unworthiness so much as when in the presence of a hotel clerk or waiter." [41]

It would be interesting to determine how much of this self-depreciation was due to the unfavorable impression that Lincoln often made upon those who saw him for the first time. By all accounts he must have been, in those days, anything but an object of beauty. His six-feet-four of homely, awkward angularity apparently owed little to the clothier's or the haberdasher's art. For in matters of dress as in other respects, he was still the plebeian, carrying about him, so to say, the broad-axe air which suggested, if it did not actually revive, the crudities of frontier customs. He no longer, it is true, wore, as in his youth, a coon-skin cap or birch-bark moccasins with hickory soles. His shirts were no longer of linsey-woolsey, nor his trousers of butternut jeans or untanned skins. Yet he never quite outgrew the image of himself so arrayed. What appears to have been particularly vivid in his memory, moreover, was a picture of flat-boat times on the river, when his buckskin breeches — the only pair — happened to fall into the water with their owner inside of them. Relating such an experience once, he said: "Now, if you know the nature of buckskin, when wet and dried by the sun, it will shrink, and my breeches kept shrinking until they left several inches of my legs bare, between the tops of my socks and the lower part of my breeches; and whilst I was growing taller they were becoming shorter, and so much tighter that they left a blue streak around my legs that can be seen to this day." [42]

Similar tendencies, in Lincoln's later, more modern apparel, to leave a sort of neutral zone unoccupied between trousers and shoes, recurred with atavistic persistence long after he became accustomed to better things. In fact, such misfits troubled him but slightly during the period of his career at the bar. "He probably had as little taste about dress and attire as anybody that ever was born," writes one attorney who saw him often in those days. "He simply wore clothes because it was needful and customary. Whether they fitted or looked well was entirely above or beneath his comprehension." The same observer says: "When I first knew him his attire and physical habits were on a plane with those of an ordinary farmer. His hat was innocent of a nap. His boots had no acquaintance with blacking. His clothes had not been introduced to the whisk-broom. His carpet-bag was well worn and dilapidated. His umbrella was substantial, but of a faded green, well worn, the knob gone, and the name 'A. Lincoln' cut out of white muslin and sewed in the inside. And for an outer garment, a short circular blue cloak, which he got in Washington in 1849, and kept for ten years." [43]

Another friend and colleague, James W. Somers, recalling a first photographic glimpse of Mr. Lincoln during the earlier days on circuit, said: "His dress was the most peculiar thing about him. The trousers were several inches too short and illy fitted. The coat was the old-style swallow-tail, and was also too small. His head was surmounted by an antiquated silk hat, battered and rusty, as was his entire suit of broadcloth, originally black. In his hands or under his arm he carried a faded green gingham umbrella. He wore a black silk or mohair stock around his neck, two and a half or three inches wide, buckled at the back, but with no tie or bow in front. At the fall term court he usually wore a short circular cloak, extending down to the hips, and much the worse for wear."

Disregard of fine apparel, moreover, was not limited by any means to Lincoln's younger days at the bar. As late as 1858, after he had achieved a prominent place at the bar, his appearance made a similar impression upon Carl Schurz, who drew this graphic thumb-nail sketch of him: "On his head he wore a somewhat battered 'stove-pipe' hat. His neck emerged, long and sinewy, from a white collar turned down over a thin black necktie. His lank, ungainly body was clad in a rusty black dress-coat with sleeves that should have been longer; but his arms appeared so long that the sleeves of a 'store' coat could hardly be expected to cover them all the way down to the wrists. His black trousers, too, permitted a very full view of his large feet. On his left arm he carried a gray woolen shawl, which evidently served him for an overcoat in chilly weather. His left hand held a cotton umbrella of the bulging kind, and also a black satchel that bore the marks of long and hard usage." [44]

Evidently the age or condition of a garment was no reason, in Lincoln's eyes, for discarding it. On the contrary, he appears at times to have cherished an old article of dress as one would an old friend. But such attachments have their penalties. And we find him in the court-room, — yes, on one occasion, in the very presence of the court, — making hasty repairs to ward off untoward accidents. Still other inconveniences grew out of Lincoln's inattention to dress. He had not been practicing long before his partner, Major John T. Stuart, received a retainer to defend one John W. Baddeley, against whom a suit was pending in the McLean County Circuit Court. When this case came to trial, the major, finding that he could not attend, sent the junior member of the firm, with a letter of introduction, to act as counsel in his stead. Baddeley gave one glance at the letter, and one at the ungainly, ill-dressed bearer of it. That a man who presented so unpromising an appearance should come offering to be his representative in the august precincts of the law irritated him beyond measure. He discharged a volley of abuse at the astonished Lincoln, paid his respects, in similar terms, to the absent Stuart, and straightway hired another lawyer, James A. McDougall, to defend the suit. What reply, if any, was made by the innocent object of all this wrath is not known. He endured it, we are told, however, without resentment; and later on, when these first unfavorable impressions had given place to warm appreciation, counted that very client among his stanchest admirers.[45]

Nor was Baddeley the only one to be deceived by Lincoln's unprepossessing garb. So keen an intellect as Edwin M. Stanton's wholly misjudged him, many years thereafter, on the occasion of their first meeting at Cincinnati, in the famous McCormick *versus* Manny reaper case; and that, too, notwithstanding the eminent position which the Springfield lawyer had by that time attained among his professional brethren at home. For this critical associate could see no promise of forensic ability in the man, to whom he contemptuously referred as a "long, lank creature from Illinois, wearing a dirty linen duster for a coat, on the back of which the perspiration had splotched wide stains that resembled a map of the continent." [46] Stanton's disdainful treatment rankled in the gentle soul of Lincoln. He began, some time after the affair, to wear better clothes — better in texture if not in fit. But he never learned to take an interest in fine linen, or to spend on his person more than was necessary to satisfy the ordinary demands of society.

Thus much for the man's simple habits. A lawyer whose immediate wants were, all in all, so moderate, certainly had no personal incentive — whatever may have been his standards of honesty — for any but upright methods in his practice. Like Manius Curius, over that historic dinner of turnips at the chimney-side, he prized honor with modest living above meretricious wealth and the luxuries it might buy.

To assume, however, that there were not numerous demands upon Lincoln for what money could procure, would be far from the fact. A kind husband and indulgent father, it distressed him to refuse his family anything. All their reasonable wants he did, in truth, cheerfully provide for, as she who knew him best bore affectionate testimony. And once, when he was contrasted in her presence with a certain well-favored rival, the little wife retorted: "Mr. Lincoln may not be as handsome a figure, but the people are perhaps not aware that his heart is as large as his arms are long."

Still, there were many who had good reason to believe in such a consonance between length of limb and breadth of sympathy. Nor was their number limited, by any means, to those on whom, as we have seen, he conferred professional kindnesses. For others frequently felt the sustaining grip of that sinewy helping hand; and the hospitality dispensed in the modest little home made a lasting impression upon the circle of friends, who were favored from time to time with coveted invitations. Then, too, among the uses that Lincoln had for money must be reckoned those numberless little charities which are of the same blood as great and holy deeds. A typical instance, eloquent in its brevity, is supplied by a slip of paper, dated September 25, 1858. It reads:

My old friend Henry Chew, the bearer of this, is in a strait for some furniture to commence housekeeping. If any person will furnish him twenty-five dollars' worth, and he does not pay for it by the 1st of January next, I will.

A. LINCOLN.

With this scrap has been preserved the obvious sequel:—

HON. A. LINCOLN, *Springfield, Illinois.*

MY DEAR FRIEND: I herewith inclose your order which you gave your friend Henry Chew. You will please send me a draft for the same and oblige yours,

S. LITTLE.

URBANA, *February* 16, 1859.[47]

Another generous act, of a different character, is gratefully recalled by an old resident of Springfield, Dr. William Jayne. He tells how the "Phi Alpha" Society at Illinois College, in Jacksonville, arranged a series of lectures, the profits from which were to be expended on books for the library. One of the lecturers during 1857 was Mr. Lincoln. On the night of his appearance, after his address had been delivered, and the rather meager audience had departed, he said, with a kindly smile, to the president of the society: "I have not made much money for you to-night."

At which the young officer who was in charge of the finances interposed: "When we pay for rent of the hall, music, and advertising, and your compensation, there will not be much left to buy books for the library."

"Well, boys," replied Lincoln, "be hopeful. Pay me my railroad fare and fifty cents for my supper at the hotel, and we are square." [48]

The speaker's benevolence on other occasions must have been carried to extremes; for partner Herndon was repeatedly heard to murmur his disapproval and a student in their office reports him as saying: "Lincoln would n't have a dollar to bless himself with if some one else did n't look out for him. He never can say 'No' to any one who puts up a poor mouth, but will hand out the last dollar he has, sometimes when he needs it himself, and needs it badly." [49]

This view was apparently shared by the plucky little woman at home. She doubtless had found, as many housekeepers have before and since, that money should be conserved, not alone because of what it procures for people, but still more because of what it saves them from. The proverbial "rainy day," with its provident demands, was therefore frequently urged upon the attention of her open-handed helpmate without, however, appreciably modifying his habits in this regard. And when remonstrance became too insistent, he replied: "Cast thy bread upon the waters." [50]

That the lady preferred to make sure of bread upon the dining-room table is not surprising, nor should it be remembered to her discredit. Yet a certain characteristic little scene between the two may not be omitted here; for, trivial though it seems, the incident throws a vivid side-light upon this phase of Lincoln's nature. The story was related to the author by John F. Mendonsa, now of Jacksonville, Illinois. His father Antonio, a poor immigrant, after arriving in Springfield sometimes did odd jobs for the Lincolns. As the older man could not speak English, he took the little son John with him to be his interpreter; and that boy never forgot the many kindnesses which he received from the master of the house. More than half a century has elapsed since then, yet among his most cherished recollections are these visits to Mr. Lincoln's home.

Recalling the great man's manner, Mr. Mendonsa writes: "He would invariably walk up to father, shake his hand most cordially, and utter some little pleasantry which I would interpret. This interpretation seemed to amuse him very much. In every way he was most considerate. If the day was hot, the maid was instructed to prepare cooling refreshments of some sort, and *vice versa*. Knowing our reduced circumstances, he would take me by the hand, after father had been paid, and place a quarter therein, saying, 'Sonny, take this to your mother to buy meat for dinner.'"

The narrator goes on to say:—

"At one time, during an extremely hot summer, father, my brother-in-law, and I went to the woods for berries. It was in July, 1856, and the berry season was all but over. We got back to town at eleven A.M., having only three pints. My brother-in-law had two quarts. We took them to Lincoln's. Mrs. Lincoln met us and asked what we wanted for the berries. Father thought they should be worth fifteen cents per quart, considering the scarcity of berries and the length of time consumed — from four A.M. until eleven. Mrs. Lincoln thought this price outrageously high, and said she would not pay more than ten cents. Father had me explain our long walk through the heat, but she was inexorable.

"We met Mr. Lincoln at the gate as we were leaving. He asked us what we had to sell. I told him, and he said, 'Does n't Mrs. Lincoln want them?' 'Yes, sir, but she will only allow father ten cents per quart, and he feels they're worth fifteen cents.' He patted me on the head, smilingly and said, 'Sonny, you tell your father we'll take them.' Mrs. Lincoln had joined us, and on hearing Mr. Lincoln's remark, said, 'No, we won't have them. I won't give that much for them.' And when she was angry, she screamed what she had to say. Mr. Lincoln quietly said, 'Mary, they have earned all they ask for them. Get me a pan in which to put them.' She refused, saying, 'No, I won't! I won't have them! I don't want them!' He then called to the maid. She brought a pan. He paid father twenty-five cents and brother-in-law thirty cents. He chatted awhile, and as he bade us good-bye, gave me a quarter, telling me to be a good boy." [51]

But Lincoln, like the skillful tactician that he was, usually contrived to avoid so violent a clashing of wills. His method, on one occasion at least, seems to have foreshadowed the diplomatic triumphs of later times. What happened is related by the Chevalier Henry Haynie, who lived in Springfield during the old days. He was torch-bearer to a volunteer fire-company which needed a new hose-cart. Making a canvass for subscriptions among the citizens of the town, young Haynie and a fellow member called upon Mr. Lincoln. That gentleman at once expressed his sympathy with the project, but thought it best, before setting down any amount, to consult "a certain little woman" about it.

"I'll do so, boys," he continued, "when I go home to supper, — Mrs. Lincoln is always in a fine, good humor then, — and I'll say to her — over the toast — 'My dear, there is a subscription paper being handed round to raise money to buy a new hose-cart. The committee called on me this afternoon, and I told them to wait until I consulted my home partner. Don't you think I had better subscribe fifty dollars?' Then she will look up quickly, and exclaim, 'Oh, Abraham, Abraham! will you never learn, never learn? You are always too liberal, too generous! Fifty dollars! No, indeed; we can't afford it. Twenty-five's quite enough.'"

Mr. Lincoln chuckled, as he added: "Bless her dear soul, she'll never find out how I got the better of her; and if she does, she will forgive me. Come around to-morrow, boys, and get your twenty-five dollars."[52]

Fallible human nature, viewing this man's uncompromising truthfulness with perhaps a trace of chagrin, may derive some consolation from the thought that now and then, when domestic skies were overcast, even he sought refuge in equivocation. His sin, on one occasion at least, speedily found him out, as he himself confessed by means of the characteristically frank letter which follows: —

Private.

SPRINGFIELD, *Feb.* 20, 1857.

JOHN E. ROSETTE, ESQ.

DEAR SIR: — Your note about the little paragraph in the *Republican* was received yesterday; since when, till now, I have been too unwell to answer it. I had not supposed you wrote, or approved it. The whole originated in mistake. You know, by the conversation with me, that I thought the establishment of the paper unfortunate; but I always expected to throw no obstacle in its way, and to patronize it to the extent of taking and paying for one copy. When the paper was first brought to my house, my wife said to me, 'Now, are you going to take another worthless little paper?' I said to her evasively, I had not directed the paper to be left. From this, in my absence, she sent the message to the carrier. This is the whole story.

Yours truly,

A. LINCOLN.[53]

Meanwhile, there were other, far heavier drafts upon that meager purse. Its strings reached all the way to the little cabin on Goose Nest Prairie, in Coles County, where, after repeated migrations, Thomas and Sarah Lincoln had taken up their last abode. The family, or what remained of it, was not more prosperous then, we need hardly add, than of yore. In fact, financial embarrassments appear to have increased, and frequent were the calls upon Abraham for aid. How he responded may be inferred from what he once wrote to his stepbrother, John D. Johnston: "You already know I desire that neither father nor mother shall be in want of any comfort, either in health or sickness, while they live."[54]

A fitting pendant is furnished by a letter which had been sent to Thomas Lincoln, himself, some years previous. It read: —

WASHINGTON, *December* 24, 1848.

MY DEAR FATHER: — Your letter of the 7th was received night before last. I very cheerfully send you the twenty dollars, which sum you say is necessary to save your land from sale. It is singular that you should have forgotten a judgment against you; and it is more singular that the plaintiff should have let you forget it so long, particularly as I suppose you always had property enough to satisfy a judgment of that amount. Before you pay it, it would be well to be sure you have not paid, or at least that you cannot prove that you have paid it. Give my love to mother and all the connections.

Affectionately your son,

A. LINCOLN.[55]

When occasion served, moreover, the writer's customary contributions to the family fund were supplemented by the proceeds of some near-by case. This happened in 1845, when he won a Coles County slander suit that had been tried at Charleston. His client, in lieu of fees, assigned thirty-five dollars of the judgment to Mr. Lincoln, who, instead of collecting the money, instructed the clerk of the court to turn the entire sum, when it was r
over to his father. The old gentlem
came in from Goos
his stepson, to g
at a time when
donor, whose t
one of his partn
exceed fifty doll

More generous still was Lincoln's course in the matter of two hundred dollars which, it is said, his parents were sorely in need of. Having paid over the money, he determined to make sure that at least part of the property held by them should not slip through their fingers. To this end, forty acres of the home place were deeded to him by Thomas and Sarah, with a reservation to the effect that the old folks should have "entire control of said tract . . . during both and each of their natural lives."[56] This was doubtless done, in the main, for the protection of his dearly beloved stepmother. To give her money or to supply her with comforts failed, as he thought, to balance the long account of affectionate service which stood between them. He went further, and secured her this piece of property at his expense for as long as she lived: secured it, indeed, against her own fond forgetfulness of self. For no sooner had Thomas Lincoln died than Sarah's own son, the good-natured, idle, happy-go-lucky John, tried to sell the place, and only Abraham's firmness in maintaining his rights as the owner kept the land under the old lady's feet. Still there was no ill-will between the brothers. When Johnston, who appears to have been perpetually impecunious, appealed for assistance on his own account, Lincoln usually responded with the desired funds. And once, when for obvious reasons the money was not forthcoming, a generous proposition accompanied the kindly refusal.[57] This warm-hearted man, then, meeting the claims of the old home as well as of the new, smoothing out from year to year a coil of debts, and indulging his fancy, at the same time, for occasional little acts of benevolence, might surely have used a much larger income to advantage.

Yet apparently none of these demands upon Lincoln's resources quickened in him, to the least degree, any tendency toward cupidity. Even certain notable ventures on the uncertain seas of politics, that brought up now and then, as we shall learn, financial straits, failed to disturb his perfect poise with regard to money matters. Nor did he attempt to better the range of his professional opportunities, and when Judge Grant Goodrich, one of the leading Chicago lawyers, offered him a partnership in a highly lucrative practice, Lincoln declined the flattering proposal. He preferred his life on the circuit, with its freedom and smaller fees, to the grind of a wealth-producing hopper in that rapidly expanding city. As a result of all this Lincoln naturally failed to attain a competency. After more than twenty years of active practice at the bar, during which his services were eagerly sought for in the Federal Courts, as well as throughout the Eighth Judicial Circuit; after a record of labors unsurpassed, if indeed it was equaled, by any of his contemporaries who attended the Illinois Supreme Court, the highest appellate tribunal in the State; after enjoying a standing that brought him important cases to be tried in distant places, and retainers to appear before the United States Supreme Court, — this powerful advocate, successful in every respect but one, closed his legal career a poor man. The circumstance once led Judge Davis to remark: "I question whether there was a lawyer in the circuit who had been at the bar as long a time whose means were not larger."

How much Lincoln might, then, be considered actually worth, as the phrase goes, has been variously estimated. It is safe to say, however, that his estate consisted, for the most part, of his home with its contents at Springfield, a tract of land comprising one hundred and sixty acres in Crawford County, Iowa, granted by the United States Government for military service during the Black Hawk War, and a lot in the new town of Lincoln.[58] If there were other similar possessions of importance, they must have escaped notice, and ready money was evidently far from plentiful. Mr. Lincoln, himself, rated his net assets, it is said, low enough. While in New York, during the month of February, 1860, he met, so the story goes, one of his former Illinois friends, who, when questioned as to how the fickle goddess had treated him, replied that she had only yielded up one hundred thousand dollars.

"Is n't that enough?" asked Lincoln. "I should call myself a rich man if I had that much. I've got my house at Springfield and about three thousand dollars."

Somewhat larger amounts figure in other versions of this interview, but at best the total sum must have been comparatively small.[59] Indeed, such scattering indications as can now be collected all warrant the inference that a banker's balance-sheet, struck in those days between Mr. Lincoln's debits and credits, would have disclosed no very sizable net surplus.

But there is another system of accounting which results in quite a different showing. It deals not with dollars and cents, nor with real estate, nor securities; yet until this method too has been applied, no such appraisement can be deemed complete. Its values are expressed in terms of honor, its profits are to be found in the hearts of the people; and by this reckoning, Abraham Lincoln's career at the bar was a brilliant success. He may, it is true, have had less property to show for all these years of toil than any of his colleagues; still, not one of them was so rich in the love and confidence of the entire region. The old circuit — judges, lawyers, and laymen — united to award him a prize that money cannot buy. They sent him out laden with the fine gold of a spotless reputation. They introduced him to the nation as their ideal of a true man, at a time when the true man was sorely needed; at a time when any but a true man placed where he was placed must have gone down in defeat with perhaps as great a cause as has ever been committed to a single champion; and to this day, his name remains a synonym throughout the land for honest dealing.

CHAPTER V

HONESTY IN POLITICS

SIDE by side with Lincoln's life at the bar ran a different yet kindred career — that of the politician. These twin pursuits claimed him at almost the outset, as they claim so many men who enter upon the law. But in his case the customary order was reversed, for he had been elected to public office before he became a lawyer.

Early during the spring of 1832, while still a clerk in Denton Offutt's grocery store at New Salem, Lincoln announced himself to be an aspirant for electoral honors. How this came about is not without interest. According to his own explanation, offered in a little speech made at the time, he had been "solicited by many friends"[1] to become a candidate for the State Legislature. The phrase doubtless passed more nearly at its face value on that occasion than is usual with such euphemisms of the stump. For in very truth, this young man — newcomer though he was, and but just past his twenty-third birthday — had won the good will of the people about him to a remarkable degree. Sunning themselves in the charm of his kindly nature, laughing at his jokes and applauding his feats of physical strength, admiring the scanty learning which he employed with so much common sense, and confiding, above everything, in an integrity that had already been subjected, as we have seen, to numerous little tests, the voters of New Salem might well have "solicited" Lincoln to enter the political field. They had known him, it is true, less than nine months, but may not that brief period have teemed with as many experiences as ordinarily fill the corresponding number of years in more conservative communities? For time seems measured by heartbeats, so to say, rather than by hours, when it is quickened with the stress and strain of life on a Western frontier. Under the primitive conditions that prevail there, elemental qualities push to the front, men stand revealed for what they really are, and true leadership comes speedily into its own. So the smiling young clerk, whose tall, angular form towered above Offutt's counter, impressed himself upon his customers as a suitable person to be entrusted with the not too onerous duties of representing them in the General Assembly. They had seen enough of him to believe that those ungainly lines overlay a group of faculties which might be relied on for effective political service; and, what was infinitely more important, they felt assured that whenever these faculties were exerted, they would move in harmony with the laws of honor.

Honor, in the fine, exalted sense of the term, however, hardly entered at this time into the calculations of the New Salem constituents. No far-reaching moral principle apparently claimed their attention, and such interests as they had in that particular election itself were commonplace enough. The voters desired a member who could be trusted to look loyally, with unsoiled hands, after their material needs at the State Capital. They wanted good faith there, rather than high ideals. The candidate — not less practical, for that matter, and a politician true to type in the making — wanted an office. To say that he entered upon this initial canvass with any exceptionally lofty programme, is to anticipate the full-orbed halo of later days, at a period when only the first faint prophetic glow might, perhaps, now and then have been discernible. In sober truth, as Lincoln frankly explained, "Offutt's business was failing — had almost failed." [2] It would soon become necessary to find a new job, and the pay of a Representative, though limited to day's wages for short terms, with mileage, looked sufficiently inviting. Moreover, this call from "among his immediate neighbors," [2] to quote him again, touched perhaps the most vulnerable point in Abe's character — his personal ambition. The "last infirmity of noble mind" may sometimes also be the first. From Lincoln's earliest youth the passion to surpass others had dominated him at every turn. Pitting his strength, whether of mind or body, against that of his associates, he had lost no opportunity of excelling them, until it seemed almost second nature for this homely mixture of modesty and self-assertion, of good humor and mastery, to become the central figure in every group through which he moved. So confirmed grew these habits of leadership that as Lincoln reached manhood the craving for distinction, the aspiration to be big where once he had been little, must have entered into the very core of his being. It was not overstating the case, accordingly, for him to tell his "fellow-citizens," in a printed address issued at the beginning of this canvass: "Every man is said to have his peculiar ambition. Whether it be true or not, I can say, for one, that I have no other so great as that of being truly esteemed of my fellow-men, by rendering myself worthy of their esteem." [3]

These phrases, stripped of their conventional wrappings, really meant that the writer had set his heart, above all things, upon popularity.

The very intensity of such an aspiration must have put him severely to the test. How far he went in gratifying it, and to what extent, if any, inconvenient moral scruples were allowed to impede his eager progress, are pertinent questions. Was he, in other words, under the absolute sway of the master passion, as so many eager souls have been, or did an alert conscience at crucial points apply the controlling brake? Conclusive answers to these queries can, we are aware, be given only after a survey of the man's entire career; yet back there, almost at the beginning of things, on the threshold, so to say, of his public life, one group of circumstances dimly prefigured, in a way, the whole story.

When Lincoln essayed this first short flight into politics, Democratic men and measures were supreme on well-nigh every hand. The reign of Andrew Jackson was at its height. Under his imperious leadership — he had just completed three years in the White House — "radical doctrines," so-called, commanded ever-increasing support; while his own magnetic personality attracted many followers who were as ardent in their support of him as they grew intolerant of those who opposed him. No predecessor had carried the rewarding of friends and the punishing of enemies to such an extreme. Partisanship was in the saddle. Proscription became the order of the day. Taking their cue from the despotic decrees issued, time and again at Washington, the "whole-hog Jackson men," as the most zealous among the President's adherents were not inaptly called, stationed themselves across the highways to preferment and crushed out the political lives of candidates who failed to respond with the familiar shibboleths of the party.[4] When methods so coercive are pursued by a powerfully intrenched majority, place-hunters in great numbers throng to its standard. Their huzzas may be heard above the voices of the faithful, and patronage, rather than political creed, directs — if indeed it does not control — the devious operations of partisan machinery. Such was the scene that presented itself to the young Lincoln's anxious eyes, as he looked over this new, this untried field for a point of vantage from which a beginner might try his wings.

Nor was the prospect nearer home essentially different. There, too, the uncompromising Democracy that swayed so much of the country at large seemed all powerful. Illinois, in fact, was counted by this potent majority among its rock-ribbed strongholds, and though factional differences, from time to time, disturbed local harmony, the journalist who described "Jacksonism" as dominating that State with "the strength of Gibraltar,"[5] hardly overdrew the picture. Sangamon County, it is true, contained a considerable number who did not favor the President, yet even there his majorities were decisive. So, all in all, an ambitious tyro, making a maiden appeal to the voters of that district from the obscure little village of New Salem, had every incentive, apparently, for enrolling himself in the ranks of these triumphant Democrats.

Such a course would not have run counter one whit to Lincoln's early sympathies. His father, we are told, was a Democrat, or a Democratic Republican, to use the older designation; his own youthful associations had been largely with people of the same stripe; and, like many other lads of the period, he regarded the picturesque chieftain of the party with a personal admiration which neither time nor political changes wholly effaced.[6] But as Abraham reached manhood, a greater statesman — greater in not a few requisites of leadership — had attracted his favor; and he found himself, ere long, at one with those who were enlisted under the banner of Henry Clay.

That eminent campaigner's personality captivated the younger man's imagination. It presented a magnet to which the true metal in Lincoln's nature could not but respond. There were elements, moreover, in "gallant Harry's" character, no less than in his achievements so far as they had then been unfolded, that compelled profound respect. Clay's early poverty, of which no sordid traces were perceptible in a singularly winning presence, his breadth of human sympathy and largeness of vision, a chivalrous manner that accorded well with an ardently sanguine temperament, his unswerving integrity with regard to pecuniary matters, the lofty standard that he had set himself for the practice of his profession as a lawyer, his equally lofty standards of public duty, — then still unshaken by the shifts of a beguiling ambition, — the splendid courage, not to say genius, with which he rose to the demands of great political occasions, a generous patriotism that inspired him to carry peace-winning concessions across the barriers raised by conflicting parties, his steadily expanding record which at every turn, whether in the Kentucky Legislature, the United States Senate, the House of Representatives, the Speaker's chair, the diplomatic service, or the President's Cabinet, had thus far been marked by the *élan* and dash of a brilliant intellect, an eloquence that baffled description, yet left his audiences for the rest of their days under the spell of its witchery, — all this and more had brought Lincoln to a point well-nigh bordering upon hero-worship.

Naturally, so strong a preference for "the Great Commoner" himself extended, in a way, to his public policies. Clay's political programme, comprising by that time three notable issues, — the demands for a federal bank, a high protective tariff, and a continental scheme of internal improvements, — may also be said to have left its impress upon Lincoln's mind. He was not deeply concerned, it is true, during those callow days, with national questions; yet so far as he held any views on such matters, they favored "Clay's American System" and the principles generally of the National Republican Party.

So it happened that when Lincoln came to make his first political campaign, he enlisted on the weaker side. "An avowed Clay man," to quote the candidate himself, he declared for a leader who, with all his attainments, had already been severely routed in a contest for the Presidency, and what is more, who was destined to encounter still further disasters of the same nature. Yet no heroics, no fine flourish of trumpets, so far as is known, accompanied this decision. A poor, obscure young man, in need of an office and eager for distinction, was merely following his convictions rather than his apparent interests by enrolling himself under colors doomed to repeated reverses, and in opposition to the most ruthlessly intolerant majority that the political processes of the country had thus far evolved. The result must have been a foregone conclusion. Lincoln's canvass came to grief. Commenting on the episode, twenty-eight years later, in that brief autobiography written as the basis for a "campaign life," he said: "This was the only time Abraham was ever beaten on a direct vote of the people." [7]

And even that beating looks now, in certain respects, more like a victory than a defeat. Lincoln did not, it is conceded, prevail at the polls; but in one of those astonishing reversals whereby the X-ray of history sometimes reveals material failure to be spiritual success, this experience should rank among his greatest triumphs.

There was another reason, less obscure at the

moment, for not regarding the campaign as wholly disastrous. It established Lincoln's claim to political consideration by a remarkable circumstance. Although he failed to receive the requisite number of votes throughout the county, — standing eighth on the list of thirteen candidates who ran, — his own neighbors in the precinct which contained New Salem gave him 277 marks out of the entire 290 recorded for Representatives.[8] The full significance of these figures can be appreciated only after it is added that the same citizens, a few weeks later, cast 115 more votes for General Jackson's Presidential electors than they gave to Mr. Clay's;[9] and further, that this well-nigh unanimous support of their youthful townsman, without regard to his politics, was bestowed during a period noted in our annals for its intensely bitter partisanship. Explaining the phenomenon, many years thereafter, another promising young politician of those days, wrote: "The Democrats of New Salem worked for Lincoln out of their personal regard for him. That was the general understanding of the matter here at the time. In this he made no concession of principle whatever. He was as stiff as a man could be in his Whig doctrines. They did this for him simply because he was popular — because he was Lincoln." [10]

Because — the writer might have continued — they had weighed and measured Offutt's clerk, while he was weighing and measuring commodities behind the grocery-store counter; because — what is still more to the purpose — both sets of accounts, however dissimilar they must have seemed in the making, tallied peculiarly with each other in the final reckoning. And when, with almost one accord, the Democrats among these people who knew the candidate best threw party obligations aside to register their approval of him at the polls, they placed on record the first notable judgment passed by the voting public upon his character. Favorable verdicts without number have been passed upon politicians, great and small. Merely national reputations are as common among them as printer's ink is purchasable. But one must search well through our whole list of eminent statesmen to find the few who achieved, at any time in their careers, what Lincoln started with — an almost perfect reputation at home.

Nor was this big local vote the only expression of confidence in the "avowed Clay man" manifested by Jacksonians during those militant days. Before another summer arrived, he had received an appointment from "Old Hickory" himself, as the reader will remember, to the postmastership at New Salem; and soon thereafter, John Calhoun, the surveyor for Sangamon County, an ardent local Administration leader, made him, it may also be recalled, one of his deputies. That these politicians — high and low — should so far forego the fruits of the spoils system, looks creditable not only to the object of their lenity, but to themselves as well. Still, in the case of the President, it may be doubted whether much attention was paid to the act which bestowed upon this obscure appointee an equally obscure office.

The place could hardly have been of less consequence. How insignificant it really was can be appreciated only when we bear in mind that a far from regular mail service, scheduled for twice a week, sufficed to meet the needs of this sparsely settled district; and that even then the high rate of postage, not to mention the low rate of scholarship, kept the business transacted there within meager bounds. Indeed, tradition goes so far as to picture Lincoln carrying the office, for the most part, "in his hat." Under its ample crown letters or papers addressed to outlying settlers are said to have been snugly tucked away until opportunities came for making deliveries — rural free deliveries, we should call them today — at people's doors.[11] This conscientious young postmaster may therefore be credited with having anticipated by more than sixty years a now highly esteemed branch of the postal service. Nor did his usefulness cease there. If the recipient of a letter was, as not infrequently happened, illiterate, Abe's ability to read and write was promptly called into play. If, on the other hand, our postman brought a newspaper, he usually came prepared to discuss its contents. For the privilege of reading before delivering all printed matter that passed through his hands appears to have been a cherished perquisite of the office. Lincoln certainly made the most of it. Too poor to subscribe himself for the various "organs" which professed to reflect, inform, and guide public opinion, he read with avidity such of them as appeared in the New Salem mails. This practice laid the foundation, so to say, of his political education. Indeed, what he was taught by these sheets during the three years in which he held the post constituted perhaps Lincoln's most valued returns from an otherwise poorly paid occupation.[12]

The office of deputy surveyor for Sangamon County, on the other hand, was more lucrative and of far greater importance: so much so, in fact, that Lincoln hesitated to accept it at the hands of an official whose politics were of the opposite stripe. True, he needed a job, just then, with a good day's pay attached, if any man ever did; but "man" — that is to say this kind of man — "doth not live by bread alone," nor is he content to live in pursuit of bread alone, when to do so brings his sincerity into question. Lincoln's first impulse had been to decline Calhoun's offer. It came through a common friend, Pollard Simmons, who, at the surveyor's request, had hastened from Springfield to New Salem with a tender of the appointment. Elated over what he regarded as Lincoln's good fortune, Simmons — so the story goes — sought him out in the woods, where he was splitting rails, and told the glad news. It did not meet with the reception that the messenger had anticipated. So, sitting down together upon a log, they discussed the proposition from their conflicting points of view. To Abe's mind, after a momentary flush of pleased surprise, two drawbacks presented themselves. He had no knowledge of surveying, and he would not tamper with his political principles to secure a berth however soft. The one obstacle a little study might, of course, remove. But how about the other? So they talked it all over until Lincoln finally said: "If I can be perfectly free in my political action, I will take the office; but if my sentiments, or even expression of them, is to be abridged in any way, I would not have it or any other office." [13]

When the speaker presented himself, a few days later, before the surveyor in Springfield, all of his objections were, as we have seen, brushed aside. Calhoun needed an able man of unquestioned integrity — needed him more, at that particular time, than the Democratic Party needed recruits. How he assisted Lincoln to master the rudiments of surveying, and how fully he guaranteed him his political independence, have already been told. To what a remarkable degree, moreover, this strangely chosen deputy justified the other's confidence has also been pointed out. It only remains to be said that, though most of the incidents which flecked John Calhoun's eventful career have been forgotten, he still abides in our memories as the politician who, when seeking a trustworthy assistant, could see through the mists of partisan prejudice clearly enough to appraise Abraham Lincoln, thus early, at his true worth.

The holding of these two places under the Jacksonian régime had no ill-effects — interesting to relate — upon the young "Clay man's" standing. His political sincerity apparently remained unquestioned. What was more, the good account that he gave of himself as a public servant, and the enlarged opportunities offered by those offices, — each in its own way, — contributed not a little toward the growth of an ever-increasing popularity. It is hardly surprising, therefore, to find him at the next election, in the summer of 1834, making another, and that time successful, canvass for the State Legislature. The list of candidates was as long as it had been two years before. Yet of the four who were now elected, Lincoln, running but fourteen votes behind the leader, received the second highest number cast.[14]

For this splendid victory he was again largely indebted to Democratic favor. In fact, prominent members of the opposing party had gone so far as to offer him their formal endorsement, — an honor which, after some hesitation and several anxious consultations with his colleagues on the ticket, Lincoln had accepted. There is no reason to infer that in so doing he had taken any unfair advantage of them, as has been suggested, or that his political principles had undergone any trimming whatsoever in the acquisition of this alien support. How it came about is obvious enough. The same confidence and good will which New Salem, regardless of party, had manifested toward him to so notable an extent at the preceding election, should merely be credited with having spread, during the intervening two years, though in a lesser degree, perhaps, through Sangamon County. That section, moreover, so far as local politics went, was giving a gracious hearing at the time to new ideas and new leaders. Under the influence of certain able young tacticians with whom Lincoln had become associated, Jacksonism itself grew less rampant in the county. There, as elsewhere, the swift alchemy of popular enthusiasm was at work, fusing hitherto unrelated elements into a novel political unit, and by a coalition of Clay's followers with other anti-Jackson factions, helping to form a great national fellowship — the American Whig Party. It was as an exponent of this vigorous though untried organization that the Representative-elect from New Salem took his seat in the Ninth General Assembly.

Those must have been strenuous days. The Whigs were in a minority; yet they began, from the fall of the gavel, to exert an influence upon legislation out of all proportion to their numbers. This required skillful team-play, and the leaders were doubtless wary of employing novices. At any rate, no important part on the programme, so far as now appears, was entrusted to Lincoln. His appointment to the Committee on Public Accounts and Expenditures seems appropriate enough, in view of the sobriquet with which he had entered the House; but the transactions of that committee afforded him slender scope, if the record may be followed, for displaying financial honesty or, in fact, honesty of any sort. Nor was he more active during this first session in general legislation. Several bills of no great moment, service on a few select committees, occasional routine motions, the presentation of an unsuccessful petition, and a resolution concerning monies received from the sales of public lands apparently made up the sum of his doings on the floor. For the rest, as behooved a fledgling, he kept modestly in the background. By the time this Legislature reassembled, however, at the special session of 1835–36, Lincoln's downright sincerity, his homely common sense, and a certain capacity for parliamentary work began to dawn upon his colleagues. He attracted favorable notice too, some say, by the zeal with which he labored, when the legislative districts were reapportioned that winter, toward securing for Sangamon a considerable increase of representation. Under the law then passed, his county, though not the most populous in the State, was awarded the heaviest membership in the House of Representatives. So that its delegation to the General Assembly became enlarged from four members in the House and two in the Senate to seven in the House and two in the Senate — changes which were destined to exert a memorable influence upon the political history of Illinois as well as upon the fortunes of Abraham Lincoln.

His popularity among the people had meanwhile suffered no diminution. They liked him, trusted him, and now some of them felt grateful toward him. It was to a pleased constituency, therefore, from more than one point of view, that he appealed during the following summer for reëlection. The contest appears to have been warmly waged on every side, and though the enlarged list of candidates included several doughty campaigners, — Democrats as well as Whigs, — Lincoln regained his seat with the highest vote given by Sangamon to any nominee for the House of Representatives. What is more, the entire legislative ticket of the new party in that district was elected. The Whigs, by a signal victory, had revolutionized the neighborhood; and so complete — we may add in passing — was their triumph throughout the county that the control which they then gained over its affairs could at no time, during several succeeding decades of Democratic ascendancy elsewhere in the State, be successfully disputed there.

Clean sweeps presuppose stalwart brooms. The newly elected Sangamon Representatives, together with the Senators who held over, did in fact make a notable group of men. They were as tall as they were vigorous. Their average weight is said to have exceeded two hundred pounds, and their average height six feet. When they appeared at Vandalia for the session of 1836–37, some wag dubbed them the "Long Nine"—an appellation that stuck. For even in the capital of a State dedicated, as the Indian tradition has it, to "superior men," their appearance no less than their achievements attracted attention. The stature, moreover, which one of these tall politicians eventually attained in the world's history lends peculiar interest to the whole coterie. On that account, if on no other, a chronicle of his doings would seem incomplete without the names of those eight colleagues. They comprised, in the House, John Dawson, Ninian W. Edwards, Robert L. Wilson, Daniel Stone, William F. Elkin, and Andrew McCormick; in the Senate, Archer G. Herndon and Job Fletcher, Sr. These men, fresh from the exaltation of a thoroughgoing party victory, took their seats in the Legislature with the avowed purpose of accomplishing great things. And they had need of all their courage. The particular task which awaited them was no easy one. They were expected to capture the State Capital for Sangamon County by having the seat of government transferred from Vandalia to Springfield.

The management of this enterprise was entrusted to Lincoln. He had then already evinced some of the qualities that go to make a political leader, and his associates in the "Long Nine," as if by common consent, looked to him for guidance. But the honor was apparently not welcome just then. Suffering from illness and from one of those attacks of morbid depression that at times possessed him, he entered upon the session, unlike the others, in no conquering mood. Nevertheless, under his direction the Sangamon delegation straightway began a spirited campaign to the greater glory of Springfield. That town was not by any means the favorite among some half-dozen places which actively aspired to the capital prize.[15] Yet so vigorously were its claims put forth that competitors came to regard it as their most formidable rival, and for a time the contest looked as if all the other municipalities in the field were combined against this one.

The odds bore heavily against the "Long Nine" — so heavily that some of the big men, at critical points in the unequal, at times well-nigh futile, struggle, lost heart. But their leader did not flinch. What might have dismayed more seasoned parliamentary chieftains merely stimulated Lincoln to renewed efforts. He seemed prepared to stake the entire session, if necessary, upon the success of the Springfield project. That measure was, in fact, thrown into the scales whenever the advocates of pending legislation sought Sangamon support.

And such calls came frequently enough, because well-nigh every member of this remarkable Assembly had his own particular interest to serve. It took the form, generally speaking, of some scheme for so-called "internal improvements," whereby the politicians tried to satisfy a mania for overnight development that had recently obsessed the inhabitants of the State — a mania which was now about to reach its culmination in a series of extravagant enactments. One eager statesman came charged by his constituents with the duty of securing a railroad; another must obtain an appropriation for a canal, another a State road; still another was under orders to have this stream or that made more widely navigable; and so on through the whole range of public betterments. A hungrier crowd of the people's chosen Representatives has seldom been seen to clamor around the "pork barrel." It seemed as if each man's political life depended upon securing and carrying home a generous helping. To that end, other interests were freely sacrificed, while "log-rolling," as the expressive idiom for the trading of votes sometimes phrased it, became the order of the day.

Few if any among these struggling legislators appear to have marketed their influence more profitably than did the members from Sangamon County; and the most able "log-roller" in even that proficient band is said, beyond a question, to have been Abraham Lincoln. Maneuvering his followers so as to take advantage of every turn, arraying their united strength solidly for or against the designs of other delegations, as those delegations declared themselves during the preliminary skirmishes to be allies or opponents of Springfield, winning over some members by appeals to personal interests, others by appeal to sheer good-fellowship, — adroit, tireless, unruffled, — Lincoln at last surmounted all obstacles, and brought this unique campaign to a triumphant finish. The "Long Nine" won. Springfield carried the day, and by a joint vote of both houses, in the closing days of the session, that town became their choice for the permanent capital of Illinois.

Great was the rejoicing throughout the Sangamon region over this achievement. And no less elated — need we add? — were the citizens of the little prairie burg so suddenly raised to prominence. They welcomed the returning delegation as they might have welcomed a band of conquering heroes. Nothing was too good in Springfield for the men who had brought it this coveted civic honor. Members of the "Long Nine" were fêted and lauded on every hand, while their leader particularly came in for grateful attentions. At one complimentary dinner sixty guests are said to have joined in the toast: "Abraham Lincoln: He has fulfilled the expectations of his friends and disappointed the hopes of his enemies."[16]

But "his enemies," or, more correctly speaking, the enemies of Springfield, were still, in a way, to be reckoned with. Some of them took their defeat hard. They affected to believe, if they did not indeed actually believe, that the Sangamon interest had won unfairly. In fact, above the notes of triumph with which the victors celebrated their joyful homecoming might be heard the discordant voices of these chagrined opponents, charging trickery and corruption.

The brunt of such assaults naturally fell upon Lincoln. He it was who had guided the activities of the "Long Nine," and against him were now directed the severest blows of their assailants. Yet the Sangamon chief, by all accounts, proved equal to the occasion. Whenever his conduct or that of his colleagues in the contest for the Capital was publicly attacked, he is said to have replied with telling effect — so much so, in truth, that before long all detractors were silenced, efforts to repeal the act failed, and the Springfield forces, rejoicing in Lincoln's prowess, remained undisputed masters of the situation.[17] They applauded without stint, as might have been expected, the man to whom this was mainly due; but their enthusiastic approval of him is not by any means the last word.

His course throughout the affair can hardly be deemed creditable in every particular. The trading of votes between lawmakers may be defensible, perhaps, under certain rare, not to say peculiar, circumstances. Still, as such transactions are usually conducted, the practice calls for condemnation. And when a group of Representatives, like the "Long Nine," go so far as to traffic through an entire session in one concerted effort to secure the passage of a bill for the special benefit of their constituents, the proceeding becomes grossly reprehensible. In this bargain and sale of legislation, the extravagant expenditure of public money is not by any means the most pernicious feature. Among men so engaged, votes speak louder than conscience, — yes, louder, on occasion, than all the Ten Commandments taken together. For your true "log-rollers" are prone — if we may paraphrase the words of a famous statesman — to consider themselves in politics, not in ethics. Their first few lapses from correct parliamentary principles open the way too often for further and still further deviations, until the standards of nearly a whole legislature seem warped out of their accustomed grooves; an indefinable laxness creeps into actions which have no concern whatever with these "log-rolling" measures, and the let-down in moral tone, brought about by repeated departures from the loftier plane of disinterested lawmaking, hardly stops short, at times, of general demoralization. To what extent this actually happened in the Tenth General Assembly of Illinois is not now definitely known. But prevailing conditions there were manifestly far from ideal; and as some of the fault, at least, was chargeable to the "Long Nine," he who stood at their head must take his share of the blame.

In fairness to Lincoln, however, it should be said — for what such a plea is worth — that any idea of wrongdoing probably never entered the young man's mind. He and his colleagues had merely pursued tactics tolerated, if indeed they were not sanctioned, by the customs of the period. During those raw pioneer days, not a few politicians looked upon votes as legitimate objects of barter; and to so flagrant an extreme, it will be remembered, were their views carried in the Illinois Legislature of 1836–37, that the Assembly became a veritable market-place. Amidst this whirl of chaffering the member from

New Salem was seen to move with steady tread. True, he had shown himself to be a poor business man at home; yet here his faculty for one peculiar kind of commerce apparently fell little short of genius. So it turned out that when the last trade was made, when the deals had all been closed, and Speaker Semple's gavel sounded for final settlements, the big winning was disclosed — as we have seen — in Lincoln's grasp. Then it was that his defeated antagonists set up those cries of outraged virtue. Then only did they discover the depths of moral turpitude into which he had fallen. But their censure came with painfully diminished effect from men who had themselves employed, though unsuccessfully, the very methods for which they now condemned him; and one is curious to know by what system of ethical adjustments they thought to reconcile their own acts with these tardy expressions of principle. In any event, the accusers may be said to have come into court, as the phrase goes, with unclean hands — at least, with hands no cleaner than those of the associate whom they denounced. Indeed, when all is said, the head and front of his offending, as far as these angry politicians were concerned, will be found to lie in the fact that he had beaten the gentlemen at their own game.

Here again let the chronicle do justice to Lincoln. He had indeed played this game — if game it may be called — for all that was in him, but he certainly had not evinced the reckless disregard of public interests that the fault-finding losers tried to lay at his door. On the contrary, he believed himself to have been serving the whole State, no less than Springfield, with every trade whereby the "Long Nine," in exchange for what they wanted, lent their votes and their influence, as has just been narrated, to establish a comprehensive, if lavish, system of "internal improvements." Such undertakings had, in fact, engaged Lincoln's imagination from the very beginning of his public life. Pledged to them, in a sense, and convinced of their value, he aimed at associating himself in the West, as other politicians had done elsewhere through the country, with some splendid scheme for public development. It was during this period that Lincoln, emulating the example of the man to whom the Empire State was chiefly indebted for its Erie Canal, confided to his friend Joshua F. Speed an ambition to make himself "the De Witt Clinton of Illinois." [18] The aspiration looks futile enough now in the light of what ensued. Still, at that time all observers, with rare exceptions, confidently expected to see this single Legislature, by passing a series of Utopian enactments, swing the young prairie Commonwealth into a millennium of prosperity; while the politicians, regardless of party, outvied one another in doing the people's bidding. Demands for these wonder-working measures were heard on every side. An influential lobby invaded the capital to urge their adoption. Petitions poured in upon the members. Their newspapers from home came full of buoyant — not to say flamboyant — articles advising liberal action. Mass meetings and conventions, voicing the general infatuation with sonorous resolutions, went so far as to issue parliamentary orders to their Representatives. In fact, the Sangamon delegation itself had been instructed by citizens of the county assembled at such a gathering to give the much-discussed "system" unqualified support. Obviously, therefore, when Lincoln exchanged improvement votes for Springfield votes, he put a price upon aid which would finally have been given, in any event. Circumstances merely enabled him, as he doubtless thought, to serve his constituents, indeed the whole State, by what he gave no less than by what he received. And if his tactics deftly took toll of legislation going, so to say, as well as coming, the process was, in its political aspect, at least, consistent enough. From all of which, those who cannot bear to contemplate a good man overstepping the narrow path ever so little will derive such comfort as they may; while others who seem inclined to insist upon a hero, immaculate no less than great, must bring themselves to realize that the best of men are sometimes — particularly during their formative years — seen to walk in the shadows.

This one cloud, moreover, on Lincoln's early political record was not without the proverbial silver lining. "Honest Abe's" better self still held sway. Indeed, ideals of public service as he then conceived them were never quite lost sight of, even amidst the temptations incident to a fiercely waged parliamentary campaign. His fault began and ended with the trading of votes. Beyond that, neither the low-leveled practices which prevailed on every hand, nor the pressure of colleagues, eager to triumph at any cost, could carry him. The Machiavellian doctrine that victory brings glory, whatever the method of achieving it, evidently formed no part of the creed which directed his "log-rolling" ambitions. And, ardently as he longed to win the day for Springfield, no questionable proposals, however alluring, were allowed to blunt in any further degree his fine sense of moral values.

A notable instance, aptly illustrating this, occurred when the struggle over the seat of government was at its height. An effort had been made to combine the friends of removal with those who were laboring for a certain measure of dubious character. What that measure entailed is not now definitely known, but Lincoln regarded it with strong disapproval. He had so expressed himself and the negotiations languished. At last, a number of Representatives, who were severally interested on both sides of the projected deal, met to discuss it in a private caucus. Their deliberations lasted, we are told, nearly all night; yet as the Sangamon leader refused to forego his objections, they finally adjourned without having reached the desired agreement. It takes more than one such repulse, however, to discourage politicians. Another conference was presently arranged, and, as if to make sure that sufficient pressure would be exerted upon the recalcitrant member, a number of prominent citizens, not in the Legislature but anxious for Springfield's success, were craftily invited to attend. An earnest discussion ensued. Those who favored the compact employed every argument that they could frame in its behalf.

Some of the speakers, deploring Lincoln's inconvenient scruples, begged him to lay them aside, join his friends, and make sure of the capital for Sangamon County, but without avail. Finally, after midnight, when the candles were burning low and the talk had well-nigh run its course, he arose to close the debate. What Lincoln said has not been preserved entire, but an admirer, who described the speech as "one of the most eloquent and powerful" to which he had ever listened, has handed down these concluding words: "You may burn my body to ashes and scatter them to the winds of heaven; you may drag my soul down to the regions of darkness and despair to be tormented forever; but you will never get me to support a measure which I believe to be wrong, although by doing so I may accomplish that which I believe to be right." [19]

How much provocation the speaker had for this burst of perfervid oratory cannot now be determined, yet whatever one may say about his rhetoric, there can be no doubt concerning his good faith. That meeting adjourned, as its predecessor had done, without taking the questionable step so warmly advocated by most of the persons present; and one of the participants, at least, must be credited with having made clear that even a "log-roller" may set conscientious bounds to the scope of his operations.

Nor was this the only occasion on which Lincoln vetoed the unseemly devices to which some of his too eager partisans would have resorted. They had accepted willingly enough, while the contest for the capital lasted, such conditions as were imposed by the general act upon whatever place might become the seat of government. But after the victory went to Sangamon, these conditions did not appear quite so attractive. One of them, in fact, gave the Springfield people some uneasiness. This was a clause which required the successful community to raise fifty thousand dollars, by private subscriptions, in order that a corresponding amount, appropriated under the act for the erection of needful public buildings, might be refunded to the State. What looks like a small sum now, must have loomed large in those days on the financial horizon of a struggling little frontier town. And its task of collecting the required donations, difficult under normal conditions, became doubly so during the hard times which were ushered in this same year by the historic panic of 1837.

The situation seemed to call for relief of some kind. So a way out suggested itself to an ambitious young politician who had recently taken up his residence in Springfield. This was Stephen A. Douglas, the newly elected Register of the Land Office. His scheme, prefiguring many adroit political shifts to come, had the characteristic merit of being at once simple and efficacious. It proposed, in a word, repudiation. By means of an innocent little legislative amendment, deftly applied, Springfield was to step out from under this burden and let the cost slip back to its original place, on the shoulders of the State. But Lincoln again barred the way.

"We have the benefit," said he. "Let us stand to our obligation like men."[20]

And so they did. Yet money for the first two payments — there were to be three in all — was scraped together with some difficulty; and worse still, when the third installment came due, no funds whatever seemed collectible. Many of the subscribers had become impoverished, while none of them were flush. So the required sum, $16,666.67, was borrowed from the State Bank of Illinois on a note that bore the signatures of one hundred and one citizens. They took eight years to discharge the debt. How hard it came for some of them to meet their share, what economies were practiced, what sacrifices made, can, in the nature of things, never be known. The episode itself, stripped of all these romantic details, — a simple tale of plain good faith, — must suffice for history. And it does suffice. For now, after more than two thirds of a century has elapsed, that painfully liquidated note is still extant. Framed and displayed in a banking-house at Springfield, where all who enter may see, it serves as a memorial to the rectitude of the community during those trying times.

They were trying times, indeed, and to none of these one hundred and one signers more so, perhaps, than to him who had written the name, "A. Lincoln." When he came to the recently chosen capital, as we have seen, shortly after adjournment of the General Assembly, to seek his fortunes at the bar, this young politician's financial condition was, in a sense, worse than penniless. The burden of "the national debt" lay upon him, and the few dollars in his pocket did not suffice — the reader will recall

— to supply his most pressing wants. How those wants were met, first by a seat at Butler's table, then by a place in Speed's bed, may also be recalled. And possibly it is as well to add — for all these circumstances are of peculiar significance now — even the horse which carried him, a few weeks later, on his first trip around the circuit was borrowed from a colleague, Robert L. Wilson, of the "Long Nine." That a man who had been one of the leading actors in an orgy of extravagant legislation should emerge from the session so impoverished as to be dependent momentarily upon the hospitality of one friend for food, of another for shelter, and of still another for the means of gaining a livelihood, is its own commentary on his probity. Nor does this appear less noteworthy, in the light of a commonly accepted belief that the "internal improvement" measures were tainted with personal corruption. The whirl of enticing opportunities during those rapid days is said to have swept more than one legislator off his feet. Yet the Sangamon chief stood steadfast. He could see nothing attractive in the illicit, or at least dubious, gains which were garnered by perverting official duties to selfish ends. In fact, then and thereafter — during that sinister period, as well as throughout his entire four consecutive terms in the Illinois House — Lincoln's record, so far as such matters went, was spotless. Like certain other political leaders to whom private fortunes have been lacking, he followed the rule laid down in one of Daniel Webster's aphorisms: "The man who enters public life takes upon himself a vow of poverty, to the religious observance of which he is bound so long as he remains in it."

There was, however, nothing ascetic, we hasten to add, about "the godlike" Daniel's life — public or private. Improvident and debt-ridden, he indulged himself, to the point of reckless extravagance, in a mode of living beside which the Illinoisan's simple habits formed a striking contrast. They were both poor, it is true, but from very different causes. What some of these were, in Lincoln's case, the stories recounting his hapless business ventures and his unprofitable methods at the bar have already disclosed. For the rest, an engrossing interest in politics with its resultant sacrifices, as the years went on, of time, attention, even money, hardly served to improve the situation. One is prepared, therefore, to learn that when funds ran low he too made shift to eke out his resources by applying the familiar mathematical formula, — three from two we cannot take so I borrow.

Lincoln's very entrance into public life had been made, it must be confessed, through the drab doors of debt. After his first election to the Legislature, while still at New Salem, he was confronted by a perplexing question. How could a countryman, wholly without means, acquire presentable clothes, travel all the way down to the seat of government at Vandalia, and maintain himself there until pay-day in a manner befitting the dignity of a lawmaker? This particular countryman was not long contriving the answer. Calling on Coleman Smoot, a prosperous farmer in the district, he asked: "Smoot, did you vote for me?"

The answer was a prompt affirmative.

"Well," said Lincoln, "you must loan me money to buy suitable clothing, for I want to make a decent appearance in the Legislature."

Here was a whimsical reversal of the course that funds too often take in passing between candidate and voter. But Smoot, who had a warm admiration for the new member, entered cordially into the humor of the affair. He handed out two hundred dollars—enough it would seem to meet all of Lincoln's prospective expenses; and these two hundred dollars—we have the lender's own statement for the fact—were some time thereafter repaid, "according to promise." [21]

The same amount of money, taking the same unaccustomed direction, figured in another peculiar election episode. On the latter occasion, however, a contribution was made to further the office-seeker's election, rather than to help him out afterwards. And this is how it happened. During a vigorously contested canvass, the Whigs raised a purse of two hundred dollars which Joshua F. Speed handed Lincoln to defray his expenses. When the election was over, the victorious candidate brought back one hundred and ninety-nine dollars and twenty-five cents. Giving this to his friend, with a request that it be distributed again among the subscribers, he said: "I did not need the money. I made the canvass on my own horse. My entertainment, being at the houses of friends, cost me nothing; and my only outlay was seventy-five cents for a barrel of cider, which some farmhands insisted I should treat them to." [22]

Lincoln's failure to find a use for these funds was in keeping with the simple honesty which prompted their return. Yet throughout this very period he must have been harried, not only by his old business debts, but also by the several successors to the Smoot loan that his necessities, from time to time, brought into being. Nor were such accommodations always from friends. We catch a glimpse, early in 1839, of a maturing note at the bank that had to be renewed, and the interest charges on which had to be paid.[23] Indeed, many years were destined to elapse before Lincoln could wholly free himself from the meshes of these carking obligations. They held him meanwhile fast-bound among the debtor class, and what he endured, intensifying a natural tenderness for all unfortunates, stirred his sympathies to their very depths in behalf of other men who might be similarly circumstanced.

The situation, however, called for more than mere sympathy. Victims of exorbitant interest charges were to be met with, during the first third of the nineteenth century, on every hand, in Illinois. There, as elsewhere, capital when staked against the hazards of pioneer ventures exacted heavy tolls. Banks and "moneyed institutions," so-called, were restricted, it is true, by an act passed in 1819, to returns not exceeding six per cent; but under that same law other investors expressly had leave to make contracts without any limitations upon the extent of their charges, and for the most part — needless to say — they took advantage of the privilege. Rates running all the way from one hundred and fifty to three hundred per cent were not uncommon in the placing of loans, while the customary figures hovered about fifty per cent. The oppression and suffering which these burdens entailed gave rise to clamorous demands for relief. Yet the way out seemed far from plain. How borrowers could be protected against ruin due to extortion, without being plunged as hopelessly into disaster through ill-advised legislation which, by discouraging lenders, might cut off all supplies, was the form which the problem took.

It appears to have been presented from many angles during the canvass of 1832; and Lincoln, as a raw candidate for the Legislature, had taken a hand, even then, in the solution. What he proposed was thus set forth among the postulates of that first formal political document, his "Address to the People of Sangamon County": —

"It seems as though we are never to have an end to this baneful and corroding system, acting almost as prejudicially to the general interests of the community as a direct tax of several thousand dollars annually laid on each county for the benefit of a few individuals only, unless there be a law made fixing the limits of usury. A law for this purpose, I am of opinion, may be made without materially injuring any class of people. In cases of extreme necessity, there could always be means found to cheat the law; while in all other cases it would have its intended effect. I would favor the passage of a law on this subject which might not be very easily evaded. Let it be such that the labor and difficulty of evading it could only be justified in cases of greatest necessity." [24]

A singular programme, truly, yet what could one expect, in those times of loose financiering, from an embryo prairie politician just pipping his shell? Older heads — in fact, seasoned lawmakers and economists without number, from the very beginning of commercial history down to the present day — hardly make a better showing when it comes to devising how this "tooth of usury," as an eminent Lord Chancellor once said, may "be grinded that it bite not too much." Lincoln's naïve plea that means could be found, when necessary, "to cheat the law, while in all other cases it would have its intended effect," reveals a certain uneasy sense of the fatal weakness running through all such legislation. And one is at a loss what to marvel over most, — the candor with which he admits this defect, or the childlike disregard of public ethics involved in his awkward attempt to meet the difficulty by suggesting occasional violations of the statute.

That subterfuge reminds us of a story, as Abe himself used to say, — one of his own, in fact. He told it, not long afterwards, on the stump, at the expense of an opponent who gave equivocal answers to some searching questions. This man, Lincoln said, was like a hunter he had once known. Boasting of his marksmanship on a certain occasion, and telling how he brought down an animal during the season when a calf might easily be mistaken for a deer, the fellow concluded his recital with the fine flourish: "I shot at it so as to hit it if it was a deer, and miss it if a calf."

What might pass for a hit-or-miss bill, limiting the rate of interest to not more than twelve per cent, became a law during the following winter. But as Lincoln had failed of election to the Legislature which enacted this statute, none of its shortcomings can fairly be laid, except in a remote sense, at his door. Such was not the case, however, with several important financial measures adopted by the succeeding sessions that he did attend. We have seen how he plunged into the excesses which grew out of the "internal improvement" craze, and though many fellow-members of both parties are also chargeable with what took place, few if any of them were more active than he in shaping the course of this hapless legislation. It was under his leadership that the "Long Nine" exerted their very considerable influence, as has been told, to put the so-called "system" through. And a merry dance they had, without too much thought concerning who should pay the fiddler. Soberer men, trying here or there in small numbers to block the way, were swept aside. An infatuated Assembly, hardly stopping to count the cost, voted appropriations for public works aggregating over ten millions of dollars; [25] and interest-bearing securities were authorized to an amount not exceeding eleven millions. Of this sum, eight millions were to be borrowed for the works, two millions for the State Bank of Illinois, and one million for the Bank of Illinois at Shawneetown. These two institutions became the fiscal agents of the State, with a proviso that their net earnings should be applied to the payment of interest, as it accrued, on "improvement" bonds. Nothing could have been simpler and — less dependable. The debt so created — at least such part of it as found a market — was out of all proportion to the young State's proper credit or resources. Consequently, when financial ruin swept over the continent in the spring of 1837, not many Commonwealths were, relatively speaking, more deeply involved than Illinois.

To meet what looked like an impending crisis, Governor Duncan called a special session of the General Assembly in the following July, and urged either modification or repeal of the "internal improvement" acts. But his efforts were fruitless. The Legislature refused to destroy or mar its handiwork. Most of those jocund castle-builders could not bring themselves to believe that the ambitious structure which they had begun to rear with so much pride was, after all, a mere house of cards, shaking in the first gust of bad weather and ready to fall about their ears. Prophecies of such a disaster met, as might have been expected, with stubborn optimism, especially from the ranks of the Whig minority. They stood pledged as a political unit to the policy of munificent public works; and enough Democrats felt similarly committed to join them in bringing about a rejection of the Governor's plea.

More than that, during the following sessions, under Lincoln's guidance — for he had meanwhile become the recognized leader of his party in the House — these "improvement" men, still bat-eyed, reached the climax of their folly, and actually enlarged the scope of the enterprise by nearly one million dollars. The rest is soon told. Hardly had this last reckless step been taken when a wave of that utter demoralization which marked the panic struck Illinois with crushing force. Improvement bonds could no longer be sold except at ruinous discounts. Some of the securities had been entrusted to bankers who failed, while other parcels were moved under circumstances which smelt strongly of fraud.

Collections, moreover, seemed impossible. The treasury of the State was nearly empty. Its credit, if not quite gone, was badly shaken, and so were all its fond illusions. The dazzling game had, in fact, come to an end. Without funds or prospects for raising any, the famous "system" collapsed. Obviously what the situation now required left but slender choice of action. The mischief already done had to be undone, as fully as circumstances would allow, and the "internal improvement" laws must be repealed. Yet the Whigs did not take kindly to this programme. They gave ground sullenly, Lincoln voting against repeal with the rest of his party through several sessions, until at last the logic of events forced them to help their Democratic colleagues put the whole deplorable business "down in a lump," as he himself expressed it, "without benefit of clergy." [26]

Unfortunately there was one detail that could not be put down so summarily. The public debt, which had been piled up with such assurance, remained to perplex its crestfallen creators. They discovered, too late, that bonds can be more easily voted than annulled; and while casting about for a way out of their dilemma, they found themselves facing an interest day with no adequate balance in sight to pay the bill. For a brief period Illinois honor hung in the balance. Some of these precious legislators wished to repudiate the entire indebtedness outright — principal as well as interest; others, not quite so shameless, proposed that the Government, disregarding face values, should deal with the bonds on the basis of what it had received for them when they were sold; while still others favored discrimination against such of the securities only as had been disposed of illegally or acquired by questionable means.

With the last of these Lincoln agreed so far as concerned bonds held by those who had themselves been parties to fraudulent transfers. Otherwise, none of the suggested expedients won his approval. He evinced no sympathy for repudiation, in whatever form it presented itself, nor was his unmercenary mind greatly exercised over the money that had been misspent. What did concern him mightily at this juncture, though, was the unmistakable trend toward dishonesty and bad faith into which such ideas were luring the State. To head off that tendency, he set himself the task of raising somehow at once sufficient funds for the accruing interest. It seemed, in a sense, peculiarly his affair. As a member of the Committee on Finance for three successive terms, and as the acknowledged leader of those who had been most active in passing this wild-cat legislation, Lincoln's share of the responsibility was no small one. He frankly admitted it. Yet here, again, the man's sterling character redeemed the faults of his business training. However blindly he may have groped with the others among the mazes of these financial and economic ventures, when the time came at last to settle for their mistakes, he saw, with crystal clearness, that anything short of payment in full would spell dishonor. The very language of the "improvement" act itself fixed this standard, unless indeed we are to regard as a mere stock-jobber's flourish the words, "for which payments and redemption, well and truly to be made and effected, the faith of the State of Illinois is hereby irrevocably pledged." [27]

But how were the needed funds to be obtained? A short-time loan secured by hypothecated bonds had been proposed, and the idea met with favor. But Lincoln objected. It would, he claimed, carry them along merely a few months, and leave the problem still unsolved. His solution, "after turning the matter over in every way," was to issue "interest bonds" which should be met eventually by taxes derived from public lands.[28] Both these plans were far from ideal. They are suggestive of the shifts resorted to by that impecunious old gentleman who thanked God because he had succeeded, at last, in borrowing enough money to pay his debts.

The alternative presented to Illinois, however, of meeting its obligations by laying a heavy direct tax upon the impoverished people of the State was, as Lincoln truly said, out of the question. Consequently we find him, when his own measure failed of adoption, helping to put through the short-time loan. In fact, by that means the interest charges payable during 1841 were met, as they became due; and one ugly crisis was, for the time being, averted. Still, the inevitable crash had merely been postponed, not prevented. Illinois defaulted on its bonds during the following year. By that time, however, Lincoln, having attended his last session as a Representative, was spared the humiliation of officially facing this disgrace.

Other ordeals growing out of the general disaster were less easy to avoid. A notable instance had run through several of Lincoln's preceding terms, when the State Bank of Illinois found itself in deep water. Compelled, like so many similar institutions, to suspend specie payment through the panic days of 1837, that enterprise seemed doomed to certain destruction, because under the law such a suspension for sixty days together was to be followed by forfeiture of its charter and liquidation of its affairs. But those affairs, the reader will remember, were concerned, to an intimate degree, with the recently adopted scheme for "internal improvements." In fact, the two interests had become so closely interlocked that whatever menaced the stability of the bank might well have been deemed a source of danger to the State.

Naturally, no time was lost in providing the remedy; and an Assembly, convened during the summer of 1837, extended the period during which specie could legally be withheld "until the end of the next general or special session." The fateful day came, but not the resumption of specie payment. So the Legislature that met in December, 1839, after listening to the several reports made by a joint select investigating committee of which Lincoln was a member, revived the forfeited charter and granted still further grace to "the close of the next session." Conditions, however, so far as available specie went, became worse rather than better. Accordingly, when the following Assembly — a special one — was called in November, 1840, at Springfield, to provide funds for defraying interest on the bonded debt, that brief sitting alone seemingly intervened between the bank and ruin.

This prospect mightily gratified the Democrats. They had grown hostile toward the "rag-barons," as these delinquent capitalists were then frequently called; while the Whigs, on the contrary, saw in their plight nothing short of a public calamity. So Lincoln and his followers determined to keep the House, which met at that time in the Methodist Church, from finally adjourning until the approaching regular Assembly, within a few days, might enable them to give the bank a new lease of life. An earnestly contested parliamentary struggle ensued. The Whig minority cannot be said to have made much headway save toward the close of the session, after attendance in the House had thinned out, and the Democrats were ready to vote adjournment without day. Then the friends of the bank, under Lincoln's leadership, set about warding off that stroke by absenting themselves in sufficient numbers to break the quorum. This procedure required alert team-play. While Lincoln and his colleague Joseph Gillespie remained to demand the ayes and noes, their associates left in a body. Directly afterwards, when the opponents of the bank tried to vote a final adjournment, they were halted, as had been planned, by the point of order, "No quorum." A call of the House having been ordered, the sergeant-at-arms rounded up a number of the absentees and brought them in. Amidst much excitement Lincoln hurried to the church door. It was locked. Turning as quickly to a window, with the faithful Gillespie and Asahel Gridley, of McLean County, at his heels, he jumped out, but not before the House had succeeded in adjourning.

There seemed still to be a chance for the State Bank, however. That ill-starred enterprise had not quite reached the closing stage. Within a few weeks its flickering life was again prolonged by legislative means, and the end was again postponed, but not, we should add, for long. Final dissolution presently set in. And after clinging to existence against desperate odds, through some very trying months, the bank collapsed, at last, beyond all hope of recovery. As for Lincoln, the lengths to which he had gone in his futile efforts to save it left him penitent. He would gladly have relegated that discreditable exit through the church window to the limbo of things best forgotten. But the public memory is tenacious of such picturesque misdeeds, and long after what really mattered in the State Bank's tragic story had passed from men's minds, the ghost of this little escapade returned at times to trouble its inventor.[29]

There were not many disquieting recollections of that sort to vex Lincoln's peace of mind; and happily so, for he became sensitive in later days concerning them. When all is said, however, the few lapses just disclosed — lapses which his admirers might well have wished otherwise — should perhaps be charged to a callow excess of legislative ardor rather than to a deficiency in correct political principles. For Lincoln's conduct as a politician — that is to say his conduct regarded from the personal rather than the parliamentary point of view — was above reproach. Indeed, he bore himself where his own interests were concerned with an attention to the niceties of honor that evoked admiring comments. How far these encomiums went may be inferred from a typical one by Judge Samuel C. Parks, who wrote: "I have often said that for a man who was for the quarter of a century both a lawyer and a politician, he was the most honest man I ever knew." [30]

That same rectitude, in fact, which debarred him from taking a shabby case at law when cases were not too plentiful, kept his politics unsoiled. The man's ambition was keen, keener by far than even his need of fees; yet the closest scrutiny reveals no personal let-down anywhere in his code while following either pursuit. Lincoln failed to conceive, despite certain commonly accepted tenets to the contrary, among public men the world over, why there should be one kind of conscience for the private citizen, and another, of a wholly different variety, for the politician.

How punctilious a campaigner this man could be is illustrated by a little incident that took place on one occasion when he was running for the Legislature. A candidate for another place — an office-seeker of whom he did not approve — accompanied Lincoln to the polls on election day, and ostentatiously voted for him with the hope, no doubt, of securing a similar compliment in return. But his cast went far wide of its mark. For Lincoln, ignoring the bait, greatly to the admiration of those who saw the occurrence, voted against him. Log-rolling to increase his own vote at election time and log-rolling to further the passage of a bill were acts so dissimilar in the eyes of the young member from Sangamon that he would not stoop to the one, while he made almost a fine art of the other.

Lincoln looked with disfavor, even during those ill-regulated days, upon the methods employed by unscrupulous politicians to attain their ends. He denounced the whole class as "a set of men who have interests aside from the interests of the people, and who, to say the most of them, are, taken as a mass, at least one long step removed from honest men." The "holier-than-thou" tone of this criticism must have flashed at the moment through his mind, for he hastened to add: "I say this with the greater freedom because, being a politician myself, none can regard it as personal." [31]

Somewhat of that same disapproval was more pithily expressed in another country, at a later date, by no less a personage than Benjamin Disraeli when, after sounding the depths and scaling the heights of English public life through a period of strenuous years, he remarked to a colleague: "Look at it as you will, ours is a beastly profession."

Benjamin and Abraham had not many traits in common: they were the products of vastly different systems; yet a striking resemblance runs through their fine sense of personal honor, their prolonged struggles with debt, their disregard for money, and their contempt of those engaged in politics to serve corrupt private ends. Venality among office-holders early aroused Lincoln's indignation. He could sympathize with nearly any human weakness but dishonesty, and the dishonesty of trusted public servants seemed to him doubly reprehensible. Consequently, in dealing with such thieves, this gentle man, usually so tender of other men's sensibilities, smote and spared not. In fact, so severe could be his blows that the scholarly English leader — expert at sarcasm though he was — is credited with no more scathing utterance than the Illinoisan pronounced against certain rogues who had robbed the American Government. Their castigation furnished a stirring incident to the famous debate on "Subtreasuries" that took place at Springfield, during December, 1839. Seven participants — four Democrats and three Whigs — had spoken, when Lincoln closed the series in what some considered the best effort of all. Addressing himself to the argument made by a predecessor in the opposing camp, he said: —

"Mr. Lamborn insists that the difference between the Van Buren Party and the Whigs is that although the former sometimes err in practice, they are always correct in principle, whereas the latter are wrong in principle; and, better to impress this proposition, he uses a figurative expression in these words, 'The

Democrats are vulnerable in the heel, but they are sound in the head and the heart.' The first branch of the figure, — that is, that the Democrats are vulnerable in the heel, — I admit is not merely figuratively, but literally true. Who that looks but for a moment at their Swartwouts, their Prices, their Harringtons, and their hundreds of others, scampering away with the public money to Texas, to Europe, and to every spot of the earth where a villain may hope to find refuge from justice, can at all doubt that they are most distressingly affected in their heels with a species of 'running itch.' It seems that this malady of their heels operates on these sound-headed and honest-hearted creatures very much like the cork leg in the comic song did on its owner; which, when he had once got started on it, the more he tried to stop it, the more it would run away. At the hazard of wearing this point threadbare, I will relate an anecdote which seems too strikingly in point to be omitted. A witty Irish soldier, who was always boasting of his bravery when no danger was near, but who invariably retreated without orders at the first charge of an engagement, being asked by his captain why he did so, replied, — 'Captain, I have as brave a heart as Julius Cæsar ever had; but, somehow or other, whenever danger approaches, my cowardly legs will run away with it.'

"So with Mr. Lamborn's party. They take the public money into their hand for the most laudable purpose that wise heads and honest hearts can dictate; but before they can possibly get it out again, their rascally 'vulnerable heels' will run away with them." [32]

These thieving officials were of a type common — far too common — among the spoilsmen billeted upon their country by the party in power during those easy-going days. Yet, numerous as the grafters must have been, Lincoln did not allow mere weight of numbers to unbalance his sense of their guilt. Nor was he less keenly alive to other forms of dishonesty that manifested themselves, from time to time, among certain self-seeking politicians, who, trimming their sails deftly at critical moments between conflicting breezes, somehow turned up, with charters revised to date, in any snug-harbor which, by an odd coincidence, happened to contain the lucrative offices.

How hard he could be upon such gentry may be inferred from the oft-related retort to George Forquer. It was uttered early in Lincoln's career, before he had attained any considerable public standing, against a man, moreover, who as a lawyer, Representative, State Senator, Attorney-General, and Secretary of State, appears to have ranked for years among the ablest leaders in Illinois. Forquer, having recently swung over from the Whigs to the Democrats, had just been rewarded with an appointment to the Registry of the Land Office at Springfield. He cut a wide swathe, and his newly erected mansion, the finest in the city, attracted attention, not alone for its beauty, but also because, conspicuously displayed on the structure, rose the only lightning-rod to be seen throughout the community. It was at about this time that the two men crossed swords. Lincoln, making the canvass of 1836 for his reëlection to the Legislature, spoke at a Springfield meeting with such effect as to stir the listening Forquer, an acknowledged master of invective, into a reply. The Register felt obliged to vindicate his recently acquired Democratic principles, but what moved him most was a conviction, as he explained it, that "this young man would have to be taken down." With a lofty assumption of superiority, the orator went on to express regret over the unpleasant task which a sense of duty had imposed upon him; yet the sentiment was apparently not allowed to dull the keen edge of his sarcasm. For the onslaught is said to have been uncommonly severe.

At its conclusion Lincoln, who had stood near, laboring under manifest excitement while attentively regarding his assailant, remounted the platform and made a rejoinder that has become historic. The final words lingered for many years in the memories of those who heard them. One listener, a devoted friend, has thus recalled what he believes to be substantially Lincoln's language: "Mr. Forquer commenced his speech by announcing that the young man would have to be taken down. It is for you, fellow citizens, not for me to say whether I am up or down. The gentleman has seen fit to allude to my being a young man; but he forgets that I am older in years than I am in the tricks and trades of politicians. I desire to live, and I desire place and distinction; but I would rather die now than, like the gentleman, live to see the day that I would change my politics for an office worth three thousand dollars a year, and then feel compelled to erect a lightning-rod to protect a guilty conscience from an offended God." [33]

The effect was electric. Forquer's rod had not averted the lightning. He had, in fact, received a grievous stroke. His antagonist was borne from the court-house on the crest of an enthusiastic crowd; and during the brief remainder of the turncoat's life, Lincoln's reproach stuck in the man's fame like a burdock on a woolly goat.

Forquer was not the only patriot of his peculiar stripe to arouse Lincoln's slow-rising ire. It reached the boiling point against another politician who apparently placed a literal construction on that rather loose epigram whereby party has been defined as "the madness of many for the gain of a few." In this particular instance, "the gain" fell short of what at least one among the favored "few" considered his just share. The malcontent, Charles H. Constable by name, lawyer by profession, and Whig by election, was intensely dissatisfied with his political associates. They had twice elected him to the State Senate; but considering his talents, which are admitted to have been of no mean order, he felt himself entitled to more substantial recognition. So insistent became this feeling that habits of disloyalty grew with it; and he lost no opportunity of denouncing the policy pursued by the party toward its younger supporters. These fault-findings, moreover, waxed especially censorious if Whig leaders happened to be present, as was the case one day on circuit when Constable, with others, visited Judge Davis and Lincoln in a room at Paris that the two occupied together.

On this occasion the man with a grievance lost no time in taking the floor. He characterized the Whigs as "old-fogyish," and charged them with indifference to rising men; while the Democrats were lauded for their progressive methods in these respects. What the grumbler said was hardly borne out by the facts; and perhaps none of those present realized this more keenly than Lincoln, whose own experience proved quite the contrary. He listened in silence, however, for he was standing at the time before a mirror, with his coat off, shaving. But when the speaker went on to instance himself as a victim of political ingratitude and neglect, Lincoln turned upon him sharply and said: "Mr. Constable, I understand you perfectly, and have noticed for some time back that you have been slowly and cautiously picking your way over to the Democratic Party."

An exciting scene ensued. Both men became so incensed that only the combined efforts of all the others who were present sufficed to prevent a fight, though Lincoln, as one of the spectators expressed it, seemed for a time to be "terribly willing." The quarrel was patched up, however, but not Constable's resentment against the Whig Party; for shortly afterward, he revealed how just had been Lincoln's rebuke by deserting to the Democracy.[34]

These shifty place-hunters were doubly blamable in "Honest Abe's" eyes. He despised politicians who forsook their colors to secure promotions under the standards of the enemy, not only because such acts were dishonorable in themselves, but also, it must be confessed, because they involved treason to political associates. For Lincoln was a partisan. His temperament, no less than his fidelity to principle, made him a champion eager and ever ready to battle for cherished convictions. But the feudal days of single combat had passed. He did not believe in battling alone. Like so many other public men of recent modern times, he did believe in the organized expression of economic opinion which is called a party. To him, as to them, it appeared obvious — almost elemental — that voters who accept the same cardinal doctrines should associate themselves together for united action, and that when several such associations with conflicting views, tempered, however, by the sober restraints of intelligent patriotism, confront one another in the field of politics, there is an approach at least to well-balanced government. The party in power deems itself answerable to the entire nation for a successful administration, the party or parties out of power feel an equal responsibility for watchful criticism; while the system itself, though far from ideal, provides a practical solution to some perplexing problems, and a safeguard of constitutional rights. As for the rest, Lincoln's common sense told him that within such organizations alone was efficient political action possible. Explaining this idea on one notable occasion, and speaking from the politician's not too lofty point of view, he said: "A free people, in times of peace and quiet, — when pressed by no common danger, — naturally divide into parties. At such times the man who is of neither party is not, cannot be, of any consequence." [35]

The speaker did, at an early day, become of "consequence." It was as a party man that he received the vote of the Whig minority for Speaker of the Illinois House in 1838, and again in 1840.[36] During those stormy sessions, the parliamentary leadership which went with this distinction could have been held by a zealous partisan only. Lincoln was that, but of course, be it said, he was abundantly more than that. For he commended himself also to his colleagues by signal qualities of a different character. In the first place, his remarkable talent for mastery had come into play betimes. To quote Governor Reynolds: "As soon as he got his bearings, got acquainted, and found how things were drifting, he took the Legislature good-naturedly by the nose, and led them, just like he did his township on the Sangamon." [37]

Then, too, under this easy assumption of control were developing the traits that draw men to a political chieftain. A ready grasp of public questions, an equally ready skill in presenting them to the people or in discussing them with an opponent, the never-failing humor which could raise a laugh when a laugh was needed without too often leaving a sting behind, an almost infallible intuition for the trend of the popular will, certain charms of personality which endeared him to friends and won over enemies, a natural aptitude for contriving measures of attack and defense, an uncommon degree of courage, — moral as well as physical, — and an even rarer fidelity to a high standard of honor, — all these doubtless had their influence upon the vote. But that the choice centered in him, apparently without a dissenting voice from among his fellow Whigs, was also highly significant. For such a compliment furnishes the measure of a leader's devotion to his party. It was as a partisan, moreover, that Lincoln figured prominently in Illinois affairs during the succeeding twenty years, amidst a clash of men and principles theretofore unparalleled for political rancor. The issues presented by the problems of those stirring times had to be fought out vigorously on party lines; and the Sangamon chief, plunging into the thick of the fray, appears to have relished the zest of combat day by day, no less than the occasional victory.

A man usually does best what he likes best to do. Lincoln loved politics. It was the one pursuit outside of his profession that he thoroughly enjoyed and in which he felt thoroughly at home. Almost any time during those twenty years, with possibly one interval, people might have said of him, as was said of another public man, "he eats, he drinks, he sleeps politics." But at no time could Lincoln have truthfully forestalled Bismarck's lament, "Politics has eaten up every other hobby I had"; for in his case there were no other hobbies. From early manhood to the end of his career, the art of government with its kindred activities was Lincoln's sole avocation. It is hardly surprising, therefore, all in all, to observe what consummate skill he brought to the service of the party. Indeed, a mere glance over this period in his career reveals how proficient he must have been. For we see him installing a system of nomination by convention among the Whigs, despite prejudice and opposition; making the keynote speeches, as they were called, in several warmly contested campaigns; drawing up the official election circulars and appeals to the people; stumping the field in his own behalf or in that of other local candidates; canvassing the State on the electoral tickets of successive Presidential nominees; adroitly taking advantage of dissensions in the opposing camp, while striving with rare tact to compose the differences in his own; planning, advising, controlling, until he became the ablest political manager, and at last, — to anticipate somewhat, — the recognized authority in his section on matters affecting the welfare of the organization.

Lincoln was what is commonly termed a "practical" politician. He knew the ins and outs of vote-getting as only a seasoned campaigner can know them. In fact, nothing of political significance seemed to escape his notice. He could say, for the most part, where the big men of the State would be found on any public question; nor was he less accurately informed as to what might be expected from local magnates of lesser degree. While if one of them did depart from his wonted course, in principle or tactics, Lincoln's intuitions might be trusted to prefigure, with some nicety, the effect of that departure upon the man's popularity. For his grasp of political probabilities amounted almost to genius. How this or that district would go under given circumstances was repeatedly forecast by him on the eve of an election with unerring precision; and when the returns came in, he manifested equal skill among the figures. Every column had some story to tell him. Every gain or loss was promptly noted, often, indeed, by the aid of his well-stored memory alone; and at times, before the tables were completed, he would place a prophetic finger on the changes which presaged defeat or victory.

That such a man stood high in the party councils goes without saying. As a member of the County Committee or the State Central Committee, his views held full sway; and when he happened to be relieved of official responsibility in the management of a campaign, those who were in charge sent for him, at important junctures, to help them out. Speaking of Lincoln's services at these conferences, Horace White, who once acted as secretary at State headquarters during a spirited canvass, said: "The Committee paid the utmost deference to his opinions. In fact, he was nearer to the people than they were. Traveling the circuit, he was constantly brought in contact with the most capable and discerning men in the rural community. He had a more accurate knowledge of public opinion in central Illinois than any other man who visited the committee rooms, and he knew better than anybody else what kind of arguments would be influential with the voters, and what kind of men could best present them." [38]

Moreover, when it became necessary to meet or head off some critical move on the part of their opponents, Lincoln brought to the fore, just as he did in the courts, that crowning gift of worldly shrewdness which not infrequently goes with simplicity of nature and downright honesty. He did not mislead himself any more than he did his associates, for he saw things as they actually were. He could put himself in the other man's place, and that is why he could make so close a calculation as to what the other man, under given circumstances, would presumably do. "The other man," during one campaign, at least, appears to have been wanting in such foresight. And when on that occasion the projects of the Democrats miscarried, because they had failed to anticipate how Lincoln's side might act, the occurrence called forth one of his little Menard County stories.

"This situation reminds me," said he, "of three or four fellows out near Athens, who went coon hunting one day. After being out some time the dogs treed a coon, which was soon discovered in the extreme top of a very tall oak tree. They had only one gun, a rifle; and after some discussion as to who was the best shot, one was decided on. He took the rifle and got into a good position. With the coon in plain view, lying close on a projecting limb, and at times moving slowly along, the man fired. But the coon was still on the limb, and a small bunch of leaves from just in front of the coon fluttered down. The surprise and indignation of the other fellows was boundless. All sorts of epithets were heaped on 'the best shot,' and an explanation was demanded for his failure to bring down the coon. 'Well,' he said, 'you see, boys, by gum, I sighted just a leetle ahead, and 'lowed for the durned thing crawling.'"[39]

When Lincoln, in the course of a political contest, allowed for something to happen, it usually did not fall very far short of taking place. A fatalist as to the great impelling current whereby a nation is carried toward its destiny, he believed that social and civic causes, however they may be impeded or diverted for a time in their operations, must at last inevitably lead to corresponding effects. His fatalism, however, was of the robust type. It recognized how important a part men play in creating these forces, as well as in bringing about the results. Miracles formed no part of his political creed, and he waited for none to do his work. So we find him repeatedly in the thick of the conflict, straining every nerve to gain a party victory. Such of his election-time letters as have been preserved furnish illuminating evidence of how industrious he could be. Appealing to this man, arguing with that, advising one inquiring supporter in the rural districts, praising another, warning a colleague of some aggressive step contemplated by their opponents here, heartening a hard-pressed brother there, figuring, explaining, forecasting, Lincoln pulled apparently every straight wire which a vigorous use of the mails brought within his reach.

He appreciated the appeal direct at its full value. And to this, Gibson W. Harris, one of the young men who sometimes assisted him, thus bore witness in later years: "The duty fell to me of writing letters, at his dictation, to influential men in the different counties, down to even obscure precincts. Finding the task not only burdensome, but slow, I suggested the use of a printed circular letter, but the proposal was vetoed offhand. A printed letter, he said, would not have nearly the same effect. A written one had the stamp of personality, was more flattering to the recipient, and would tell altogether more in assuring his good will, if not his support. So for several days the clerk was kept busy in writing more letters. Young and inexperienced as I was, I could not help noticing how shrewdly they were put together, and no two exactly alike. He approached each correspondent in a different way, and I soon reached the conclusion that the necessity he felt for doing this was his weightiest reason, after all, for discarding type." [40]

Lincoln did not lose sight, however, of the wider opportunities for influencing voters presented by the printing-press. A tireless student of newspapers himself, reading them in fact, during this period, almost to the exclusion of all other general publications, Lincoln became so familiar with the journals issued throughout the State that their several party affiliations were, whenever he had occasion to recall them, at his tongue's end. Many an article from his pen, purporting to be an expression of editorial opinion, appeared from time to time in various Illinois sheets. Whether the respective editors, when they adopted these contributions as their own, wholly eliminated the element of deception that enters into such transactions, is perhaps a moot question. One editor, at least, by a simple course avoided any misunderstanding on the subject. This was Jacob Harding who published a country newspaper in the southern part of the State. To him Lincoln once wrote: "*Friend Harding:* I have been reading your paper for three or four years, and have paid you nothing for it." Enclosing ten dollars the writer adds: "Put it into your pocket, say nothing further about it."

The journalist did as he was bid. But soon thereafter, when the generous subscriber sent him a political article with the request for its publication in the editorial columns of his "valued paper," Harding promptly declined, "because," he explained, "I long ago made it a rule to publish nothing as editorial matter not written by myself."

The joke was on Lincoln. Laughing heartily over the letter, he read it aloud to his law-partner, and said: "That editor has a rather lofty but proper conception of true journalism." [41]

This experience was exceptional, however. For in the main, Lincoln's newspaper contributions, like his personal missives, reached their intended goals, as indeed did most of his projects over the still wider ranges of party management. A practical politician, he employed practical methods. That much-decried scheme of coördinated effort, which for lack of a better term is commonly called "the machine," owed its development among the Whigs in Illinois more perhaps to him than to any other leader. As early as 1840, upon the eve of the Harrison campaign, he put forth a plan for thoroughly organizing the party within the State. Four other men, it is true, were associated with him on the Central Committee that had this matter in hand, but the enterprise was largely his work. He wrote the circular letter which explained the system they had adopted, and which announced explicitly what would be required thereafter of each party worker. From the several county committees that were arbitrarily appointed by the terms of the circular, down through district committees and sub-committees, — even to the individual voters, — every Whig was assigned to his part in the undertaking.[42] A more complete programme for the control of political operations is not easily conceived. Nor do we often meet with a document of this class so frankly expressed in the imperative mood. Its language is that of a master to his men. The crack of the party whip seemingly still rings, even at this late day, through the whole performance; and the hand which grasped the whip did so with a vigor not unlike that customarily displayed, in more recent decades, by the leader to whom political idiom has given the title of "Boss."

But the parallel goes no further. Lincoln was not a boss. And nothing else in his leadership even suggests the mercenary autocrats whose intrigues have, from time to time, brought reproach upon the whole field of politics, — yes, upon republican institutions themselves. His organization was, in fact, a very different affair from the corrupt local machine of a later period. For even political machines have no vices of their own. They are what the men who run them make them. The modern ring with its spoilsmen, grafters, heelers, blackmailers, thugs, and what-not, — all held together by the cohesive power of public pelf and patronage, — could not have existed for a moment where Lincoln was in control. Nor can we conceive of him packing primaries, manipulating pudding ballots, falsifying election returns, or taking part in any of those numerous other criminal acts whereby the wishes of honest voters have, on notorious occasions, been systematically frustrated.[43] "He could not cheat people out of their votes any more than out of their money," writes Horace White, who enjoyed the exceptional opportunities for close observation already spoken of. "Mr. Lincoln never gave his assent, so far as my knowledge goes, to any plan or project for getting votes that would not have borne the full light of day." [44] He never, it is safe to add, so far as anybody's knowledge goes, allowed his passion for a triumph at the polls to blur an uncommonly clear vision of what was right and what was wrong. Virtue, they say, wears the garb of no party. Yet a Lincoln could evidently be loyal to his organization, — loyal, if you will, to the machine itself,— without losing sight of what he owed, in the last event, to his own ideals and to the national well-being.

There was still another obligation, of a less lofty character, however, that neither parties nor principles could make this alert politician wholly forget. No matter how freely he gave himself up to the public, his thoughts were rarely withdrawn long from what seemed due, as the phrase goes, to number one. The appetite for distinction, so frankly avowed in that maiden address sent out from New Salem, had grown by the very efforts made to satisfy it. For those efforts were of no laggard quality. When a young man, eager to rise in the world, must first free himself from the triple clog of so many youthful aspirations, — lowly birth, ignorance, and narrow fortunes, — he sometimes acquires a degree of momentum that is not diminished even after the need for it has ceased. This happened to Lincoln. The "little engine that knew no rest" stirred him to political action through the greater portion of his life, and when he did not hold a public place, he appears to have been engaged, with occasional lulls, in hot pursuit of one. Here was no reluctant patriot of the Washington-Marshall order, waiting in dignified retirement for the office to seek the man. On the contrary, Lincoln went out to meet his honors more — much more — than halfway. And of all the faulty pictures presented by intrepid eulogists to a trustful world, none perhaps is further from the fact than that which depicts him as regretfully interrupting the practice of the law in order to enter public life at the call of duty. The sober, unromantic truth presents quite another view. It reveals the real Lincoln who ardently desired political preferment, and, with characteristic candor, said so. Indeed, few, if any, among the vote-getting campaigners of his time plunged into the ruck of a canvass with more spirited self-assertion. "Do you suppose," he once wrote to a grumbling young politician, "that I should ever have got into notice if I had waited to be hunted up and pushed forward by older men?" [45]

No! Lincoln saw to his own pushing — coat off and sleeves rolled up. He did so, moreover, in the downright, honest way we should expect from him.

And some idea of how it was done — in one direction, at least — may be gathered from an illuminating little anecdote told recently by John W. Bunn, another fledgling during those early Springfield days, who sought office, to use his own phrase, "under the political wing" of that same energetic leader.

"A day or two after my first nomination for city treasurer," writes Mr. Bunn, "I was going uptown and saw Mr. Lincoln ahead of me. He waited until I caught up and said to me, 'How are you running?' I told him I did n't know how I was running. Then he said, 'Have you asked anybody to vote for you?' I said I had not. 'Well,' said he, 'if you don't think enough of your success to ask anybody to vote for you, it is probable they will not do it, and that you will not be elected.' I said to him, 'Shall I ask Democrats to vote for me?' He said, 'Yes; ask everybody to vote for you.' Just then a well-known Democrat by the name of Ragsdale was coming up the sidewalk. Lincoln said, 'Now, you drop back there and ask Mr. Ragsdale to vote for you.' I turned and fell in with Mr. Ragsdale, told him of my candidacy, and said I hoped he would support me. To my astonishment, he promised me that he would. Mr. Lincoln walked slowly along and fell in with me again, and said, 'Well, what did Ragsdale say? Will he vote for you?' I said, 'Yes; he told me he would.' 'Well, then,' said Lincoln, 'you are sure of two votes at the election, mine and Ragsdale's.' This was my first lesson in practical politics, and I received it from a high source." [46]

The source may indeed be called "high," from

more than one point of view. For that term does not overstate the matter when it applies to a politician who could zealously press his own interests or those of his party amidst the hurly-burly of many a closely contested field, as Lincoln did, and at the same time keep clear of the mud in the low places. Confuting a common fallacy, he demonstrated, once for all, that there is no essential connection between public life and personal corruption. His career puts to shame those smug gentlemen who, cloistered in spotless self-love, hold themselves aloof from active civic service, on the plea that politics would contaminate them. Of course, in their cases such fears may not be groundless. Perhaps these respectable citizens may know themselves to be weak-kneed. Perhaps their stumbling feet could not avoid the mire. In any event, they may as well be reminded that merely to keep clean, while shirking the work, is to practice a virtue of doubtful value. This man, on the other hand, spending his best years in the thick of things, and giving to each task what the task demanded, came through it all unsullied.

But to infer from these activities that Lincoln was unduly obtrusive in advancing his political interests would be wide of the mark. When he did blow his own trumpet, it struck a note which gave no offense. For from an early day he had mastered the art, so difficult to acquire, of pushing one's self forward without overstepping the bounds of decorum. There was an air of reserve in his demeanor at the very moment when those rising fortunes were urged upward most eagerly. In fact, whatever he did seemed tinged with the lambent modesty that serves, under some conditions, to light up rather than to obscure true merit. It clearly helped Lincoln to know himself and his deserts. One might say that the insight which made the man conscious of extraordinary powers left him painfully aware, as well, of their limitations. He could look himself in the face with a certain detached candor not often found among ambitious politicians. What is more, he could stand erect against other men and check off his own shortcomings. Conceit in any form — need we add? — cannot thrive under such clarity of vision. At the same time, if this faculty for seeing things squarely as they are had failed Lincoln, an abiding simplicity of character — to say nothing about an ever-ready sense of humor — would doubtless have saved him from any exaggerated opinion of his own importance. He certainly manifested no craving for what might be called honorary distinctions. Purely formal or ornamental functions, such as the chairmanship of a meeting, the leading part in a civic ceremony, and the like, were exceedingly distasteful to him; while the master of ceremonies at some social entertainment, strutting about "drest in a little brief authority," aroused his good-natured disdain. With all the politician's fondness for public life and public office, he shrank from the mere display of himself on public occasions. At times, moreover, some of those personal tributes, so dear to the hearts of professional big-wigs, actually distressed him. He seemed annoyed, to cite an instance, by a tendency to name children for him that set in among certain admirers long before his fame had become more than local. And even the honor of standing sponsor to a whole community apparently brought this unassuming man no elation. For, when his friend Whitney asked whether the town of Lincoln was named after him, he answered dryly: "Well, yes, I believe it was named after I was." [47]

Obviously, all this is not of a piece with the oft-quoted pride that apes humility. It should be described rather as the genuine modesty which had its origin down deep in the man's honest soul, in his own appraisal of his true value, made on his own sensitive scales. He could not mislead himself or others by false pretensions, during those aspiring times, any more than he had found it possible, in the old grocery-store days, to cheat customers with false weights. He frankly rated his merits quite as low as those around him were likely to have placed them; and it may be doubted whether even his intimates had a less exalted opinion of Abraham Lincoln than in the last analysis had Abraham Lincoln himself.

This freedom from egotism impressed, sooner or later, all who came in contact with the man. His political associates, somewhat after the manner, as the reader may remember, of his colleagues on circuit, bore witness to the almost humble spirit in which he ordinarily conducted himself. That such a course is likely to win popular support, disarm criticism, and turn aside the shafts of envy, might lay almost any politician so behaving open to the suspicion of assuming a pose — any politician but a Lincoln. In his case, the posture accords too closely with what we have seen of him from other angles to leave any doubt concerning its sincerity. For instance, the same kindly fellowship that encouraged beginners in the law, when they happened to approach him after he had become a leader of the bar, was manifested under parallel circumstances toward budding politicians. Among the most brilliant of these may be ranked the young German refugee, Carl Schurz, who had interested himself in American public affairs even before he could have been eligible to American citizenship. Having made some speeches in Lincoln's behalf during a memorable canvass, the newcomer improved an early opportunity for meeting the Sangamon chief; and much to his surprise, found himself received, as he relates, with "offhand cordiality, like an old acquaintance."

This must have made a vivid impression on the tyro's mind. Recalling the interview toward the close of his life, Mr. Schurz tells us, with renewed wonder, how unreservedly Lincoln discussed the campaign, and then goes on to say: "When, in a tone of perfect ingenuousness, he asked me — a young beginner in politics — what I thought about this and that, I should have felt myself very much honored by his confidence had he permitted me to regard him as a great man. But he talked in so simple and familiar a strain, and his manner and homely phrase were so absolutely free from any semblance of self-consciousness or pretension to superiority, that I soon felt as if I had known him all my life and we had long been close friends." [48]

Among strangers, Lincoln carried himself, it is

perhaps needless to say, equally free from any suggestion of the grand air. His commonplace — at times uncouth — appearance, together with his unassuming ways, gave the chance comer no hint of the man's importance, even after he had obtained some measure of fame beyond the State border. On more than one occasion he might have exclaimed, as did the famous Achæan general when they found him meekly cutting up firewood for the hostess of Megara: "I am paying the penalty of my ugly looks."

So different, in truth, was Lincoln's manner from the breezy, bumptious swagger not seldom seen among the public personages of his day, that only an observer of rare discernment would have taken him, at first glance, for a prominent politician. Even nimble-witted members of the guild themselves "smelt no royalty," as he once quaintly expressed it, in his presence. And one of them has handed down an amusing tale which relates how the big man's modest bearing hoaxed a brace of jocund statesmen to the top of their bent. Here is the story, as Thomas H. Nelson of Terre Haute, tells it on himself: —

"In the spring of 1849 Judge Abram Hammond, who was afterwards Governor of Indiana, and I arranged to go from Terre Haute to Indianapolis in the stage-coach. An entire day was usually consumed in the journey. By daybreak the stage had arrived from the West, and as we stepped in we discovered that the entire back seat was occupied by a long, lank individual, whose head seemed to protrude from one end of the coach and his feet from the other. He was the sole occupant, and was sleeping soundly. Hammond slapped him familiarly on the shoulder, and asked him if he had chartered the stage for the day. The stranger, now wide awake, responded, 'Certainly not'; and at once took the front seat, politely surrendering to us the place of honor and comfort. We took in our traveling companion at a glance. A queer, odd-looking fellow he was, dressed in a well-worn and ill-fitting suit of bombazine, without vest or cravat, and a twenty-five-cent palm hat on the back of his head. His very prominent features in repose seemed dull and expressionless. Regarding him as a good subject for merriment we perpetrated several jokes. He took them all with the utmost innocence and good-nature, and joined in the laugh, although at his own expense.

"At noon we stopped at a wayside hostelry for dinner. We invited him to eat with us, and he approached the table as if he considered it a great honor. He sat with about half his person on a small chair, and held his hat under his arm during the meal. Resuming our journey after dinner, conversation drifted into a discussion of the comet, a subject that was then agitating the scientific world, in which the stranger took the deepest interest. He made many startling suggestions and asked many questions. We amazed him with 'words of learned length and thundering sound.' After an astounding display of wordy pyrotechnics the dazed and bewildered stranger asked, 'What is going to be the upshot of this comet business?' I replied that I was not certain, in fact, I differed from most scientists and philosophers, and was inclined to the opinion that the world would follow the darned thing off!

"Late in the evening we reached Indianapolis, and hurried to Browning's Hotel, losing sight of the stranger altogether. We retired to our room to brush and wash away the dust of the journey. In a few minutes I descended to the portico, and there descried our long, gloomy fellow-traveler in the center of an admiring group of lawyers, among whom were Judges McLean and Huntington, Edward Hannigan, Albert S. White, and Richard W. Thompson, who seemed to be amused and interested in a story he was telling. I enquired of Browning, the landlord, who he was. 'Abraham Lincoln of Illinois, a member of Congress,' was the response. I was thunderstruck at the announcement. I hastened upstairs and told Hammond the startling news, and together we emerged from the hotel by a back door and went down an alley to another house, thus avoiding further contact with our now distinguished fellow-traveler." [49]

As these two wags sneak sheepishly away from their recent butt, they present a comical reminder of that time-honored aphorism: "The world receives an unknown person according to his appearance; it takes leave of him according to his merits." True, our crestfallen Hoosiers did not themselves sense the worth concealed under Lincoln's homespun manners; yet for this the man who had so neatly gulled them could hardly be blamed. He paid the merry jesters in their own coin, so to say; and if they failed to notice the twinkle of his keen gray eyes as he made change, no one was at fault but themselves. The ethics of practical joking had been observed fairly enough. At all events, the gentlemen from Indiana, so far as is known, set up no claim to the contrary.

Lincoln's energies were not confined, however, to such encounters. Within the party itself occasionally arose contests between rival leaders that differed widely from the usual election campaigns against the common enemy; and it is of interest to see how "Honest Abe," under these more delicate circumstances, conducted himself. A typical instance was that of his canvass for Congress. This began as early as 1842 when, upon the completion of a fourth term in the Illinois House of Representatives, he declined the proffered renomination, but not because he wished to retire from public life. "His ambition," as one intimate friend declared, "was a little engine that knew no rest." It seemed always speeding him toward higher levels. A seat in the National House had now become his goal; and with characteristic directness, he announced himself as a candidate for the promotion. An attempt, obviously not so direct, was made to turn him aside; for we find among his letters this word of warning, addressed at the time to a correspondent in Cass County: "If you should hear any one say that Lincoln don't want to go to Congress, I wish you, as a personal friend of mine, would tell him you have reason to believe he is mistaken. The truth is I would like to go very much." [50]

In those days the Springfield District, as it was

sometimes called, had become a Whig stronghold to such a degree that whoever received the endorsement of the party there on the Congressional ticket might well feel assured of his election. Naturally the prospect attracted other ambitious young politicians besides Lincoln. He found himself strongly opposed for the nomination by Edward Dickinson Baker, of his own county, and General John J. Hardin, of Black Hawk War fame, from Morgan County. The preliminary canvass was uncommonly warm. It appears to have reached a white heat, at almost the very outset, between Lincoln and Baker in their struggle for the control of the delegation which Sangamon should send to the nominating convention. Both men were popular, but Baker's longer residence in the State, his charm of manner, his dashing personality, and his remarkable talent for impromptu oratory gave him an advantage, which enthusiastic friends sought still further to improve by tactics manifestly open to criticism, especially when employed in a party contest. For, strange to relate, a personal campaign of an abusive nature was waged against the man from New Salem. His recent faithful leadership on the floor of the Legislature had, for the moment, in some quarters at least, apparently been forgotten; while his marriage during the year to Mary Todd, whose religious affiliations — unlike those of the Bakers — were not with the potent Campbellite Church, became by cunningly contrived suggestion an adverse issue of seeming importance. Moreover, his own alleged irreligion, slyly hinted at, a duel that had been talked of but had never been fought,[51] an unpopular temperance address recently delivered, and, above all, his connection through the young wife with her prominent, perhaps too self-satisfied, relations, were severally urged in various directions as good reasons for withholding the desired support.

What particularly pained Lincoln was this last count in the indictment. For one who had so recently been a "friendless, uneducated, penniless boy working on a flat-boat at ten dollars per month," to be "put down" — we are quoting his own protest — "as the candidate of pride, wealth, and aristocratic family distinction," must have felt odd beyond measure.[52] It is not surprising that, with all his political acumen, he was at a loss for an adequate reply. What reply, indeed, can one make to such a charge! He tried to laugh it off, meeting the story of those high-bred relatives with the whimsical remark: "Well, that sounds strange to me. I do not remember of but one who ever came to see me, and while he was in town he was accused of stealing a jew's-harp." [53]

Still the canard persisted, though the fact that it ever received serious attention must be counted among the mysteries of Illinois politics; unless perhaps a faint suggestion of an explanation is to be found in Lincoln's own demeanor. He was, it is true, a commoner, a man of the people, if there ever has been one in American public affairs. His democratic ways, unpretentious garb, and homely fashion of speech were as truly expressive of the man as were his sympathetic dealings, in all the essentials of life, with the plain citizens around him. But he neither flattered them nor catered to their prejudices. Lincoln was no demagogue. Coming upon the scene with a generation of pioneers whose antipathy toward the so-called aristocrats naturally had its corresponding reaction in a fondness for men of their own kind, he made it a point, nevertheless, to ask for support wholly on his merits; and practiced none of those crude arts whereby politicians of that day too often courted popular favor.[54] In fact, he went at times as far the other way, and bluntly declined so to cheapen himself.

A case in point occurred on the occasion of his address before an agricultural society, when he said: "I presume I am not expected to employ the time assigned me in the mere flattery of the farmers as a class. My opinion of them is that, in proportion to numbers, they are neither better nor worse than other people. In the nature of things they are more numerous than any other class; and I believe there really are more attempts at flattering them than any other, the reason for which I cannot perceive unless it be that they can cast more votes than any other. On reflection, I am not quite sure that there is not cause of suspicion against you in selecting me, in some sort a politician and in no sort a farmer, to address you." [55]

These words — we must add — were uttered some years later, but they nicely illustrate the speaker's bearing throughout his political career. The compelling candor which led him to speak so was, in truth, the very essence of the man. He could not do otherwise. And therein, perhaps, lay some explanation of why it was difficult for him, during this congressional contest, to meet the charge of having joined the so-called privileged class, — particularly as the accusation came from members of his own party.[56]

That Baker himself had anything to do with the misconduct of these overzealous partisans, Lincoln refused to believe.[57] Still he could not close his eyes to the inroads which their attacks made upon his strength in the county. And when the Sangamon Whigs met, in the spring of 1843, to elect delegates for the District Convention, Baker was clearly their choice. The meeting so voted. But its confidence in the rejected candidate was evinced, to a noteworthy extent, by his selection as a member of the delegation, instructed to cast Sangamon's ballot at the convention for his successful opponent. This placed Lincoln in an embarrassing position; and he tried, though without avail, to be excused. Commenting on the singular occurrence to his absent friend Speed, he wrote: "The meeting, in spite of my attempt to decline it, appointed me one of the delegates; so that in getting Baker the nomination, I shall be fixed a good deal like a fellow who is made a groomsman to a man that has cut him out and is marrying his own dear 'gal.'"[58]

There was this difference, however. The groomsman usually renounces his hopes at the church door; whereas Lincoln, for a time at least after the meeting, still considered himself, in some degree, a candidate. Expecting his old neighbors in the New

Salem-Petersburg vicinage to instruct a Menard County delegation for him, he figured out a combination whereby they might, under certain conditions, cast the deciding votes in the convention. "It is truly gratifying to me," he wrote Martin M. Morris, one of these supporters, "to learn that while the people of Sangamon have cast me off, my old friends of Menard, who have known me longest and best, stick to me."

After outlining the situation, with the terse, firm strokes of a skilled politician, he continued: "You say you shall instruct your delegates for me, unless I object. I certainly shall not object. That would be too pleasant a compliment for me to tread in the dust. And besides, if anything should happen (which, however, is not probable) by which Baker should be thrown out of the fight, I would be at liberty to accept the nomination if I could get it. I do, however, feel myself bound not to hinder him in any way from getting the nomination. I should despise myself were I to attempt it. I think, then, it would be proper for your meeting to appoint three delegates, and to instruct them to go for some one as a first choice, some one else as a second, and perhaps some one as a third; and if in those instructions I were named as the first choice, it would gratify me very much." [59]

This letter furnishes another revelation of how tight a grip Lincoln's ambition, carrying him along at top speed, had upon his movements; and by that same token, of how tight a grip he meant to keep, in any event, upon the restraining brake, which was so rarely allowed to leave his watchful hand. Whether he could have maintained his moral equilibrium, however, in the District Convention, as a delegate instructed for one candidate while he permitted his friends to support another candidate, and that candidate himself, raises, under all the circumstances, a delicate question in political ethics. Happily, Lincoln was not called upon to try it out. By the time the delegates gathered at Pekin, he and Baker were both outdistanced by General Hardin, who promptly became the choice of a far from harmonious convention.

Then ensued an incident which, besides having a controlling influence toward the shaping of local politics for some years to come, caused controversies later of more than local importance. This is how it came about. No sooner had the vote been taken than Lincoln walked across the room to James M. Ruggles, one of the Hardin delegates, and asked him whether he would favor a resolution recommending Baker for the succeeding congressional term. Ruggles, who was fond of that gentleman, readily consented, so Lincoln said: "You prepare the resolution, I will support it, and I think we can pass it." [60]

The motion is said to have "created a profound sensation, especially with the friends of Hardin." Some of them warmly objected, but it was passed, nevertheless, by a very close vote. The proposition should, indeed, have been well received. It belonged to that class of convention devices which is sometimes designated as "good politics." The contest had stirred up much feeling, and Lincoln, like the alert party leader that he was, took this means of placating a disgruntled faction. "So far as I can judge from present appearances," he declared, "we shall have no split or trouble about the matter. All will be harmony." [61] And when the nominee wrote a letter, after the convention, expressing some doubt as to whether the Whigs of Sangamon would support him, Lincoln replied: "You may, at once, dismiss all fears on that subject. We have already resolved to make a particular effort to give you the very largest majority possible in our county. From this, no Whig of the county dissents. We have many objects for doing it. We make it a matter of honor and pride to do it; we do it, because we love the Whig cause; we do it, because we like you personally; and last, we wish to convince you, that we do not bear that hatred to Morgan County, that you people have so long seemed to imagine. You will see by the *Journal* of this week, that we propose, upon pain of losing a Barbecue, to give you twice as great a majority in this county as you shall receive in your own. I got up the proposal." [62]

This magnanimous treatment of Hardin, like the resolution in Baker's favor, is noteworthy. Yet here again — of a truth, in neither case — did Lincoln wholly neglect his own aspirations. Though he regarded both these men with sincere good-will, and stepped aside for them with unruffled temper, it was in the hope that his turn would come next. Some of the party leaders, in fact, eventually worked out an arrangement whereby John J. Hardin, Edward Dickinson Baker, Abraham Lincoln, and Stephen

Trigg Logan succeeded one another in the Whig nomination of the district, for a single congressional term each. That this bargain or deal — to use familiar political expressions — existed has been vehemently denied. And in the nature of such affairs, it may well be doubted whether there was a definite agreement to which the parties in interest gave their formal approval. The Hardin following, for one, appears to have acquiesced unwillingly, if indeed it actually assented at all. Still, no less an authority than Lincoln himself tells us of "an understanding among Whig friends," whereby each of these men received the nomination in turn.[63] And this understanding, in part at least, had its public ratification, if not its origin, as we have seen, with his resolution endorsing Baker. Although politicians usually conceal such transactions, because they are looked upon by the voters with disfavor, and although some through-thick-and-thin eulogists, trembling for the fair fame of their hero, have refused to believe that Lincoln did anything at this point which savored of intrigue, he himself manifestly made no secret of the matter nor of his hand in it. A thoroughgoing candidate from start to finish, this man, honorable as he was, played his game according to the standards of the aggressive political school in which he had been bred. But he played it openly. He saw no harm in that group of aspirants "making a slate," as the process is sometimes called; and under all the circumstances, neither do we.

The Sangamon chief, true to his pledge, loyally supported the nominee of the convention. General

Hardin, triumphant at the polls, went to Congress. And when, by reason of a change in the time for holding the next election, it became necessary, during the following year, to name his successor, he gave way in Baker's favor, as the Pekin resolution had provided. Naturally Lincoln, the father of that measure, did likewise. In fact, he worked no less faithfully for rival number two than he had for rival number one, and Baker was duly chosen.[64] Then at last, in 1846, came Lincoln's turn. Expecting to reap the reward of his patience, he struck out vigorously for the nomination. But to his chagrin, Hardin, ready to make the race for another term, threatened again to block the way; while Judge Logan, the remaining claimant on the slate, had also entered the field, demanding precedence over Lincoln on the ground of seniority as well as of valuable services to the party. Whether this latter candidature was entirely sincere, or whether it should be deemed one of those back-firing devices to head off other aspirants, so often employed by political strategists, cannot, at this late day, be determined. True, the dissolution of partnership at law between Logan and Lincoln, several years before, had been due, in a degree at least, to the conflicting congressional ambitions of its members. Still, nothing that then took place was rasping enough, so far as is known, to keep them from entering into an "understanding" for their mutual benefit. At all events, Logan can hardly be said to have made a very vigorous start and, after a brief reconnoissance of the district, he withdrew gracefully in Lincoln's favor.

Hardin was not so easily disposed of. Denying that there had been any agreement personally on his part to rest content with one term, he declared himself betimes a candidate for another nomination. Lincoln's rejoinder was the maxim, — "Turn about is fair play." He called this his "only argument," and proceeded in effect to make it the slogan of an energetic campaign. A less inspiring issue on which to ask for political support is not often presented. Yet this was the issue, and Lincoln candidly said so. With a freedom from the customary cant of "public servants" that is really refreshing, he canvassed the party on personal grounds, but without personalities. His supporters were cautioned against saying anything unkind about Hardin; and when he himself made any reference to his adversary, it was in terms of friendly appreciation. Lincoln wanted that office. He wanted it badly. But his ever-present sense of fairness saved him from resentment toward the Bakers and Hardins who wanted it, too. They were entitled to a place in the sun. And even the fact that one who had basked in its warmth for a season was trying now to elbow him back when his turn came, did not ruffle the man's good humor. Yet he stood his ground firmly, while insisting, with winsome naïveté, on "a fair shake." So when General Hardin made a crafty suggestion that the candidates should agree respectively to "remain in their own counties," Lincoln promptly declined, with the obvious explanation: "It seems to me that on reflection you will see, the fact of your having been in Congress has, in various ways, so spread your name in the district, as to give you a decided advantage in such a stipulation."

His reasons, given in the same letter, for refusing to walk into the general's other cunningly contrived pitfalls, were equally cogent; while the temper of the missive, as a whole, may be inferred from the pretty little apology: "I have always been in the habit of acceding to almost any proposal that a friend would make, and I am truly sorry that I cannot in this." [65]

Hardin, on his part, was apparently not so amiable. The general's supporters were allowed to assail Lincoln in somewhat the same manner that Baker's friends had done three years before. Indeed, they may have been even less scrupulous. For one of Lincoln's youthful lieutenants, G. W. Harris, tells us how, disheartened by their methods, he went to his chief in the heat of the canvass, and declared that it was useless to proceed any further unless the object of these assaults was willing to adopt similar tactics. Without any show of feeling, Lincoln replied: "Gibson, I want to be nominated; I should like very much to go to Congress; but unless I can get there by fair means, I shall not go. If it depends on some other course, I will stay at home." [66]

"That settled it," Harris adds. But things hardly went as he had predicted. Not long thereafter his leader's scruples were vindicated, on even the politician's narrow ground, by Hardin's withdrawal from the contest, in a generous letter, which left the field to our Springfield friend unopposed. So it came to pass that when the Whig District Convention met early in May, 1846, the name of this sole remaining candidate was duly presented by Judge Logan and Lincoln received a unanimous nomination.

The Democrats put forward as their candidate the well-known Methodist circuit-rider, Peter Cartwright. He gave promise of making a formidable antagonist. Few men had more friends throughout the district, and indeed, throughout the State. His robust ministry, as he traveled on horseback undaunted by frontier hardships from place to place, brought him into intimate, at times even sacred, relations with the people. They cherished, in their rough way, a fondness for the man whose piety and never-failing human sympathy had made him through all the shifting years, whether at weddings, christenings, sick-beds, or funerals, the dependable partner of their joys and their sorrows. A preacher, moreover, of the church-militant, he compelled respect among these sturdy pioneers by his physical, no less than by his spiritual, qualities. As became one who patrolled in autocratic fashion "the country of superior men," he was wont, when occasion served, to pound out a sermon or knock out a service-disturbing brawler, with equal force, and — if the truth must be told — with equal relish. But the aggressive elements in Cartwright's make-up found still freer vent on the several occasions when he sought to transmute all this popularity into votes. For somewhat after the manner of the high priests in Israel, the "Apostle of the West," as he was sometimes called, aspired to combine religion with statecraft. A Jacksonian Democrat of the uncompromising type, his politics like his theology belonged to the hard-shell variety; and few campaigners could give a better account of themselves on the stump. If rugged eloquence failed to produce the desired effect, a certain nimble-witted humor might be depended on to carry the day for him. He had, in fact, been elected or, more precisely speaking, reëlected, to the State Legislature when Lincoln suffered his first, his only, rebuff at the polls, fourteen years before; and with the two men now pitted against each other again — this time on a larger field — the Democrats naturally expected to bring about a repetition of that defeat.

But the Lincoln who faced Cartwright in 1846 was a different adversary from the comparatively unknown novice who had gone down before the famous preacher in 1832. Since then the younger man must have learned many practical lessons in the school of politics, and learned them well, for his congressional canvass is described as a model of skillful electioneering. It left unturned, in all the district, no stone beneath which might lurk a favorable vote; while it met, with similar alertness, every issue raised by the enemy, or more accurately speaking, every issue but one — that of religion.

The charge of impiety, covertly made in former primary contests, as we have seen, by Lincoln's own Whig associates, was now publicly urged against him with far greater earnestness by his Democratic opponents. What ground they had for their accusations cannot conveniently be considered at this point. The assailed candidate himself shrewdly refrained from taking any public notice of the matter, and he impressed upon his lieutenants the wisdom of exercising similar forbearance. Here was one of those rare junctures in which your true leader may be recognized, not so much by what he does as by what he omits to do. Lincoln confidently left this issue in the hands of the people. They have on repeated occasions been known to meet it with appropriate vigor, yet nearly every generation of politicians must be taught the lesson anew. The man who lays Religion by the heels, and drags her through the mire of a political campaign for the votes that may adhere to the soiled vestments, usually bends so low over his narrow course that he does not see, until too late, the shocked devotees, on the one hand, deserting him because he has profaned a scared thing, nor the indignant citizens on the other, turning from him because he would obtrude sectarian influences where they have no business — in purely secular affairs. Even the popularity of a Cartwright sags under such a strain. Moreover, his sterling character gave him no countervailing advantage in that particular contest. For when it came to the weighing of these opposing candidates — cleric against skeptic, saint against sinner — by almost any voter's own work-a-day standards, the rectitude of Lincoln's life at the bar, no less than the notable honesty of his politics, dressed the balance between the two champions, so far as practical ethics went, to a nicety. This left the revulsion from bigotry that touched broad-minded men in both parties, together with the normal preponderance of the Whigs and the superior campaigning tactics of their leader, to tip the scales finally in his favor. As the canvass drew near its close, not a few of the Democrats are said to have looked upon him with kindly eyes. But party feelings ran so strong in those days that to support a candidate on the opposing side involved a wrench to cherished traditions from which these alien well-wishers, these friends the enemy, naturally, for the most part, recoiled. One of them, doubtless a typical instance, coming to Lincoln in such a dilemma, declared himself willing to cast a Whig ballot if it were needed to defeat Cartwright. The sacrifice, he thought, should be required only in the event of a very close struggle; and the Whig captain, accepting this view, agreed to let him know how the contest stood. Accordingly, right before election-day, Lincoln having made one of those clever forecasts for which he was noted, released his provisional recruit with the announcement: "I have got the preacher, and don't want your vote." [67]

He certainly did have the preacher. When returns came in, it was found that a considerable number of Democrats, setting public spirit above partisan prejudice, after all, had given their adherence to the Whig nominee. Lincoln led Cartwright at the polls by 1511 votes. How splendid a victory this was, and how much of it may be credited to Democratic defections, will be understood when it is recalled that the same district had, in the preceding presidential campaign, given electors for Henry Clay, the popular Whig standard-bearer, a plurality of but 914. "Lincoln's election by the large majority he received," said Governor Reynolds, commenting on the congressional contest some years later, "was the finest compliment personally and the highest political endorsement any man could expect, and such as I have never seen surpassed." [68] These superlatives hardly overstated the case. No previous Whig campaigner of the district had in fact achieved such results; and so fully did they justify Lincoln's persistent demands upon his party for the nomination that his election must have brought him a double measure of gratification.

Then, however, came the all but inevitable reaction. That triumph, so long deferred and so patiently wrought out, fell short of what his ambitious fancy had pictured. The sub-acid tang, which detracts too often from our complete enjoyment of life's sweetest morsels, entered into the victor's spirit at the moment of achievement, and left him disappointed. Addressing his sympathetic friend Speed — the other self of those days — in much the same vein as the great Roman politician Cicero was wont to employ toward his intimate Atticus, when eclipsing shadows of depression marred the joy of some brilliant exploit, Lincoln wrote: "Being elected to Congress, though I am very grateful to our friends for having done it, has not pleased me as much as I expected." [69]

THE END

ALONZO ROTHSCHILD

ALONZO ROTHSCHILD

ALONZO ROTHSCHILD

THE morning that my father finished that concluding paragraph — the last that he ever wrote — he called mother into the study. With an air of mysterious solemnity, belied by the twinkle in his eye, he beckoned her to the desk.

"Meta, if you promise not to tell a soul, I'll tell you a state secret," he said. "I've got Lincoln to Congress at last." Then more earnestly he continued: "It was n't an easy job either. I've fought all his battles side by side with him, and the world will probably never know how hard we toiled and moiled together."

These words exactly expressed his relationship to his work. During the twenty-three years that he devoted to the study and interpretation of Abraham Lincoln, he lived with him in spirit as the great novelists have lived with the children of their fancies. Lincoln's sorrows and triumphs and defeats were as real to him as those of his own life. It is small wonder, therefore, that when men who had known Lincoln read *Lincoln, Master of Men,* they frequently mistook its author for an intimate contemporary of the great President.

Though not of the same generation as Lincoln, my father's life was, in a trivial way, associated with it at the start. He was born in New York City on the evening of a Lincoln rally at Cooper Union, October 30, 1862. The family physician was at the meeting when the time became ripe for his services, so my grandfather followed him there, somehow found him in the vast crowd, and worked upon his sense of duty so that he consented to forego the speeches, and returned with my grandfather to the Rothschild home.

One is tempted to speculate whether or not, as the

doctor looked down at the boy whose birth had prevented him from hearing eminent men discuss the President, — whether or not some confiding Fate whispered to him a half-articulate prophecy that that same boy was one day to be among the most deep-seeing interpreters of Abraham Lincoln.

Interesting as this coincidence is, in the light of succeeding developments, it is, of course, quite devoid of significance. Not until some years later did Abraham Lincoln actually become an influence in my father's life.

Probably it was his father who first planted the seed of admiration for Lincoln in his mind, for John Rothschild came to America with an influx of German revolutionists — men of the Carl Schurz stamp — and to him, as to so many of those who came in that wave of immigration, "Lincoln became an ideal, — a prophet."

Just as some knowledge of my father's parentage helps to an understanding of his interest in Abraham Lincoln, it enables one better to comprehend several of his personal characteristics. The thoroughness that fortified all his undertakings may be attributed to his unmixed German blood. For his mother as well as his father was German. She was known as "Beautiful Kate," but a remarkable amiability that poverty and the raising of a large family never impaired was her outstanding characteristic. The evenness of disposition that my father inherited from her combined strangely with a certain fiery impetuosity and violence of temper that was of paternal origin, so that his ordinary mildness and long-suffering sometimes blazed out into a Jovian wrath. From both parents equally, he derived a sturdy honesty, common sense, and humor, while to his father in particular he owed a ready wit and skill in repartee.

Beyond the excellence of his parentage, there was nothing particularly auspicious about the conditions of my father's early life. John Rothschild was an invalid, and his various attempts to get on in the world were unsuccessful. Furthermore, there were six complications in the bread-and-butter problem of which my father was the fourth. But nature had equipped him splendidly for the upward battle that those must wage who would rise from the ranks. While there cannot have been much suggestive of the fighter in the frail little chap who was "Lonny" Rothschild, yet a cool sureness of purpose and virile resourcefulness often won him the palm in unequal encounters with bullies as well as in the subtler battles of school and daily life.

There is a story that testifies to his resourcefulness and at the same time indicates his literary instinct. "Lonny's" family lived on Fifty-fourth Street and his school was at Thirteenth Street, two miles away. He could afford the horse cars only on his way to school, and used to return afoot. His chum, however, whose parents were in better circumstances, received two car fares daily and was expected to ride both ways. One day, by the promise of a story, "Lonny" inveigled the youngster into walking home with him. The story proved to be an exciting serial that never ended, so that henceforth the author always had company on these journeys. And what is more, not only were his spirits fortified by company, but his inner being was regaled with the refreshments that he persuaded young Crœsus to buy along the way with the misappropriated car fares.

Generally speaking, "Lon" did not care much for the company of his schoolmates or for their games. He preferred a book to a game of ball. In fact he used habitually to get his one pair of shoes wet so that he might be allowed to curl up in an armchair before the kitchen stove with a biography or some standard novel.

There was a periodical shop in the neighborhood, where he spent part of his spare time, helping the proprietor and, in lieu of pay, gorging himself indiscriminately on the literature that lined the walls. Heterodox as it may be to say so, "Jack Harkaway" and the other yellow-backs which he read there, had a beneficial effect on his style. They developed the virility and feeling for dramatic sequences that later constituted his main literary charm.

But perhaps the most germinal of all these early literary habits was his daily custom of reading the newspaper to his invalid father. Those were the Reconstruction days, when the blunders of certain of Lincoln's successors called forth constant editorial comment on "How Lincoln would have done it." The spirit of reverence and admiration for the great President that the press exhaled must have stimulated tremendously the hero-worship that had already taken root in the enthusiastic mind of the lad.

Somewhat of an idealist, as this would suggest, almost from the first, Alonzo Rothschild was never a mere dreamer. The same balance that contributed so to his success throughout later life was already ingrained in his make-up. He was earnest, but fun-loving; frail, yet red-blooded; youthful, and still mature; idealistic, but none the less practical.

His practical powers had an opportunity to expand as soon as he was old enough to run errands. From that time on until he left college, his summer vacations were spent in the employ of some firm, earning a little money and learning something of business methods. The first of these summer positions was with a leather importer, who, largely in jest, set him the task of making a cable code. What the merchant meant in fun, my father took in earnest, and some time thereafter he handed his employer a code so well worked out, and so beautifully written, that for weeks the man proudly exhibited it to every member of the trade who entered the office.

Such precocity often engenders superficiality, but his was the rare brilliance that does not catch at sunbeams, but is content to labor. This appeared in school as well as in his summer work, for the abstract desire to do effectively whatever might come to hand was reinforced, in school, by ambition and directed by a passion for knowledge.

At the age of fourteen he entered the College of the City of New York, where he took his first independent step into journalism. One of his summer positions had been with an art magazine which employed him as "office boy, devil, and General Utility, — his only military distinction." The force was small and the office boy's functions corresponded with the range of his abilities. He ran errands, received visitors, read proof or compiled articles for publication, as occasion demanded.

With this varied experience, as a background, the lad started a college publication called *The Free Press*. The paper was intrinsically modest, but when one considers that the bulk of the work was borne by one boy and that the publication was successful enough to pay that boy's expenses, the matter appears in a wholly different light.

He did almost everything connected with *The Free Press* save the printing. He wrote the jokes, editorials, stories, and news items. But so effectively did he attack certain obnoxious faculty measures that he was compelled to work behind a mask of anonymity, thus forfeiting the prestige that his achievement would normally have given him in the eyes of his fellow students.

Although his connection with the paper remained a secret during his college years, it caused his downfall. So much of his time did the undertaking absorb that in his junior year, he failed to pass his examinations. This slump from honors to failure, however, did not destroy the confidence that his teachers had in his inherent worth, for when he decided to finish at Cornell, the president of the College gave him a warm letter of introduction to the president of the other institution.

The plan to transfer to Cornell was never consummated. His brother Meyer, who favored it strongly and who was furnishing him the means, went to Europe that summer on business, and in his absence my father decided that the hour had come for him to assume a share in his brother's burdens. Acting upon this decision, he turned to newspaper work, and his brother upon his return found him reporting for the *Commerical Advertiser.* Yet, even with the college doors closing behind him and the bitter, dubious, financial battle ahead, my father determined to return to college in ten years. His first news assignment cannot have cast much of the sunshine of hope upon his ambitions. It was a dog-show. But he soon demonstrated his ability so conclusively that it became the rule to billet him for important assignments. And a few months later he was selected to interview Thomas A. Edison.

He had notable success as an interviewer, a success that he owed to his scrupulous accuracy. He recognized two obligations,— an obligation to the newspaper and an obligation to the person who had entrusted him with the publication of his opinions. But it did not take him long to discover that in the newspaper world faithful service such as his waits long for even meager rewards, so after a few months with the *Commercial Advertiser*, he turned his back on journalism and entered the employ of a wholesale gem company. There his promotion was steady and he even learned the business well enough to travel for the firm. After several years, however, he decided that early financial independence and consequent freedom for literary pursuits could not come to him if he remained a "hireling." He therefore cast about until he found what seemed an opportunity, and having matured his plans with the precision of a military strategist, he started out at the age of twenty-two to be his own employer.

His new venture carried him back again into the field of journalism. The jewelry trade publications of the day were monthlies or semi-monthlies and though better than the common run of their contemporaries in trade journalism, they were contemptible when judged by twentieth-century journalistic standards. Their only aim was to sell advertising space and they subordinated everything to that one purpose. Their pages were given over to "puffs" and inadequate news items, and to dull technical articles. They published the news or suppressed it at the will of powerful advertisers.

Mr. Rothschild planned a weekly which was to publish the jewelry news with the impersonal completeness of a daily newspaper; whose editorial comment was to be "brief, conservative and absolutely independent of advertisers"; and in which "puffs" were to be confined to a single column where brevity and moderation were to obtain. As a partner in the enterprise, he chose a man whose previous experience in the field led him to value his services.

A class publication conducted on such principles was an innovation and the graybeards shook their heads. Their belief that the whole thing was the disordered dream of a Don Quixote and his Sancho was strengthened into certainty when it became known that Mr. Rothschild allowed none of his agents to treat customers. In the light of their experience it was as necessary to clinch a contract with a drink as it was to ingratiate one's self by a judicious suppression of news, and a lavish use of "puffs."

Had the founder of *The Jewelers' Weekly* been merely an idealist, their prophecies would have been justified. But so completely did his new paper cover the activities of the jewelry world that no jeweler could keep abreast of the trade without reading it. Such an indispensable organ was logically a valuable advertising medium, and before long disgruntled advertisers came trooping back with contracts, quite willing to let the young editor determine his own policies. What those policies were may be inferred from a law which owes its presence on the statute books of New York to the activities of *The Jewelers' Weekly*. The law is that which forbids a pawnbroker to receive a pledge from any one under sixteen years of age. The need for it was first revealed by an exposé in *The Jewelers' Weekly* and its passage was due largely to Mr. Rothschild's efforts.

Not only was the *Weekly* a power for good, but its

editor, though not much more than twenty, became the recognized "guide, philosopher, and friend" of the trade. He took a friendly interest in the affairs of all his customers, particularly the small men whom it was his delight to nurse along with advice and assistance, helping them often to achieve great success.

In this respect and in several others, Mr. Rothschild showed himself to be no mere seeker after wealth. It is true that he was in business with the avowed purpose of making a competency rapidly, but while in the game he played it as much for its own sake as for the prize. Writing in his diary concerning the famous "Birthday Number," the finest thing of its day in trade journalism, he said: "My ambition is to make this the handsomest and most readable volume ever issued by a trade publication." That and similar utterances indicate that his interest in the *Weekly* was not focused entirely on its money-getting powers.

Because of ill health, his partner withdrew from the firm after a few years, leaving him a free hand in all departments, editorial and financial, and he was able to test his theories to the limit. In the six months following he made the *Weekly* a landmark in trade journalism besides increasing its value five times. The principle which built his success at this time will surprise most business men. It was: "Give the other fellow a chance to make something too." In testing this thesis, he worked out what was probably one of the first profit-sharing plans, which, like his other attempts to humanize business, justified itself in dollars and cents.

It was partly this policy of liberality and partly his desire to pave the way for his farewell to business that induced him, at the zenith of his success, to take his one-time partner back into the firm, and with him two other men.

The Jewelers' Weekly Publishing Company, as it was called, with Mr. Rothschild as president, then took over *The Jewelers' Weekly* and the allied publications that he had either started or projected. As long as he remained an active member of the firm, success continued to crown its undertakings, but after he ceased to have a hand in its conduct the splendid publication of which he was so proud, languished.

The failure of his colleagues to continue the work he had so successfully carried on almost single-handed, throws into strong relief his achievements. He had attained financial independence in six years — an independence won at cost to no one else and with incidental benefit to many; he had shown that profits and ethical principles are not at opposite poles of human endeavor; he had proved the feasibility of the profit-sharing plan; he had elevated the tone of the jewelry trade; and he had set new standards in trade journalism.

One would ordinarily feel safe in concluding that a young man who in six years accomplished so many things had not been able to do much else. Yet Alonzo Rothschild found opportunity, also, to keep alive his intellectual interests, to do literary work, and to take an active part in city politics.

While still in newspaper work he had begun making an elaborate card index of his reading in the belief that it would be useful in later literary undertakings. This he continued to enrich during the years that he was building up the *Weekly*, finding time somehow to do a vast amount of general reading. His active literary work comprised a very excellent monograph on Nathan Hale which appeared subsequently in *America*, a patriotic journal of the day. The research requisite for the work was considerable and it was only by dogged persistence that Mr. Rothschild could make any headway. All through his chronicle of those busy days one comes across references to the Hale manuscript, triumph at having found time to progress or chagrin at being delayed. One of these passages throws so much light upon his character that it is worth quoting. He writes: "The Hale notes hardly seem to move. I get so little time for them. I am tempted to discontinue them for the present, but I have never yet failed in anything I started to accomplish and I will not begin now. We'll crawl ahead as best we can."

Despite the conflicting interests that he complains of, he still found time to do his part in politics. He was one of the founders of the Good Government Movement — "Goo-Goos," as they were called — and the youngest member of its Executive Council. When the organization was forming, a body of naturalized Germans asked to be affiliated, proposing to designate their branch as German-American. Without any heed to the possible political consequences of such a course, Mr. Rothschild argued against affiliation with any society that maintained a hyphenated character. He said: "There is no such thing as a German-American. These men are either American or they are not. If their patriotism is equivocal and they persist in tying strings to it, we must have nothing to do with them." Such an attitude in one whose tenderest associations were all in some sense German is strikingly indicative of an unbiased, logical mind.

Mr. Rothschild's activities were not even confined to politics, study, and literary work. He was also prominent among the younger members of the Society for Ethical Culture. He had a way of giving an original turn to a discussion or of putting a question in a clearer, more spiritual light that attracted Dr. Adler and the latter asked him to write a book on the *Morals of Trade* and to become a member of the society's lecture staff.

Few young men would have been dissatisfied with a lot so varied and rich as his, yet this many-sided man longed for something different. Neither was this a vague dissatisfaction. Ever since he left college he had hoped, one day, to make good the deficiencies of his education. Somewhere in these days came also the ambition to write about Abraham Lincoln.

One of the marvels of his career is that he should have realized his ideals. Other men have tried to do what he did and have failed because money, instead of remaining a means to them, became the object. Yet at no time did he let the brilliant present loom large enough in his mind to shut out the future. At the flood-tide of his success, one finds this passage in his diary: "How I long for the day when, free from business cares, I can give my whole time and attention to literary work!" Another, further on, shows that with increased prosperity he grew even more restive. It reads: "Five more months of my last money-grubbing year have passed. They were more agreeable than I expected them to be. I long for the day when some other sound than the chink of the golden guinea will charm my ear. It is siren music. . . . Let me steer my bark through the high seas of moral and intellectual progress toward — well, we shall see! How I long for the day of my freedom!"

Finally the day of freedom did come and then my father made good his old vow to return to college, entering Harvard University as a special student at the age of twenty-eight. His year there was one of almost cloister-like tranquillity and yet it was marked by achievement. In addition to his studies he found opportunity to write a series of newspaper articles on the Elective System, then being introduced by President Eliot. The latter evinced great interest in his work and went far out of his way to furnish him with data.

Shortly after his return to New York from Harvard, Mr. Rothschild met Miss Meta Robitscheck, who subsequently became his wife. She was heartily in sympathy with his aspirations and agreed with him that the work he planned could be done better away from the distractions of the metropolis. Accordingly, they went, immediately after their wedding, to Cambridge, wrenching themselves away from lifelong associations. This action seemed to others even more unjustifiable than my father's premature withdrawal from business, but neither he nor his partner in the enterprise ever regretted their course.

The two years at Cambridge were an auspicious beginning for the intellectual life. There my mother took special courses at Radcliffe until my birth increased her responsibilities, and there my father began his study of Abraham Lincoln. It was his plan at first to write a set of monographs on Lincoln and his Cabinet, but an investigation of the material revealed possibilities for more ambitious work, and gradually the great scheme matured of which *Lincoln, Master of Men*, and this book are merely parts, the whole to have been a cycle of books treating Lincoln's character from all angles. Having set himself this monumental task of reconstructing a personality, my father decided to find a quiet spot where he might settle down to work and where his family could grow up. He finally discovered in the village of East Foxboro, twenty-two miles south of Boston, a hundred-year-old house surrounded by more than one hundred acres of land that suited him and my mother, and there they moved in the fall of 1897. It was in this place that Ruth and Miriam were born and that my father passed the last eighteen years of his life in the happy realization of the dreams of his youth.

Though absorbed in his chosen work, he somehow found time to foster other interests, just as in the New York days. From the very first, he was a guiding voice in the town councils. He gained the confidence of the people by his absolute straightforwardness and their support by his sound judgment. Only once did he consent to hold office, but he never withheld his assistance, serving on many committees and doing all manner of valuable work. He might as well have been a town official, for usually, when there was constructive work to be done, the selectmen came to him for guidance. People seemed instinctively to turn to him for assistance. Shortly after he moved to East Foxboro, the inhabitants asked him if he would be their leader in a legislative fight for independence from Foxboro. For years they had nursed their grievances and waited for a Moses to lead them out of bondage. They complained, very justly, that they had been paying taxes and asking in vain for their share of the appropriations. The streets were in bad condition, the schoolhouse falling to decay, and on every hand were evidences of a very palpable wrong. Somewhere, somehow Mr. Rothschild had got a remarkably sound knowledge of law. He drew up a petition of separation and led the fight against the parent town, in the legislature. The facts of the case were plainly in favor of the petition, and it would have been granted, had not the member from Foxboro log-rolled long before the bill came up. Although defeated in his effort to make East Foxboro a separate town, Mr. Rothschild virtually won a victory, for ever since that time the village has enjoyed fair treatment from the parent town.

A number of years later East Foxboro called upon Mr. Rothschild to go before the state authorities to procure a water district charter. He drew up the charter and saw to its enactment, thus saving the district several thousand dollars in attorneys' fees. And, what is more, his charter embodied such improvements that it has since been the model for new water districts in Massachusetts.

Nor were Mr. Rothschild's public services confined to his own community. He was instrumental in procuring the passage of a law that compels every town in Massachusetts to employ the services of a superintendent of schools. He was also one of those who tried, with partial success, to get the State to compel the railroads to burn crude oil in their locomotives and thus put an end to the forest fires caused by flying coal sparks.

Save for such public services to his community and to the State, my father devoted most of his time to his study of Abraham Lincoln. It is true that he was vice-president of the Lincoln Fellowship, a director of the Free Religious Association, a member of the Anti-Imperialist League, of the Massachusetts Peace Society, and of the Massachusetts Reform Club, but none of these organizations claimed much of his time.

In 1901 he was a delegate to the Anti-Imperialist Convention at Indianapolis, but barring this and occasional short business or pleasure trips, he spent his time quietly at "Brook Farm" educating his family; entertaining his friends; farming a little; helping those who turned to him for advice from all sides; and carrying on his work. In 1906 this study bore its first fruit in the volume *Lincoln, Master of Men.*

His premature death at the age of fifty-three prevented him from quite completing *Honest Abe.* Had he finished this book, however, he would merely have taken Lincoln a little further in his political career and added to proof that already amply sustains his thesis.

It is given to few to meet death so exquisitely as he did, — alone, without suffering, in the presence only of Nature. On the morning of September 29, 1915, after a game of tennis with my mother, he went down to the lake alone for a plunge. He was missed some hours later, and a search discovered him dead in the water — a victim of heart failure caused by the icy shock.

His life was a candle that, burning with an unusually generous and beautiful flame, consumed itself before the appointed hour.

One of my father's friends used to say, "The real thing never looks the part." Like most epigrams his is too inclusive. My father, for example, did most thoroughly look the part. Literary admirers who met him in the flesh were not disillusioned and those other persons who came in casual contact with him rarely hesitated to class him as a student, —though beyond that point opinions diverged. Some set him down for a physician, others for a lawyer, still others as a college professor, and a few of the keenest for what he really was, — a man of letters. His physical traits, clothes, and manner were — contrary to his friend's epigram — true indices to his personality and occupation.

A trifle below the medium stature, my father had a distinction of air that many a taller man might have envied.

That dignity — courtly at times — was due to a subtle blending of distinct characteristics. To say that he owed it to his well-built, muscular figure, or to his erect carriage, would be palpably inaccurate. Such a description might fit many a substantial bourgeois, whereas Alonzo Rothschild, despite his plain tastes, was far more the patrician. One would have had to imagine him with another head and other hands to consider him bourgeois. Such long, white, blue-veined hands belong to the proverbial gentleman; such delicate skin is an attribute of gentle birth; such a head is seen only on those who do the world's thinking. Admirably moulded, it put one in mind of a well-built house, — good in its lines and roomy inside. The broad, dome-like forehead — exaggerated by partial baldness — and the full, gray-brown beard were almost unmistakable indications of the scholar. Yet quite as distinctly were the silkiness of his black hair, the well-set, finely cut features, the sparse eyebrows, and the curling nostrils, marks of the aristocrat. But it was the kindliness and swift intelligence of his hazel eyes that gave his face its mobility of expression. Passions and moods played across it as freely as the lights and shadows of the sky are reflected on the surface of a summer meadow.

As his appearance bespoke, my father was physically and nervously of delicate fiber. His sense of touch, for example, was hypersensitive, and it was amusing, at table, to see how gingerly he handled hot plates. He was, however, in no sense unmanly and too often suffered acutely in silence. In fact he could much better bear suffering himself than witness it in others. Not infrequently when some member of the family was in pain, he became similarly afflicted through sheer sympathy.

Sometimes his constitutional intensity manifested itself in quite a different manner. Ordinarily mild-tempered and patient, he was capable of a withering wrath. Relentless, and concentrating in itself all his physical and intellectual forces, it could flare up without warning, or wait years for an opportune moment, and then sweep upon the chosen enemy like a rain of fire. Crushing as the effect of such an outburst was upon its victim, it was hardly less disastrous in its physical reaction upon himself.

Irritability and violence of temper constituted in his case the enemy that every man carries within himself. It is evident that he recognized his cardinal fault, for he kept a little card perched on his inkstand bearing this proverb in his own handwriting: "Mensch ärger dich nicht."

Usually people so highly organized are difficult to live with, but my father was a striking exception. Save for such occasional outbursts as have already been alluded to, he was of a sunny disposition and most considerate in his personal relationships. Those whose duty it was to minister to his comfort and physical well-being found him easy to please. He was austerely plain in matters of dress and neither knew nor cared what he ate. Indeed, when mentally absorbed, he forgot his meals, and it is said that while he was editing *The Jewelers' Weekly* he ate lunch only if one of his friends came and dragged him out. Even had he been more exacting and given freer rein to his moods, his personal charm would have been sufficient counterbalance. His resonant voice, buoyancy, and ready sympathy would alone have made him a pleasant companion. Then, too, he had an almost magical influence over all who came within his range of acquaintance, stimulating the best that they had in them, and bringing it to the surface.

His interest in humanity was not limited by age or sex. He had a great tenderness for children and a power over their affections that was but another phase of his diverse nature. He made a capital playmate, as his own children well remember, and the serious concerns of the grown-up world never so shackled him that he could not shake them off for a romp, or a song, to invent a new game or to play some old favorite. Like many other men who have done big things, he never entirely lost a certain boyishness that cropped out occasionally in whimsical little pranks. One of these is so superior to the general run of practical jokes that it bears narrating.

It was in *The Jewelers' Weekly* days. He was returning to New York from a trip to Albany and some friends had accompanied him to the train. While they were waiting, my father accidentally dropped a half-dollar and one of the young ladies, picking it up, vowed that she would keep it as a remembrance. My father pleaded with mock concern that he needed it to complete his fare, but she, disbelieving him, clung to it the more firmly. She was correct in her assumption that he had plenty of money with him, but on the train he decided that the fifty cents should earn him some fun and not be a total loss.

On arriving in New York, he went to his printer and had him strike off a mock newspaper clipping which narrated how a young man, giving his name as Alonzo Rothschild, had been ejected from the Chicago Limited because he lacked part of the fare; how he maintained that it had been stolen from him by a Miss L—— of Albany, and how he was last seen trudging toward New York.

Not only was the young lady contrite over her playful theft, but she was enraged at the newspaper that would print such a story about her, and for a long time she begged my father to divulge the name so that she might bring suit.

This story well illustrates the exuberant, playful humor that brightened his whole life and that made our dinner table more famous for puns, jokes, and repartee than for good cheer of the other sort. But there is another anecdote of this period which throws more light on his character.

One day a gentleman who knew the family was walking through Mount Morris Park, in New York, when he noticed a bareheaded young man seated on a park bench and absorbed in a book. Approaching along the path he was surprised to recognize my father, and on reaching the bench he was still more astonished to see that his forehead swarmed with mosquitoes.

"Did n't expect to see you here, Lon," he sang out. My father started at the unexpected sound of the voice as if he had been shot, and looked up. "Why, hello, Sid, I'm just studying," he said. "It looks more as if you were mosquito farming," his friend replied. "Why don't you brush them off?" "Oh, I want them there," my father answered. "I don't concentrate the way I ought to and I'm learning how."

The discipline must have been effectual, for while interruptions annoyed him exceedingly, the mere presence of people in the study while he worked never disturbed him. For years my youngest sister spent her mornings on the rug beside his desk, and while she cut out paper dolls and crooned to herself, he wrote.

My father was capable, not only of great concentration, but also of unity of purpose. Gifted with a variety of talents and innumerable opportunities to exercise them, he remained — save for unavoidable digressions — a one-job man. He consistently refused tempting offers to address audiences, to undertake other literary labors, or to go into politics, and always with the same answer, that he had a task to do and must not stop until he had finished. He could have made himself a prominent figure in the public eye, but he found greater satisfaction in quietly doing work of permanent value.

Singleness of purpose and concentration were only two of the several qualities that made Alonzo Rothschild a man of strength. What had been willful stubbornness in his childhood crystallized, later in life, into dogged persistence. How great a factor it was in his successes may be judged from his own words. Once in speaking of his past life he said, "I have never really wanted a thing without getting it."

In addition to this driving force he had the gift of silence. Not that he was what is known as a man of few words, nor that he was loath to express definite opinions, but he knew how to keep his own counsels. He rarely discussed a plan until its success was assured, and concerning his literary work, he was almost secretive. This reticence in discussing himself was due somewhat to discreetness, somewhat to good taste, but largely to his doctrine of work and to his constitutional objectivity. He believed that the world's interest should focus on the work, not on the author. He despised the man whose personality was more discussed than his work and seemed to have little sympathy for him who made his pen a vehicle for expression of self. In this prejudice one can read the influence of Addison, and others of the classical school, — the masters whom he followed in forming his style.

Almost equal to his admiration for literature that definitely "gets somewhere" was his impatience with leisurely, descriptive, digressive writing, however charming its meanderings might be. The full measure of his scorn, however, was reserved for "precious" writers such as Walter Pater, whose involved, mannered style and somewhat luscious thought were peculiarly offensive to one who prized virility, lightness of touch, and lucid directness, as he did.

Between his literary work and his fine business instinct there was a connecting bond. He applied to research the methods of a highly trained business expert. The results can best be described by quoting his own words: "I can," he said, "go into my study and at a moment's notice lay my hand on the references covering any point in Lincoln's life."

Such a complete mastery of the subject bespeaks a laborious thoroughness that one associates with such names as Stradivari; a striving for perfection suggestive of the days of hand-made things. With the care of a master cabinet-maker choosing his woods, he collected facts, subjecting them to the same searching scrutiny to which the cabinet-maker subjects the woods in a hunt for hidden flaws. Then having tested his materials, he put them together — fitting, readjusting, and polishing, with all the care of the cabinet-maker — until he had done a work that would stand for all time. He wrote with a deliberateness that might seem laughable to those unacquainted with the art of authorship, never permitting a sentence to stand until every word rang true even though it were to take hours in the writing. Like Ben Jonson he realized that, "Who casts to write a living line must sweat." It may seem a trivial matter, but none the less it is significant of the spirit in which he worked, that the printers who set up *Lincoln, Master of Men*, found the manuscript one of the most faultless that they had ever handled.

The grasp of detail here exemplified, supplemented by clearness of judgment, originality, and foresight, constituted a rare intellectual fitness. It is not uncommon to find a man of constructive ability or one who is a good administrator, but the two qualities are rarely found together. Where they are associated, one has a man equipped for high service. With such an endowment of all-round effectiveness, Alonzo Rothschild could have attained leadership in any one of many fields of human endeavor.

There were lines, however, along which my father was little developed. His tastes in music and art were plain, not to say plebeian. Nor was he of a deeply poetic or metaphysical cast of mind. The older he grew, the more he centered his attention upon international, ethical, and social questions, and the less upon abstract metaphysical inquiries. A Jew by birth, he early settled down to agnosticism, though never quite contentedly. As a young man he had been strongly attracted by Theosophy, but finding nothing substantial on which to base a belief he sadly gave it up and lapsed back into agnosticism. Still all through his life Theosophy flitted before his eyes as an unattained desire and he often expressed the wish that he could accept its beautiful philosophy. That he had a strong religious instinct is further testified by his own words about sacred music. He writes: "Irreligious as I am, sacred music when well played on the organ has a powerful influence on me. It makes me feel sometimes as if I were inspired — as if I could seize my pen and write something worth reading."

Though too much a man of the world to be a poet in the strict meaning of the word, he was one in the larger sense of magnificence of conceptions, elevated thoughts, and high purposes.

It is interesting in this connection to consider what influence his almost lifelong study of Abraham Lincoln may have had on his character. It would seem that in his great simplicity, he must have been directly influenced by Lincoln. Like him, he considered himself a plain man, and he contented himself with a plain man's share of the world's luxuries. He rarely rode in a parlor-car and could satisfy his hunger as contentedly at a dairy lunch as in a hotel dining-room. He cared nothing for the appearance of things.

The last eighteen years of his life he spent in a plain old farmhouse. There was nothing about its exterior to distinguish it from thousands of other New England farmhouses, but once inside, the visitor found himself in "a city of books." In other respects he found the house as unpretentious inside as it appeared from without. It lacked no comforts or conveniences, but there was no studied attempt at decoration. It was quite evidently the home of a man who valued only the genuine things of life.

And yet, with all its simplicity, that house was a Mecca toward which turned many feet. All sorts of people came there, knowing that none ever went away without being enriched. For one it was new inspiration; for another the solution of some vexing problem, or perhaps a fresh grasp on his whole life. They knew that the man who dwelt there was never too busy or too weary to help his fellow men, and they came like tired children for comfort or for help. They knew him to be a man of warm sympathies, a brave man, an honest man, and a man strong enough to help shoulder their burdens. How many realized as they sat there, quietly talking with him, smiling with him, laughing with him, that this man who seemed so like themselves was — in the language of one grateful old lady — a "prince of men" in whom were all the elements of true greatness.

JOHN ROTHSCHILD.

CAMBRIDGE, MASSACHUSETTS
April, 1917.

A LIST OF BOOKS CITED

A LIST OF BOOKS CITED

WITH THE CORRESPONDING ABBREVIATIONS USED IN THE NOTES

Archer's Ethical Obligations: Ethical Obligations of the Lawyer. By Gleason Leonard Archer. Boston: Little, Brown & Co. 1910.

Arnold: The Life of Abraham Lincoln. By Isaac N. Arnold. Seventh Edition. Chicago: A. C. McClurg & Co. 1896.

Atkinson: The Boyhood of Lincoln. By Eleanor Atkinson. New York: The McClure Company. 1908.

Banks: The Lincoln Legion. The Story of Its Founder and Forerunners. By Rev. Louis Albert Banks, D.D. Illustrated with Drawings by Arthur I. Keller and Photographs. New York: The Mershon Company. 1903.

Barrett, New: Abraham Lincoln and His Presidency. By Joseph H. Barrett, LL.D. Illustrated. In Two Volumes. Cincinnati: The Robert Clarke Company. 1904.

Barrett: Life of Abraham Lincoln. Presenting his early history, political career, and speeches in and out of Congress. By Joseph H. Barrett. Cincinnati: Moore, Wilstach & Baldwin. 1865.

Bartlett: The Life and Public Services of Abraham Lincoln. With a Portrait on Steel. To which is added a biographical sketch of Hon. Hannibal Hamlin. By D. W. Bartlett. New York: H. Dayton. 1860.

Bateman: Abraham Lincoln; an address. By Newton Bateman. Galesburg, Ill.: Cadmus Club Publications. 1899.

Binney: The Life of Horace Binney, with selections from his letters. Philadelphia: J. B. Lippincott Company. 1903.

Binns: Abraham Lincoln. By Henry Bryan Binns. London: J. M. Dent & Co. New York: E. P. Dutton & Co. 1907.

Boyden: Echoes from Hospital and White House. A Record of Mrs. Rebecca R. Pomroy's Experience in War-Times. By Anna L. Boyden. Boston: D. Lothrop & Co. 1884.

Brady: Washington and Lincoln. A comparison, a contrast, and a consequence. An address delivered on June 18, 1904, at Valley Forge, Penna. before the Pennsylvania Society of Sons of the Revolution: to commemorate the abandonment of the camp by the continental army in 1778. By Cyrus Townsend Brady. Philadelphia: Sons of the Revolution, Pennsylvania Society Publications. 1904.

Brockett: The Life and Times of Abraham Lincoln, Sixteenth President of the United States. By L. P. Brockett, M.D. Philadelphia: Bradley & Co. 1865.

Brooks: Abraham Lincoln and the Downfall of American Slavery. By Noah Brooks. New York: G. P. Putnam's Sons. 1896.

Brougham's Works: Works of Henry Peter Brougham, First Baron Brougham and Vaux. Seven volumes. Edinburgh: Adam and Charles Black. 1872.

Browne: The Every-day Life of Abraham Lincoln. Lincoln's life and character portrayed by those who knew him. Prepared and arranged by Francis F. Browne. St. Louis: William G. Hills. 1896.

Browne's Lincoln and Men: Abraham Lincoln and the Men of his Time. By Robert H. Browne, M.D. Two volumes. Cincinnati: Jennings & Pye. New York: Eaton & Mains. 1901.

Campbell's Reports: Reports of cases determined at nisi prius in the courts of King's Bench and Common Pleas, and on Circuit. Four Volumes. By John, Baron Campbell. New York: Riley. 1810–1816.

Carpenter: The Inner Life of Abraham Lincoln. Six Months at the White House. By F. B. Carpenter. New York: Hurd & Houghton. 1867.

Caton: Miscellanies. By John Dean Caton. Boston: Houghton, Osgood & Co. 1880.

Chiniquy: Fifty years in the Church of Rome. By Father Chiniquy, the apostle of temperance in Canada. 3d Edition. Chicago: Craig & Barlow. 1886.

Chittenden: Recollections of President Lincoln and his Administration. By L. E. Chittenden, his Register of the Treasury. New York: Harper & Bros. 1891.

Clarke: James Freeman Clarke. Autobiography, Diary, and Correspondence. Edited by Edward Everett Hale. Boston and New York: Houghton, Mifflin & Co. 1891.

Coffin: Abraham Lincoln. By Charles Carleton Coffin. New York: Harper & Bros. 1893.

Curtis's Lincoln: The True Abraham Lincoln. By William Eleroy Curtis. Philadelphia and London: J. B. Lippincott Co. 1904.

Davidson: A Complete History of Illinois from 1673 to 1873. By Alexander Davidson and Bernard Stuvé. Springfield: Illinois Journal Co. 1874.

Debates: Political Debates between Abraham Lincoln and Stephen A. Douglas, in the Celebrated Campaign of 1858 in Illinois. Including the preceding speeches of each at Chicago, Springfield, etc. Also the Two Great Speeches of Abraham Lincoln in Ohio in 1859. Cleveland: O. S. Hubbell & Co. 1895.

Dodge: Abraham Lincoln, the evolution of his literary style. By Daniel Kilham Dodge. Champaign, Ill.: University of Illinois. 1900.

Douglass: Life and Times of Frederick Douglass. Written by himself. His early life as a slave, his escape from bondage, and his complete history to the present time. With an introduction by Mr. George L. Ruffin of Boston. Hartford, Conn.: Park Publishing Co. 1881.

Edmonds: Facts and Falsehoods concerning the war on the South, 1861–1865. By George Edmonds. Memphis, Tenn.: Taylor & Co. 1904.

Flower: Edwin McMasters Stanton, the Autocrat of the Rebellion, Emancipation, and Reconstruction. By Frank Abial Flower. Akron, Ohio: The Saalfield Publishing Co. 1905.

French: Abraham Lincoln, the Liberator. A biographical sketch. By Charles Wallace French. New York: Funk & Wagnalls. 1891.

Gallaher: Best Lincoln Stories, tersely told. By J. E. Gallaher. Chicago: James E. Gallaher & Co. 1898.

Gillespie: Recollections of early Illinois and her noted men. Read before the Chicago Historical Society, March 16, 1880. By Hon. Joseph Gillespie, Judge of Circuit Court of Madison County District. Chicago: Fergus Printing Co. 1880.

Greeley: Greeley on Lincoln. With Mr. Greeley's Letters to Charles A. Dana and a Lady Friend. To which are added reminiscences of Horace Greeley. Edited by Joel Benton. New York: The Baker & Taylor Co. 1893.

Gridley: The Story of Abraham Lincoln, or the Journey from the Log Cabin to the White House. By Eleanor Gridley, Secretary of the Lincoln Log Cabin Association. Copyright, 1902, by Eleanor Gridley.

Gridley's Defense: Lincoln's Defense of Duff Armstrong. The story of the trial and the celebrated almanac. By J. N. Gridley. Reprint from the Journal of the Illinois State Historical Society: April, 1910.

Hamlin: The Life and Times of Hannibal Hamlin. By his grandson, Charles Eugene Hamlin. Cambridge: The Riverside Press. 1899.

Hanaford: Abraham Lincoln: His Life and Public Services. By Mrs. P. A. Hanaford. Boston: B. B. Russell & Co. 1865.

Hapgood: Abraham Lincoln, the Man of the People. By Norman Hapgood. New York: The Macmillan Company. 1899.

Hart's Sketch: A Biographical Sketch of Abraham Lincoln. By Charles Henry Hart. Reprinted from the introduction to Bibliographia Lincolniana. Albany: Munsell. 1870.

Haynie: The Captains and the Kings. Anecdotes and biographical notes on contemporary celebrities. By Henry Haynie. New York: Frederick A. Stokes Co. 1904.

Herndon: Abraham Lincoln. The True Story of a Great Life. By William H. Herndon and Jesse W. Weik. With an introduction by Horace White. Illustrated. In Two Volumes. New York: D. Appleton & Co. 1896.

Hill: Lincoln, The Lawyer. By Frederick Trevor Hill. New York: The Century Company. 1906.

Hilliard's Memoir: Politics and Pen Pictures at home and abroad. By Henry Washington Hilliard. New York: G. P. Putnam's Sons. 1892.

Hitchcock: Nancy Hanks. The Story of Abraham Lincoln's Mother. By Caroline Hanks Hitchcock. New York: Doubleday & McClure Co. 1899.

Hobson: Footprints of Abraham Lincoln. Presenting Many Interesting Facts, Reminiscences, and Illustrations Never Before Published. By J. T. Hobson, D.D., LL.B., author of "The

Lincoln Year Book." Dayton, Ohio: The Otterbein Press. 1909.

Holland: The Life of Abraham Lincoln. By J. G. Holland. Springfield, Mass.: Gurdon Bill. 1866.

Howells: Lives and Speeches of Abraham Lincoln and Hannibal Hamlin. By W. D. Howells and John L. Hayes. Columbus, O.: Follett, Foster & Co. 1860.

Irelan: The Republic; or A History of the United States of America in The Administrations, From the Monarchic Colonial Days to the Present Times. By John Robert Irelan, M.D. In Eighteen Volumes. Chicago: Fairbanks and Palmer Publishing Co. 1888.

Jayne: Abraham Lincoln. Personal Reminiscences of the martyred President. An address delivered by William Jayne to the Grand Army Hall and Memorial Association, February 12, 1900. Chicago: The Grand Army Hall and Memorial Assn. 1908.

Jennings: Abraham Lincoln, The Greatest American. By Janet Jennings. Dedicated to the plain people of the Nation he saved — To the University of Wisconsin that honors his memory. Copyright, 1909, by Janet Jennings. Madison, Wis.

Jones: Lincoln, Stanton, and Grant. Historical Sketches. By Major Evan Rowland Jones. London: Frederick Warne & Co. 1875.

Keckley: Behind the Scenes. By Elizabeth Keckley, formerly a slave, but more recently modiste, and friend of Mrs. Abraham Lincoln. Or, Thirty Years a Slave, and Four Years in the White House. New York: G. W. Carleton & Co. 1868.

Ketcham: The Life of Abraham Lincoln. By Henry Ketcham. New York: A. L. Burt Co. 1901.

Koerner: Memoirs. Life sketches written at the suggestion of his children. By Gustav Philipp Koerner. Edited by Thomas J. McCormack. 2 Volumes. Cedar Rapids, Iowa: The Torch Press. 1909.

Lamon: The Life of Abraham Lincoln; from his Birth to his Inauguration as President. By Ward H. Lamon. Boston: James R. Osgood & Co. 1872.

Lamon's Recollections: Recollections of Abraham Lincoln, 1847–65. By Ward Hill Lamon. Edited by Dorothy Lamon. Chicago: A. C. McClurg & Co. 1895.

Larwood's Humor of Law: Humor of the Law. Forensic anecdotes. By Jacob Larwood [pseudonym for L. R. Sadler]. London: Chatto & Windus. 1903.

Leland: Abraham Lincoln and the Abolition of Slavery in the United States. By Charles Godfrey Leland. New York: Merrill & Baker. 1879.

Lewis's Great American Lawyers: Great American Lawyers. A history of the legal profession in America. (University Edition.) Eight volumes. Edited by William Draper Lewis. Philadelphia: The John C. Winston Co. 1907–1909.

Liber Scriptorum: The First Book of the Authors' Club. Liber Scriptorum. New York: Published by the Authors' Club. 1893.

Lincoln and Douglas: Abraham Lincoln. A Paper Read before The Royal Historical Society, London, June 16, 1881. By Hon. Isaac N. Arnold, F.R.H.S. Stephen A. Douglas: An Eulogy Delivered before the Chicago University, July 3, 1861. By Hon. James W. Sheahan. Chicago: Fergus Printing Co. 1881.

Lincolnics: Familiar Sayings of Abraham Lincoln. Collected and Edited by Henry Llewellyn Williams. New York and London: G. P. Putnam's Sons. 1906.

Ludlow: President Lincoln, Self-Pourtrayed. By John Malcolm Ludlow. Published for the benefit of the British Foreign Freedmen's Aid Society. London: Alfred W. Bennett; Alexander Strahan; Hamilton, Adams & Co. 1866.

McCulloch: Men and Measures of Half a Century. Sketches and Comments. By Hugh McCulloch. New York: Charles Scribner's Sons. 1889.

MacChesney: Abraham Lincoln. The Tribute of a Century, 1809–1909. Commemorative of the Lincoln Centenary and containing the principal speeches made in connection therewith. Edited by Nathan William MacChesney. Chicago: A. C. McClurg & Co. 1910.

McClure's Stories: Abraham Lincoln's Stories and Speeches. Edited by J. B. McClure, A.M. Chicago: Rhodes & McClure Publishing Co. 1899.

McClure's Yarns: "Abe" Lincoln's Yarns and Stories. A complete collection of the funny and witty anecdotes that made Lincoln famous as America's Greatest Story Teller. With introduction and anecdotes by Colonel Alexander K. McClure of the Philadelphia Times, a personal friend and adviser of the Story-Telling President. The Story of Lincoln's Life told by himself in his stories. Wit and Humor of the War, the Courts, the Backwoods, and the White House. Copyright by Henry Neil, 1901.

Magruder's Marshall: John Marshall. By Allan B. Magruder. Boston: Houghton, Mifflin & Co. 1899.

Markens: President Lincoln and the Jews. By Isaac Markens. New York: Printed for the Author. 1909.

Master: Lincoln, Master of Men. A Study in Character. By Alonzo Rothschild. Boston and New York: Houghton, Mifflin Company. 1906.

Merrick's Narrative: Old Times on the Upper Mississippi. The Recollections of a Steam-Boat Pilot from 1854 to 1863. By George Byron Merrick. Cleveland, Ohio: The Arthur H. Clark Co. 1909.

Morgan: Abraham Lincoln, The Boy and the Man. By James Morgan. New York: The Macmillan Company. 1908.

Morgan's Henry: The True Patrick Henry. By George Morgan. Philadelphia: J. B. Lippincott Co. 1907.

Morse: Abraham Lincoln. By John T. Morse, Jr. Two volumes. Boston and New York: Houghton, Mifflin & Co. 1896.

Newton: Lincoln and Herndon. By Joseph Fort Newton. Cedar Rapids, Iowa: The Torch Press. 1910.

Nicolay: A Short Life of Abraham Lincoln. Condensed from Nicolay and Hay's Abraham Lincoln. By John G. Nicolay. New York: The Century Company. 1904.

Nicolay's Boys' Life: The Boys' Life of Abraham Lincoln. By Helen Nicolay. New York: The Century Company. 1906.

Nicolay & Hay: Abraham Lincoln, A History. By John G. Nicolay and John Hay. Ten Volumes. New York: The Century Company. 1890.

Oldroyd: The Lincoln Memorial. Album-Immortelles. Original Life Pictures, with autographs, from the hands and hearts of eminent Americans and Europeans, contemporaries of the great martyr to liberty, Abraham Lincoln. Together with extracts from his speeches, letters, and sayings. Collected and edited by Osborn H. Oldroyd. With an introduction by Matthew Simpson, D.D., LL.D., and a sketch of the patriot's life by Hon. Isaac N. Arnold. Chicago: Gem Publishing House. 1883.

Onstot: Pioneers of Menard and Mason Counties. Made up of personal reminiscences of an early life in Menard County, which we gathered in a Salem life from 1830 to 1840, and a Petersburg life from 1840 to 1850, including personal reminiscences of Abraham Lincoln and Peter Cartright. By T. G. Onstot. Forest City, Illinois: T. G. Onstot. 1902.

Parkinson's Tour in America: A tour in America, in 1798, 1799, and 1800. Exhibiting sketches of society and manners, and a particular account of the American system of agriculture. By Richard Parkinson. London: J. Harding. 1805.

Paul: Massachusetts' practice with reference to proceedings before masters and auditors, and their reports. Boston: Little, Brown & Co. 1909.

Phillips's, Men who knew: Abraham Lincoln, by some men who knew him. Being personal recollections of Judge Owen T. Reeves, Hon. Jas. S. Ewing, Col. Richard P. Morgan, Judge Franklin Blades, John W. Bunn. With introduction by Hon. Isaac N. Phillips. Bloomington, Ill.: Pantagraph Printing and Stationery Co. 1910.

Pratt: Lincoln in Story. The Life of the Martyr-President told in Authenticated Anecdotes. Edited by Silas G. Pratt. Illustrated. New York: D. Appleton & Co. 1901.

Ram: A treatise on facts as subjects of inquiry by a jury. Fourth American Edition. Edited by John Townshend, and additional notes by Charles F. Beach, Jr. Also appendix. New York: Baker, Voorhis & Co. 1890.

Raymond: The Life and Public Services of Abraham Lincoln, Sixteenth President of the United States, together with his State Papers. By Henry J. Raymond. To which are added anecdotes and personal reminiscences of President Lincoln. By Frank B. Carpenter. New York: Derby & Miller. 1865.

Rice: Reminiscences of Abraham Lincoln. By distinguished men of his time. Collected and edited by Allen Thorndike Rice. New York: The North American Review. 1888.

Salkeld's Reports: Reports in French and English, containing cases heard and determined in the court of King's Bench, during the time that Sir Robert Foster, Sir Robert Hyde, and Sir John Kelyng were chief Justices there, as also of certain cases in other courts at Westminster during that time. 2d Edition. Two Volumes. Translated into English by Mr. Serjeant Salkeld and others. London: Browne. 1722.

Schurz: The Reminiscences of Carl Schurz. Three Volumes. New York: The McClure Company. 1907–1908.

Schurz's Essay: Abraham Lincoln. An Essay. By Carl Schurz. Boston and New York: Houghton, Mifflin & Co. 1892.

Scripps: Tribune Tracts No. 6. Life of Abraham Lincoln. Entered according to act of Congress in the year 1860 by Horace Greeley and Company in the Clerk's Office of the District Court of the United States for the Southern District of New York.

Selby: Stories and Speeches of Abraham Lincoln. Including stories of Lincoln's early life, stories of Lincoln as a lawyer, Presidential incidents, stories of the war, etc., etc. Lincoln's Letters and Great Speeches Chronologically arranged; with Biographical Sketch by Paul Selby (Associate Editor of the Encyclopedia of Illinois). Fully Illustrated. Chicago: Thompson & Thomas. 1900.

Sheppard: Great Americans of History: Abraham Lincoln. A Character Sketch. By Robert Dickinson Sheppard, D.D. With supplementary essay, by G. Mercer Adam. Together with Anecdotes, Characteristics, and Chronology. Milwaukee: H. G. Campbell Publishing Co. 1903.

Speed: Reminiscences of Abraham Lincoln and Notes of a Visit to California. Two Lectures by Joshua F. Speed. With a sketch of his Life. Louisville: John P. Morton & Co. 1884.

Stephens: Recollections of Alexander H. Stephens. His Diary, kept when a prisoner at Fort Warren, Boston Harbor, 1865; giving incidents and reflections on his prison life and some letters and reminiscences. Edited, with a biographical study, by Myrta Lockett Avary. New York: Doubleday, Page & Co. 1910.

Stevens's Black Hawk: The Black Hawk War, including a review of Black Hawk's life. Chicago: Stevens. 1903.

Stoddard: Abraham Lincoln. The True Story of a Great Life. By William O. Stoddard, one of President Lincoln's Private

Secretaries during the War of the Rebellion. New York: Fords, Howard & Hulbert. 1896.

Stovall: Robert Toombs. Statesman, Speaker, Soldier, Sage. By Pleasant A. Stovall. New York: Cassell Publishing Co. 1892.

Stowe: Men of Our Times, or Leading Patriots of the Day. Being a narrative of the lives and deeds of Statesmen, Generals, and Orators. By Harriet Beecher Stowe. Hartford: Hartford Publishing Co. 1868.

Sumner: The Promises of the Declaration of Independence. Eulogy on Abraham Lincoln, delivered by Charles Sumner before the municipal authorities of the City of Boston, June 1, 1865. Boston: Farwell & Co., Printers to the City. 1865.

Tarbell's Early Life: The Early Life of Abraham Lincoln. Containing many unpublished documents and unpublished reminiscences of Lincoln's early friends. By Ida M. Tarbell, assisted by J. McCan Davis. New York: S. S. McClure. 1896.

Tarbell: The Life of Abraham Lincoln. Drawn from original sources and containing many speeches, letters, and telegrams hitherto unpublished. Two Volumes. By Ida M. Tarbell. New York: The Doubleday & McClure Co. 1900.

Thayer: The Pioneer Boy and How He Became President. By William M. Thayer. Boston: Walker, Wise & Company. 1864.

Trevelyan's Fox: The Early History of Charles James Fox. By Sir George Otto Trevelyan. New York: Harper & Bros. 1880.

Ward: Abraham Lincoln. Tributes from his associates. Reminiscences of soldiers, statesmen, and citizens. With introduction by The Rev. William Hayes Ward, D.D. New York: Thomas Y. Crowell & Co. 1895.

Whipple: The Story-Life of Lincoln. A Biography composed of Five Hundred True Stories, told by Abraham Lincoln and his friends, selected from all authentic sources, and fitted together in order, forming His Complete Life History. By Wayne Whipple. Memorial Edition. Issued to commemorate the 100th Anniversary of Lincoln's Birth. Copyright, 1908, by Wayne Whipple.

White: Abraham Lincoln in 1854. An address delivered before the

Illinois State Historical Society. By Horace White. January 30, 1908. Illinois State Historical Society Publication.

White, Money and Banking: Money and Banking, illustrated by American history. By Horace White. Boston: Ginn & Co. 1896.

Whitney: Life on the Circuit with Lincoln. With Sketches of Generals Grant, Sherman, and McClellan, Judge Davis, Leonard Swett, and other contemporaries. By Henry C. Whitney. Boston: Estes & Lauriat. 1892.

Whitney's Life: Life of Lincoln. By Henry C. Whitney. Edited by Marion Mills Miller, Litt.D. Two Volumes: Vol. I., Lincoln, The Citizen; Vol. II., Lincoln, The President. New York: The Baker & Taylor Company. 1908.

Williams: The Burden Bearer, an Epic of Lincoln. By Francis Williams. Philadelphia: Jacobs & Co. 1908.

Wilson's Washington: George Washington. By Woodrow Wilson. Illustrated by Howard Pyle. New York: Harper & Bros. 1905.

Works: Complete Works of Abraham Lincoln. Edited by John G. Nicolay and John Hay. With a General Introduction by Richard Watson Gilder, and Special Articles by Other Eminent Persons. New and Enlarged Edition. Twelve Volumes. New York: Francis D. Tandy Company. 1905.

NOTES

NOTES

THE author would have wished to acknowledge his indebtedness to the many admirers of Abraham Lincoln who so cheerfully and readily replied to his inquiries. The responsiveness of all to whom he applied for information and particularly the eagerness with which collectors entrusted precious pamphlets and scrap-books to him were a constant source of gratification and encouragement.

In the following notes there are frequent references to secondary authorities. They are given, not to authenticate what has been said on direct authority, but for the convenience of readers and the service of students. The reader may find one book more available than another; and the student, who may wish to collate all that has been published on a subject, will have at hand an adequate bibliography.

CHAPTER I

1. Henry Pirtle, quoted in Herndon, i, 7. See, also, W. F. Booker, in Barrett (New), i, 6; Irelan, xvi, 21.
2. George B. Balch in Browne, 87; Samuel Haycraft in Barrett (New), i, 8; Rev. Thomas Goodwin, *ibid.*, 115.
3. Atkinson, 44–45.
4. Thomas Lincoln and Nancy Hanks were married near Beechland, in Washington County, Kentucky, on the 12th of June, 1806.
5. Usher F. Linder, who was born in Hardin County, Kentucky, became a prominent Democratic leader in Illinois. Delivering a eulogy of Lincoln in 1865 and speaking from his recollections of the old Kentucky days, he said: "They were

a good family. They were poor, and the very poorest people, I might say, of the middle classes, but they were true."

6. Sarah Lincoln was born February 10, 1807. The removal to Nolin Creek is said to have occurred in the following year.
7. Speed, 30; Browne, 489; Barrett (New), ii, 122–23; Morgan, 255–56.
8. The reader who wishes to follow Thomas Lincoln in his migrations is referred for some of the fuller accounts to: Lamon, 12–15, 19–22, 25–26, 73–75; Herndon, i, 15–18, 57–61; Holland, 24–26, 38–41; Brockett, 37–40, 51–54, 57; Barrett, 21–24, 30–34; Barrett (New), i, 9–10, 12–14, 25–26; Brooks, 6, 8–13, 44–45; Browne, 42, 45–51, 80–85; Tarbell's *Early Life*, 40, 51–55, 94–101; Tarbell, i, 13–15, 18–19, 45–49, 59; Nicolay and Hay, i, 24–30, 45–47; Whitney's *Life*, i, 21–28, 57–64; Stoddard, 10–18, 57–59; Coffin, 18–29, 46–49; Irelan, xvi, 34–40, 64–65; Curtis's *Lincoln*, 19–22, 26, 30; *Works*, vi, 26–31.
9. Gridley, 47–48. For the story of a previous speculation, of a similar nature, that resulted disastrously, see Dr. C. C. Graham in Tarbell's *Early Life*, 233; also, Hitchcock, 93–97, and Gridley, 47. The loss of the cargo by an accident to the vessel, however, as told by Dr. Graham, bears a striking, perhaps suspicious resemblance to what befell Thomas Lincoln (note 8) when he tried to move his belongings by water from Kentucky to Indiana.
10. Nancy Hanks Lincoln died at Little Pigeon Creek, Indiana, on October 5, 1818, in her thirty-fifth year.
11. Holland, 23; Arnold in Oldroyd, 33; Barrett (New), i, 16; Browne, 43–44; Coffin, 28; Ketcham, 12; Hart's *Sketch*, 5; L. S. Portor, in the *Woman's Home Companion*, February 1909, pp. 10, 64; see, also, Speed, 19. Attention is called to the slight variations in the language as reported by these several writers.
12. In the Little Pigeon Creek cabin were Abraham, his sister Sarah, and cousin Dennis Hanks, sometimes called Dennis Friend, whom luckless chance had made a member of the Lincoln family. The Johnston children comprised John D., Sarah, and Matilda.
13. Thomas Lincoln and Sarah Bush Johnston were married on December 2, 1819. The episode of the debts is related

in Barrett (New), i, 17; Herndon, i, 26; Lamon, 29; Coffin, 31; McClure's *Stories*, 272–74; Tarbell's *Early Life*, 52.

14. But see charges or surmises that Thomas Lincoln, in his anxiety to win Mrs. Johnston, had misrepresented conditions at home: Lamon, 11, 30–31; also Herndon, i, 27; Brooks, 28; French, 28; Leland, 18; Irelan, xvi, 44; Hapgood, 9; Stoddard, 21–22, 24; Sheppard, 118. These latter writers, following the lead of Lamon, have done so, apparently, to explain what needs no historical explanation — an improvident marriage; and Lamon quotes neither chapter nor verse for the faith, or, more accurately speaking, the lack of faith, that is in him. On the other hand, Cousin Dennis Hanks, though not always a trustworthy witness, offers what look like sufficient reasons for the lady's course. "Tom," he says, "had a kind o' way with the women, an' maybe it was somethin' she tuk comfort in to have a man that did n't drink an' cuss none." (Atkinson, 21.)

15. Irelan, xvi, 26–27, 41; Lamon, 32; Leland, 20; Jones, 4; Hapgood, 8; Janes, 7; E. I. Lewis in St. Louis *Globe-Democrat*, February 12, 1899.

16. Brooks, 28; Short Autobiography, in *Works*, vi, 27.

17. Danville (Ill.) *News*, February 12, 1904.

18. Probably Webster's *American Spelling Book*, Dilworth's *Spelling Book*, Pike's *Arithmetic*, Murray's *English Reader*, Scott's *Lessons in Elocution*, and the *Kentucky Preceptor*. Lincoln studied Kirkham's *Grammar* after he left home. See Dodge, 4–6; Sumner, ix, 375; Scripps, 3; Herndon, i, 34, 44–45, note, 75–76; Lamon, 37, note, 50; Hitchcock, 87; Atkinson, 18; Leland, 22; Browne, 70, 96; Brooks, 54; Morse, i, 19; Holland, 46; Tarbell's *Early Life*, 124–25, 132; Tarbell, i, 66–67; Nicolay and Hay, i, 84; Nicolay, 25–26; Nicolay's *Boy's Life*, 36–37; Ketcham, 66; Howells, 29–30; Irelan, xvi, 96–97; Stoddard, 70; Browne's *Lincoln and Men*, i, 158–59; Jones, 8.

19. Scripps, 3; Speed, 38; Herndon, i, 36; Lamon, 37, 57 note; Tarbell, i, 29–34; Binns, 18–19; Atkinson, 23–27; Selby, 45; Stowe, 15; Nicolay and Hay, i, 35; Oldroyd, 33–34; McClure's *Stories*, 22–23; Schurz's *Essay*, 4–5; Chittenden, 433–34; Nicolay, 14; Nicolay's *Boy's Life*, 23; Morse, i, 13; Swett's *Reminiscences*, in Rice, 459; Raymond, 22; Hobson, 30–31; Barrett (New), i, 23–24; Arnold, 21; Brooks,

23–24, 29–30; Browne, 66–68; Holland, 31; Morgan, 19–21; Whitney's *Life*, i, 41–42; Tarbell's *Early Life*, 69–71; French, 24–25; Hitchcock, 87–88; Leland, 22; Stoddard, 32–33, 36–37, 43; Sumner, ix, 375; Curtis's *Lincoln*, 56–58; Beach, 8–9; H. W. Mabie, in the *Chautauquan*, April, 1900, pp. 33–34, and in the *Outlook*, February 20, 1904, pp. 454–55. See also *infra*, p. 331.

20. According to most of our authorities this was the book by Mason L. Weems, entitled *The Life of George Washington; with curious anecdotes, equally honourable to himself and exemplary to his young countrymen.* But Scripps (3), Raymond (21–22), Brockett (47), and Holland (32) are apparently accurate in stating that the work was Dr. David Ramsay's *The Life of Washington.* It should be remembered that Mr. Lincoln himself, looking with uncommon care through the advance sheets of Scripps's biography, published in 1860, made no correction as to the name Ramsay there employed in connection with the anecdote. Lincoln's reference to Weems's *Life*, moreover, in the speech at Trenton (*Works*, vi, 150–51), indicates that he had read that book during his early childhood — some years before he could as a "tall and long-armed" youth have "made a clean sweep" of Crawford's fodder-corn.

21. Herndon, i, 52, note.

22. For the fuller accounts of this episode see: Whitney's *Life*, i, 42–43; Arnold, 23; Raymond, 21–22; Lamon, 38, 50–51, 55, 66, note; Scripps, 3; Holland, 31–32; Brockett, 47–48; Herndon, i, 37, 52, note; Stoddard, 37–38; French, 26; Irelan, xvi, 55–56; Brooks, 24–25; Barrett, 25–26; Browne, 67, 69–70; Bartlett, 116–17. A somewhat fanciful narrative may be read in Thayer, 120–30, 177.

23. Herndon, i, 29–31; Pratt, 11–12; Hapgood, 18–19. An instance of truth-telling by Lincoln, regardless of impending punishment, quite after the Weems manner, is related by Thayer (110–11), in his story about the broken buck's horn.

24. Lamon, 71.

25. How serious these abuses ultimately became may be inferred from Merrick's narrative (174–80), and from what Horace White says on the subject, in *Money and Banking*, pp. 351–52: —

"The bewildering state of the paper currency before the

Civil War may be learned from the numerous bank-note reporters and counterfeit detectors of the period. It was the aim of these publications to give early information to enable the public to avoid spurious and worthless notes in circulation. These were of various kinds: (1) ordinary counterfeits; (2) genuine notes altered from lower denominations to higher ones; (3) genuine notes of failed banks altered to the names of solvent banks; (4) genuine notes of solvent banks with forged signatures; (5) spurious notes, such as those of banks that had no existence; (6) spurious notes of good banks, as 20's of a bank that never issued 20's; (7) notes of old, closed banks still in circulation.

"The number of counterfeit and spurious notes was quite appalling, and disputes between payer and payee as to the goodness of notes were of frequent occurrence, ranging over the whole gamut of doubts, — as to whether the issuing bank was sound or unsound, whether the note was genuine or counterfeit, and, if sound and genuine, whether the discount was within reasonable limits."

26. For a severe, though manifestly biased comment on the bad money episode, so far as it concerned Lincoln, see Edmonds, 47–48.
27. Wilson's *Washington*, 11–12.
28. Hill, 219–20.
29. New Salem, Illinois, when Lincoln took up his residence there in the summer of 1831, was a busy little village of recent origin, near the west bank of the Sangamon River, in the county of that name. Its site — for the place has long since fallen into decay — is within the present limits of Menard County, about twenty miles northwest of Springfield.
30. The anecdote is from Parkinson's *Tour in America*, ii, 436–37 (London, 1805). Whether or not it had come under Lincoln's notice we have no means of knowing.
31. William McNeely, in Oldroyd, 393–94; Browne, 104.
32. John Rowan Herndon, in Herndon, i, 98.
33. William G. Greene, in Browne, 116–17; and in Onstot, 81–83. A more circumstantial account, based on correspondence with Greene, may be found in Coffin, 73–76. See, also, Nicolay and Hay, i, 110–11; Herndon, i, 98–99; Lamon, 136–37; Tarbell, i, 92; Tarbell's *Early Life*, 160; Holland, 54; Brooks, 66.

34. Lincoln's experience with Berry reminds one of Benjamin Franklin's trials with his partner Hugh Meredith, who was "often seen drunk in the streets, and playing at low games in the ale houses." It is an interesting coincidence, moreover, that both Franklin and Lincoln were aided, at these critical junctures, by generous friends.
35. Dennis Hanks, in Atkinson, 50.
36. Leonard Swett, in Rice, 465–66.
37. At about the time Abraham Lincoln thus spoke to his creditors in Illinois, a young man in far-away Maine named Hannibal Hamlin, destined to share his electoral honors, used somewhat similar language under corresponding circumstances. He had gone on the bond of a certain deputy sheriff for four thousand dollars. That officer became a defaulter, and the people who had claims against him looked to his bondsmen. Hamlin, having called the creditors together, said: "My friends, I have lived among you only a few years, but I think you know that I keep my word. I am poor, young, and struggling for an honest support for myself. This struggle will continue right among you, my neighbors. I am unable now to meet this just debt; but if you will give me time, and God will give me strength, I will pay off every dollar I owe you, even if it takes me a lifetime to do it."

    He redeemed his promise to the last cent; but at what cost may be inferred from his exclamation, many years later, in telling the story: "Heavens! how long it kept my nose on the grindstone."

    A fuller narrative of the incident may be found in Hamlin, 46. For another somewhat similar episode, in the early life of Andrew Jackson, the reader is referred to Brady, 56–57.
38. A patron of Samuel Hill's store, Harvey Ross who carried the mails, once told how he, as well as others, was impressed by Lincoln's straightforward methods. His narrative which belongs perhaps to this period may be found in Onstot, 76–77.

    "Mr. Lincoln," said Ross, "was very attentive to business; was kind and obliging to the customers, and they had so much confidence in his honesty that they preferred to trade with him rather than Hill. This was true of the ladies who said he was honest and would tell the truth about the goods. I went into the store one day to buy a pair of buckskin gloves, and asked him if he had a pair that would fit me. He threw down a pair on the counter: 'There is a pair of dogskin gloves that I think will fit you, and you can have them for seventy-five cents.' When he called them dogskin I was surprised, as I had never heard of such a thing before. At that time no factory gloves had been brought into the county. All the gloves and mittens then worn were made by hand, and by the women of the neighborhood from tanned deerskins, and the Indians did the tanning. A large buckskin could be bought for fifty to seventy-five cents. So I said to Lincoln: 'How do you know they are dogskin?' 'Well,' he said, 'I'll tell you how I know they are dogskin. Jack Clary's dog killed Tom Watkins's sheep, and Tom Watkins's boy killed the dog, old John Mounts tanned the dogskin, and Sally Spears made the gloves, and that is the way I know they are dogskin gloves.' So I asked no more, but paid six bits, took the gloves, and can truly say that I have worn buckskin and dogskin gloves for sixty years and never found a pair that did me such service as the pair I got from Lincoln."

39. Lincoln to George Spears, *Works*, i, 11. A facsimile of the letter is reproduced from the Menard-Salem-Lincoln Souvenir Album, in Tarbell, i, 97.

40. Tarbell's *Early Life*, 190, note.

41. This kind act is attributed to James Short and one of the Greenes, — whether Bowling or William G. appears to be in doubt. See Lamon, 138–39, 149–50; Arnold, 41–42; Herndon, i, 114–15; Leland, 43–44; Barrett (New), i, 40; Morse, i, 42; Curtis's *Lincoln*, 33–34; Stoddard, 88–89; Irelan, xvi, 109; Tarbell, i, 105–06; Tarbell's *Early Life*, 188–90.

42. William H. Herndon, Lincoln's law partner, relates (Herndon, i, 100): "He was a long time meeting these claims, even as late as 1848 sending to me from Washington portions of his salary as Congressman to be applied on the unpaid remnant of the Berry and Lincoln indebtedness. But in time he extinguished it all, even to the last penny."

According to Nicolay (36): "It was not until his return from Congress, seventeen years after the purchase of the store, that he finally relieved himself of the last installment of his 'national debt.'"

43. Several decades thereafter, when reference was made in President Lincoln's hearing to the large tracts of valuable land acquired by Surveyor-General Edward F. Beale, in California, the Executive may be said to have suffered no twinges of conscience if he remarked, as was reported: "Yes, they say Beale is monarch of all he surveyed."
44. Henry McHenry, in Herndon, i, 113.
45. The Grigsby affair. (Master, 16–17.)
46. Frank E. Stevens, in *Magazine of History*, February, 1905, pp. 86–90.
47. William G. Greene, who was present, so quotes Lincoln; but Lamon (111) and Stevens (*Black Hawk*, 283) report him to have said: "Boys, the man actually threw me once fair, broadly so; and the second time, this very fall, he threw me fairly, though not so apparently so."
48. *Magazine of History*, February, 1905, pp. 86–90. See also Stevens's *Black Hawk*, 281–83; Oldroyd, 516–17; Browne, 112–13; Lamon, 109–12; Herndon, i, 87–88; Nicolay and Hay, i, 94; Thayer, 239–40; Lincoln and Douglas, 194*a*–194*b*; Master, 39–40.
49. The whole experience left a deep impression in Lincoln's mind. After his first nomination to the Presidency, he received one day a delegation of college men, among whom was Professor Risdon M. Moore, the son of Jonathan, that quondam referee.

"Which of the Moore families do you belong to?" inquired the candidate, with a twinkle of the eye. "I have a grudge against one of them."

To which the Professor, with a still merrier twinkle, replied: "I suppose it is my family you have the grudge against; but we are going to elect you President, and call it even."

Thereupon Mr. Lincoln, narrating to those who were present the story of his defeat by Thompson, concluded with the words: "I never had been thrown in a wrestling-match until the man from that company did it. He could have thrown a grizzly bear."

Nor did the reminiscences concerning that memorable encounter cease there. Discussing former days with old friends who visited him at the White House, President Lincoln several times referred to the occurrence. One of these interviews is thus related by Mr. Greene: "During the rebellion, in 1864, I had occasion to see Mr. Lincoln in his office at Washington, and, after having recalled many of our early recollections, he said, 'Bill, whatever became of our old antagonist, Thompson, — that big curly-headed fellow who threw me at Rock Island?' I replied I did not know, and wondered why he asked. He playfully remarked that if he knew where he was living, he would give him a post-office, by way of showing him that he bore him no ill-will."

50. Henry McHenry, in Lamon, 154; Browne, 104.
51. Confidence in Lincoln as an arbitrator continued through his later career. This is evinced by the following telegram, quoted by Hill (250) from the Orendorff collection: —

To ABRAHAM LINCOLN, CHICAGO, Oct. 14, 1853.
Springfield, Ill.

Can you come here immediately and act as arbitrator in the crossing case between the Illinois Central and Northern Indiana R.R. Companies if you should be appointed? Answer and say yes if possible.

(Signed) J. F. JOY.

52. Address on Benjamin Ferguson, delivered at a meeting of the Washington Temperance Society on February 8, 1842.
53. Lincoln read this book during a series of visits that he made for the purpose to the home of David Turnham, a constable, who owned the volume. It was entitled: "The Revised Laws of Indiana, adopted and enacted by the General Assembly at their eighth session. To which are prefixed the Declaration of Independence, the Constitution of the United States, and the Constitution of the State of Indiana, and sundry other documents connected with the Political History of the Territory and State of Indiana. Arranged and published by authority of the General Assembly. Corydon: Printed by Carpenter and Douglass. 1824."
54. Herndon, i, 52; Tarbell's *Early Life*, 72.
55. Alban Jasper Conant, in *Liber Scriptorum*, 172; and in *McClure's Magazine*, March, 1909, p. 514. That Lincoln's

picture of close application was not overdrawn may be inferred from this paragraph in Lamon (140), based on the recollections of an old settler: "'He used to read law,' says Henry McHenry, 'in 1832 or 1833, barefooted, seated in the shade of a tree, and would grind around with the shade, just opposite Berry's grocery store, a few feet south of the door.' He occasionally varied the attitude by lying flat on his back, and 'putting his feet up the tree,' — a situation which might have been unfavorable to mental application in the case of a man with shorter extremities." See, also: Nicolay and Hay, i, 112–13; Herndon, i, 101–02; Browne, 121–23.

56. Report of an interview by Albert B. Orr, with C. F. Warden, in the McKeesport (Pa.) *Times*, February 12, 1909: also a letter from Mr. Orr to the author.

57. In response to the writer's inquiries Henry B. Rankin of Springfield, Illinois, at one time a clerk in Lincoln and Herndon's office, furnished a statement that is of topographical interest. The communication was addressed to the Hon. James R. B. Van Cleave of that city, through whose courtesy it is here published:

"The route Mr. Lincoln went over, in and out of Springfield from Salem when he made his home in that village was entirely on the south side of the Sangamon river, not the north as the travel from that vicinity has been for the past fifty years. There was no bridge over the Sangamon river in its entire length while Mr. Lincoln was at Salem. The first bridge over this river was built in the early '40s at the then Carpenter's Mills in this county. The next at Petersburg a few years later, in the '40s, and *via* Athens in 1843.

"Mr. Lincoln's trips to Springfield were usually made by the road as now located, for the first few miles bearing south out from Salem, — from that on into the city there have been more or less minor changes since, at various places, — on to the junction with the present 'Jacksonville and Springfield road,' and *via* it, entered the city on the west. Quite occasionally he walked from Salem to Springfield, and these trips were 'across country,' skirting the bluffs and breaks on the south bank of the Sangamon river 'as the crow flies,' — by shortest angles, some five miles shorter trip in.

"I have heard Mr. Lincoln in the old Lincoln and Herndon law office refer to these trips on foot into the city across the then unfenced prairie and woods. So many writers about Mr. Lincoln's early years have traveled over the road from Springfield to Petersburg *via* Athens, — now the nearest and always chosen one, — that you will please pardon me for the stress I place on the difference between the two roads. The road south of Salem across the 'Rocky ford' of 'Rock Creek,' and several other streams, — then called 'creeks,' had to bear westerly after leaving the Sangamon bottoms south of Salem, and cross these creeks at the most favorable places between banks best fitted to span crude bridges over. This made the 'foot-path way' from Springfield to Salem, a much shorter one than the wagon road between them. This wagon road as *then* traveled was fully twenty-five miles between Salem and the Capital City."

58. A reminder of this toilsome period is to be found, many years later, in the letter addressed to J. M. Brockman: —

SPRINGFIELD, ILLINOIS, September 25, 1860.

DEAR SIR: Yours of the 24th, asking "the best mode of obtaining a thorough knowledge of the law," is received. The mode is very simple, though laborious and tedious. It is only to get the books and read and study them carefully. Begin with Blackstone's "Commentaries," and after reading it carefully through, say twice, take up Chitty's "Pleadings," Greenleaf's "Evidence," and Story's "Equity," etc., in succession. Work, work, work, is the main thing. Yours very truly,

A. LINCOLN.

59. The Revised Laws of Illinois, edition of 1833, pp. 99–102, §1 and §9. Hill (57–58) is the only writer on Lincoln that has taken notice of this prohibition.

60. There appears to be some ground for controversy as to when Lincoln was admitted to the bar. He, himself, preparing notes of his life for the Scripps biography, sometime during 1860, wrote: "In the autumn of 1836 he obtained a law license." (See *Works*, vi, 33.)

And Jesse W. Weik, Herndon's collaborator, referring to

the records, states (*Century Magazine*, June, 1904, p. 279): "The first step in Lincoln's legal career is thus set forth in an entry found in the records of the Circuit Court of Sangamon County, Illinois, dated March 24, 1836. 'It is ordered by the Court that it be certified that Abraham Lincoln is a person of good moral character.' After this necessary preliminary, as appears from the records of the clerk of the Supreme Court, he was on September 9 duly licensed to practise in all the courts of the State."

But Hill (61) asserts: "He was legally qualified on March 24, 1836, and his professional life properly dates from that day."

Reaffirming this conclusion, Mr. Hill writes to the author: "There is no doubt that Lincoln was legally admitted to practice March 24, 1836, as is shown by the papers on file; but casting back to find out when he was admitted to the bar, Lincoln undoubtedly relied upon the rolls of attorneys for the year 1836, in which his name appeared September 9th of that year."

Summarizing the facts, Judge John P. Hand, of the Illinois Supreme Court, said in a Lincoln memorial address delivered on February 11, 1909: "He was licensed as an attorney, September 9, 1836, enrolled March 1, 1837, and commenced practice April 21, 1837." (See Illinois Reports, ccxxxviii, 13; and MacChesney, 204.)

Yet beyond a doubt, Lincoln appeared as an attorney in actions at law, previous to April 21, 1837. Following the rather offhand ways of the day, he tried some cases at the bar, as we have seen, before all the requirements for his admission had been complied with. The present writer ventures the opinion that, according to statute, three steps must have been taken before a person was, at this period, legally qualified to practice as an attorney or counselor at law, within the State. First, he had to obtain a certificate "of his good moral character," from a County Court; second, he had to secure a license signed by two justices of the Supreme Court; and third, having taken the oath of office, he had to have his name entered on the roll kept by the clerk of that court. It was not, therefore, until Lincoln had been formally enrolled that his career as a lawyer may correctly be said to have begun. (See Revised Laws of Illinois for

1833, pp. 99–100; and a decision of the Supreme Court, December Term, 1840, in the matter of E. C. Fellows, an attorney who had failed to have his name enrolled — Illinois Reports, iii, 369.)

CHAPTER II

1. Nicolay, 53. See, also, Browne, 150–51; Coffin, 94.
2. This narrative of the interview has been collated from the several accounts of it given by Mr. Speed at various times. See Oldroyd, 145–46; Whitney, 16–17; Browne, 152–53; Clarke, 341–42; Herndon, i, 175–76. See, also, Arnold, 53–54; Brooks, 80; Coffin, 95; Hapgood, 61–62.
3. There are a number of variations in the different accounts of this episode, but the essential facts appear to be as here related. Comprehensive versions are given by Arnold, 39–40; Stowe, 19–20; Holland, 55–56; Browne, 119–20; Onstot, 89–90; Brockett, 710; Jayne, 10; Noah Brooks, in *Harper's Magazine*, July, 1865, p. 226.
4. According to Major Stuart, Lincoln was his partner from April 27, 1837, to April 14, 1841; Judge Stephen T. Logan's, from April 14, 1841, to about September 20, 1843; and William H. Herndon's, from about September 20, 1843, until the death of Mr. Lincoln. There appears to be some ground for the belief that the last partnership was formed some months later than is here stated.
5. The oft-repeated statement that Lincoln disdained to keep accounts has, in his case as in that of another eminent lawyer, Patrick Henry, been confuted by the evidence of the fee-books themselves.
6. Onstot, 58.
7. The parallel between Lincoln and his running mate in the successful canvass of 1860 might be drawn at this point also. Referring to Hamlin's early days in the practice of law, his biographer says: "He handled a good deal of money belonging to his clients, and it often happened that they did not call for it until some time after it had been collected. Mr. Hamlin, therefore, had at times considerable sums of money in his possession, and on one occasion he told a friend what disposition he made of such money and his reasons. He said, 'When I collect money for a client, I inclose

it in an addressed package, and lock the package up in my trunk until it is called for. I will not touch or use that money for my purposes under any circumstances, unless, of course, the owner should authorize it. The money belongs to the owner. I have no more right to use it, even if I could replace it in five minutes, than I would have to take money that he might happen to have in his pocket-book.'" (Hamlin, 45.)

8. This principle was recognized as early as Cicero's time. In his *Ninth Philippic*, eulogizing Servius Sulpicius, that most profound of Roman advocates, the orator said, according to Forsyth's version: "He did not consider himself a lawyer rather than a servant of justice, and his constant endeavor was to temper the severity of law, by reference to principles of equity. He had less pleasure in advising that actions should be brought, than in removing all cause for litigation."

9. *Works*, ii, 142. Lincoln's comment — "the nominal winner is often a real loser" — suggests the similarity between his advice and that of Professor Porson, as expressed in that learned humorist's mock examination questions for students: —

 "What happens if you win your cause?"
 "You are nearly ruined."
 "What happens if you lose your cause?"
 "You are quite ruined."

10. Browne's *Lincoln and Men*, i, 338; Browne, 220.

11. For a few of these stories the reader is referred to Onstot, 20; Stringer, i, 218; McClure's *Yarns*, 380; Gallaher, 46–47; *Lincolnics*, 30–31; MacChesney, 299–300; Depew's *Speech*, February 12, 1909, pp. 6–7; Dr. George M. Angell, in Bloomington (Ill.) *Pantagraph*, February 12, 1909.

Lincoln was not the only great lawyer concerning whom such anecdotes might be told. The eminent New England advocate, Jeremiah Mason, is said to have been equally successful in bringing about compromises. "Mr. Mason," writes one who knew him well, "magnified his position by exerting all his influence to prevent litigation, or the commencement of suits upon mere quibbles, or for the purpose of procrastination, or to gratify personal vindictiveness, or retaliation. He was eminently a peacemaker, and was instrumental in healing many a wound, and in preventing the useless expenditure of money, by a set of litigants, who were in the habit of annoying (employing?) lawyers to aid them in schemes of malice or revenge." (John P. Lord, quoted in Hillard's *Memoir and Correspondence of Jeremiah Mason*, 46.)

12. Browne's *Lincoln and Men*, i, 339.
13. Herndon, ii, 14.
14. Browne, 218–19. Lincoln's expedient for preventing trivial litigation was similar in its essence to that of the New York attorney concerning whom Edwards, in his *Pleasantries about Courts and Lawyers*, tells this anecdote: —

"In a certain part of our State, two Dutchmen, who built and used in common, a small bridge over a little stream which ran through their farms, had a dispute concerning certain repairs which it required. One of them declined to bear any portion of the expense necessary to the purchase of two or three planks. The aggrieved party went to a neighboring attorney and placing ten dollars, in two notes of five dollars each, in his hand, said —

"'I 'll give you all dish monies if you 'll make Hans do justice mit de pridge.'

"'How much will it cost to repair this bridge?' asked the attorney.

"'Well, den, not more ash five tollars.'

"'Very well,' said the legal gentleman, pocketing one of the notes and giving the Dutchman the other, 'take this and go and get the bridge repaired. It 's the best course you can take.'

"'Yaas,' responded the client slowly, 'y-a-a-s, dat ish more better as to quarrel mit Hans.'

"But as he went home, he shook his head frequently, as if unable, after all, quite clearly to see how he had gained anything by going to the lawyer."

15. This narrative is based on two interviews, secured for the author from Henry Rice, in the autumn of 1907 and in the spring of 1908, respectively. See, also, Markens, 24.
16. Lincoln's refusal to take what he considered a bad case is in harmony, as far as civil actions go, with the practice of every high-minded lawyer. David Hoffman, of the Baltimore bar, drawing up, early in the nineteenth century, a code of ethics for the guidance of his students throughout their professional careers, prescribed as the eleventh of

fifty resolutions: "If, after duly examining a case, I am persuaded that my client's claim or defense (as the case may be) cannot, or rather ought not to be sustained, I will promptly advise him to abandon it. To press it further in such a case, with the hope of gleaning some advantage by an extorted compromise, would be lending myself to a dishonorable use of legal means in order to gain a portion of that, the whole of which I have reason to believe would be denied to him both by law and justice."

17. Holland, 126; Browne, 162. But see Lamon, 317, for McHenry's account of a somewhat similar interview that had a different termination.
18. "Never stir up litigation. A worse man can scarcely be found than one who does this." (Notes for Law Lecture, in *Works*, ii, 142.)
19. Tarbell, i, 248; McClure's *Yarns*, 359–60.
20. Lamon, 325.
21. It should, perhaps, be noted that in refusing Matteson's case Lincoln turned his back on one of his own influential clients, whom he had represented in the Supreme Court but a short time before this happened. See the appeal of Constant *vs.* Matteson *et al.*, argued at the January term of 1859, in the Second Grand Division. (Illinois Reports, xxii, 546–62.)
22. James Judson Lord to William H. Herndon, in Herndon, ii, 14–15, note; Letter of Mrs. Katherine Lord Driscoll to the author.
23. General John H. Littlefield, in *Success*, February, 1901, p. 600; *Lincolnics*, 31. An interview, somewhat like these two, culled from the practice of the eminent Southern lawyer and statesman, Robert Toombs, is thus related by his biographer: "On one occasion he said to a client who had stated his case to him, 'Yes, you can recover in this suit, but you ought not to do so. This is a case in which law and justice are on opposite sides.' The client told him he would push the case, anyhow. 'Then,' replied Mr. Toombs, 'you must hire some one else to assist you in your damned rascality.'" (Stovall, 18–19.) Another distinguished Southerner, Alexander H. Stephens, held equally conscientious opinions as to what constitutes a lawyer's duty. These views, based on a long and honorable career, occupy a notable place in his *Recollections*. (See Stephens, 383–89.)

24. Rev. John Putnam Gulliver, in the New York *Independent*, September 1, 1864. The article is reprinted in Carpenter, 309–17.
25. Atkinson, 28–29; Lamon, 40, note.
26. For details concerning these and other similar incidents the reader is referred to: Curtis's *Lincoln*, 77; Browne, 646–47; Brooks, 426; Carpenter, 78, 114–15; Hill, 131, 198; Tarbell, i, 254; Bateman, 30–32; Flower, 63; Emerson, 5–9; *Works*, ii, 70, 368; *ibid.*, iii, 32; *ibid.*, ix, 26, 84–85; *Debates*, 13, 26; *Scribner's Magazine*, February, 1878, p. 565. See, also, Speed, 18.
27. From the response by Justice David Davis, of the United States Supreme Court, to resolutions presented upon the death of Lincoln, at a session of the Federal Circuit Court held in Indianapolis, May 19, 1865.
28. Ex-Chief Justice Caton's address to the Supreme Court of Illinois, May 3, 1865, in Caton, 12; Illinois Reports, xxxvii, 13.
29. Barrett, 818; Browne, 235–36; Nicolay and Hay, i, 303–04.
30. Swett to Herndon, in Herndon, ii, 246–47.
31. Whitney, 261.
32. Lamon, 324.
33. This account of the incident is based chiefly on statements made by District Attorney Ward Hill Lamon, himself (Lamon, 322), and by Judge David Davis, who probably referred to the affair in a story which he recalled, with unimportant variations, many years later, for the entertainment of Ratcliffe Hicks, a contributor to the *Century Magazine* of February, 1894, p. 638. Henry C. Whitney, it should be added, writing after Lamon but before Hicks, contradicted the former's narrative in almost every important particular. A careful reading, however, of Whitney's book (at pages 130–32 and 534), leads to the conclusion that the error lies with him rather than with Lamon and Davis; for he obviously confused the Patterson trial, in his memory, with another Champaign County case.
34. Letter from Abraham Lincoln to H. Keeling, dated March 3, 1858, and quoted from manuscript in Herndon, i, 326.
35. Shaw's letter of June 13, 1866, quoted from manuscript in Herndon, i, 323.
36. Holland, 130; Stowe, 22.

37. Joseph Gillespie's manuscript letter of October 8, 1886, quoted in Herndon, ii, 13–14; Lamon, 321–22. Gillespie was, to a precise degree, Lincoln's contemporary at the bar. Their enrollment dates from the same year — 1837.
38. The same figure of speech was used, to describe a similar attitude of mind, by that other eminent lawyer, Horace Binney, leader for many years of the Philadelphia bar. In his private record, written for the eyes of his children, we find: "I never prosecuted a cause that I thought a dishonest one, and I have washed my hands of more than one that I discovered to be such after I had undertaken it." (Binney, 443.)
39. For the details of this anecdote the author collated the accounts in Browne, 228; Lamon, 324; and Stringer, i, 217. According to the last-mentioned authority, however, Lincoln was found, not at the tavern, but in the Postville Park, playing townball with the boys.
40. Whitney, 130–32, 262; see, also, 136. It was probably concerning this incident that the same colleague wrote in another work: "On one occasion, Swett and I sat on a bench in the extreme rear of the court-room while Lincoln closed to the jury on our side, and we were utterly astonished at the cruel mode in which he applied the knife to all the finespun theories we had crammed the jury with." (Whitney's *Life*, i, 175.)
41. The authenticity of this story has been questioned. It certainly calls for confirmation, as the first case in which Lincoln appeared before the State Supreme Court, according to the printed records (Illinois Reports, iii, 456–57), was that of Scammon *vs.* Cline. Here he was associated with another attorney, James L. Loop, of Belvidere, and represented, not the appellant, but the defendant in error. The discrepancies are striking rather than vital. From the peculiar nature of that case Lincoln may well, at the time, have made the brief oral statement attributed to him; and, as we know, the decision which followed was, in fact, against his client. On the other hand, perhaps the scene did not take place during the argument on Scammon *vs.* Cline. If Judge Treat's narrative is correct in every particular, Lincoln must have made his first bow before the Supreme Court sometime during the three and a half years of practice that

preceded this hearing. And he might have done so, too, without that fact appearing in the records. For the reporter, finding the early material incomplete, and seeking to limit the size of the published volumes, did not include all the cases. It may be added that an account of this incident has, in some form, been accepted by Herndon, i, 322–23; Lamon, 321; Schurz, 16; Leland, 61; and Stoddard, 119. All these men knew Lincoln — some of them throughout almost his entire legal career. That they believed him capable of the course described in the anecdote is, perhaps, as significant as the story itself.

An essay, giving the results of careful researches into the case of Scammon *vs.* Cline, by Richard V. Carpenter, was printed in the *Journal of the Illinois State Historical Society* for October, 1911, pp. 317–23.

42. "Judge Davis often delegated his judicial functions to others. I have known of his getting Moon of Clinton to hold court for him in Bloomington for whole days; Lincoln to hold an entire term, and frequently to sit for short times; and I even knew of Colonel Bryant of Indiana to hold court for him in Danville. All judgments rendered by these lawyers were voidable. Time has probably now cured them. It was a hazardous business for them and the sheriff and suitors in their cases." (Whitney's *Life*, i, 192.)

One of these irregular judges, it may be said in passing, more than returned the compliment, some years later, by elevating Davis to the bench of the United States Supreme Court; and the legality of that appointment has not been questioned.

CHAPTER III

1. It would not be correct, however, to say, as is sometimes said, that Lincoln won every case which he should have won. Contemporary lawyers testify to the contrary.
2. Herndon, ii, 3; Whitney, 251.
3. Hill, 225–26.
4. Whitney, 259; Whitney's *Life*, i, 177.
5. Anthony Thornton, in the Chicago *Tribune*, February 12, 1900, p. 14.
6. Illinois Reports, xxxvii, 15.

7. Whitney, 262–63; Whitney's *Life*, i, 196.

   These tributes to Lincoln's honorable methods again recall the principles that contributed not a little toward Horace Binney's preëminence. In the review of his career he wrote: "I at all times disdained to practise any stratagem, trick or artifice for the purpose of gaining an advantage over my adversary; and unless I thought him unfair, I was generally willing that he should see all my cards while I played them. I can truly say that I am not conscious of having lost anything by this candor; but, on the contrary, have repeatedly gained by it. If my client was at any time suspected, I had no reason to think that I was, by either the Court or the bar; and how many balancing cases, in the course of thirty-five years' practice, this sort of reputation assisted, I need not say." (Binney, 443.)

8. Herndon, i, 326–28; *Atlantic Monthly*, April, 1867, p. 412.

   Whatever the practice at the Springfield bar may have been, Lincoln's objection to the making of a fictitious plea was of course not finical. No less an authority than Chief Justice Holt had said: "The attorney, if he puts in a false plea to delay justice, breaks his oath, and may be fined for putting a deceit on the Court." (Pierce *vs.* Blake, Salkeld's Reports, ii, 515. See, also, Johnson *vs.* Alston, Campbell's Reports, i, 176.)

9. Whitney, 263–64; Herndon, ii, 17–18. It should be noted that April 24, 1856, fell on a Thursday, not a Saturday. Whether the 4 is a misprint for 6, or whether this term of court extended to Saturday, May 24, or whether the error lies elsewhere, cannot now be determined.

10. Browne's *Lincoln and Men*, i, 360–62.

11. Lincoln to Trumbull, December 18, 1857, in the *Century Magazine*, February, 1909, p. 620.

12. Justice David Davis from the bench of the Federal Circuit Court, at Indianapolis, May 19, 1865.

13. Holland, 130; Lamon's *Recollections*, 19–20; Stowe, 22; Browne, 162.

14. Koerner, ii, 110.

15. Recollections of Colonel Richard J. Hinton, in the Chicago *Times-Herald*, November 17, 1895.

16. Holland, 80. See, also, Nicolay and Hay, i, 307; Ward, 205, 270; Browne, 238.

17. Mrs. Norman B. Judd, in Oldroyd, 523; also, in Tarbell, i, 277–78. A report of Lincoln's argument, rather full, though far from complete, has been reprinted from the Chicago *Daily Press*, in *Works*, ii, 340–54, and Tarbell, ii, 324–30.
18. Admissions that seemed to be of a more damaging nature than those which were made in this case have at times been known to assist, rather than interfere with, the winning of a verdict. How far counsel may go, along such lines, was illustrated in the practice of Daniel Webster. A more brilliant, though less scrupulous, advocate than Lincoln, he went the limit.

    Once in Boston, defending a man who had been indicted for forgery, his first act — at the very beginning of the trial, before a witness had been called — was to arise and say: "May it please the Court, we admit the forgery, so that evidence on this point will be unnecessary. We deny that the note was uttered in this county."

    The astonishment of those present gave way to comprehension, when it became evident that the prosecution could easily have made out a case of forgery against the prisoner; but that it could not so readily have proven, what was of equal importance, the issuing of the forged instrument in Suffolk County. For want of sufficient proof, on this very point, the defendant was acquitted. He might have fared differently if both the questions of forgery and utterance had been presented to the jury. It is not unlikely that had they listened to evidence on the crime itself, those facts would have so overshadowed other considerations in their minds as to bring about a conviction. Webster's avowal prevented this, and saved his unworthy client.
19. Herndon, ii, 3; Whitney, 251.
20. Lincoln to Linder, February 20, 1848, *Works*, ii, 3.
21. Herndon, ii, 7.
22. Arnold, 84. See, also, Whitney's *Life*, i, 173; Oldroyd, 37; Nicolay and Hay, i, 307.
23. Herndon, ii, 7.
24. Gibson W. Harris, quoted in Browne, 220.
25. Letter of Justice David J. Brewer to the author; and an article by him in the *Atlantic Monthly*, November, 1906, p. 591.
26. Caton, 13; Illinois Reports, xxxvii, 13.
27. A statement made by Judge David Davis.

28. Hill, 211–12.
29. Letter of Hon. Shelby M. Cullom to the author; Bateman, 13–15. See, also, Hill, 236–37; and T. W. S. Kidd, the crier of the court, in Tarbell, i, 273–75.
30. Judge Lawrence Weldon, quoted in Hill, 212–15.
31. A letter said to have been written by Lincoln to Mrs. Armstrong, offering her his services, is published in Selby (254), and Hobson (41–42); yet neither of these writers, responding to inquiries by the author, has been able to throw any light on the question of its authenticity. According to other biographers, a communication of such a nature was received by Mrs. Armstrong, who stated, as they allege, that it had been lost. On the other hand, "Duff" himself, in his detailed narrative, makes no reference to a letter from Mr. Lincoln; and John, his younger brother, in an equally full account of the affair, taken down for the author by Thomas D. Masters of Springfield, Illinois, expresses the opinion that no written message on the subject was ever received. The Masters notes concerning this topic read: —

"Mr. Armstrong has no recollection of hearing of any letter being written by Mr. Lincoln to his mother, at the time his brother got into the trouble in question; and he requests me to say to you that he is quite sure that had such a letter been written he would have known of it. He points out to me that his mother was unable to read, and in that early day, had she received a letter from a man such as Lincoln then was, — a much-talked-about lawyer in Springfield, — that by reason of the exigencies of the occasion, and the interest such a letter would have excited in the household, he certainly would have known of it. His recollection is that his mother, probably after the cause was venued to Cass County, made a trip to Springfield, of course, knowing Mr. Lincoln, and feeling friendly to him, and having confidence in him, for the purpose of employing him to assist in the defense of her son at Beardstown."
32. A singular parallel presents itself in ancient Athenian history, where Alcibiades and his friends were charged, as Plutarch relates, with mutilating the images of Mercury, on a certain night. When one of the informers was asked how he managed to recognize the features of the accused in the darkness, he answered, — "I saw them by the light of the moon," — a palpable misstatement, as the affair hap-

pened at the time of a new moon which gave practically no light. This anecdote, however, could hardly have prompted Lincoln to consult an almanac in the Armstrong case, because he had not read Plutarch's *Lives* at the time of that trial, and only did so two years later.

33. Judge Abram Bergen, quoted by James L. King, in the *North American Review*, February, 1898, pp. 193–94. Bergen's testimony should be supplemented by a statement which "Duff" Armstrong himself made, in his respectable old age, to J. McCan Davis. It was published in the New York *Sun* of June 7, 1896. According to this report Armstrong then declared: "The almanac used by Lincoln was one which my cousin, Jake Jones, furnished him. On the morning of the trial I was taken outside the courtroom to talk to Lincoln. Jake Jones was with us. Lincoln said he wanted an almanac for 1857. Jake went right off and got one, and brought it to 'Uncle Abe.' It was an almanac for the proper year, and there was no fraud about it."

34. Ram, 269–70, note, 505. It is interesting to note that a somewhat similar tale is frequently met with among the anecdotes of the English bar. A barrister at the "Old Bailey," according to this version, secured the acquittal of a client charged with highway robbery by introducing an almanac to prove that there was darkness on a certain night, instead of the bright moonlight, in which the prosecuting witness claimed to have distinguished the prisoner's features. The almanac, however, as afterwards transpired, had been fraudulently so printed for that occasion.

35. Those who wish to collate what has been published about the Armstrong affair may find these references of service: Gridley's *Defense*, 3–23; Hill, 229–34; Hobson, 40–50; Tarbell, i, 270–73; Lamon, 327–31; Arnold, 87–89; Onstot, 98–100; Irelan, xvi, 142–44; Oldroyd, 213–15; Herndon, ii, 26–28; Barrett, 63–66; Barrett (New), i, 152–54; Holland, 128–29; Browne, 224–27; Brockett, 82–85; Selby, 94–97, 254; Phillips's *Men Who Knew*, 62–63; Stoddard, 157–60; Raymond, 29–31; Brooks, 127–29; French, 75–76; Whipple, 261–65; Bartlett, 111–15; Curtis's *Lincoln*, 75; Coffin, 162–63; Stowe, 23–25; Morgan, 102–03; Nicolay's *Boy's Life*, 94–97; Hanaford, 44–48; Pratt, 78–82; Thayer, 285–93; McClure's *Stories*, 97–99; Williams, 68–73; *Lin-*

colnics, 64–66; Jones, 15; Master, 20–22; New York *Sun*, June 7, 1896; *North American Review*, February, 1898, pp. 191–95; Kankakee (Ill.) *Republican*, February 12, 1909, Bloomington (Ill.) *Pantagraph*, January 20, 1912; also Eggleston's *The Graysons*, in which the trial and the almanac incident are used by the novelist with good effect.

36. Tarbell, i, 265; Emerson, 5.
37. From an unpublished manuscript entitled "Lincoln on the Stump and at the Bar," by Judge Scott, quoted in Tarbell, i, 253–54.
38. Judge William M. Dickson, in *Harper's Magazine*, June, 1884, p. 63; Barrett (New), i, 121–22. See, also, Alban J. Conant, in *Liber Scriptorum*, 175–76, and in *McClure's Magazine*, March, 1909, p. 516; Chauncey M. Depew, in Rice, 432; Browne, 229–30; Curtis's *Lincoln*, 85; McClure's *Yarns*, 457; McClure's *Stories*, 92; Pratt, 59–60.
39. Collated from accounts by George W. Minier, in Oldroyd, 187–89, and in Herndon, ii, 327–28; also: Arnold, 85–87; Brooks, 122–24; Coffin, 108; Pratt, 68–69.
40. Binney, 444.
41. Lincoln would doubtless have approved of David Hoffman's rule on this subject. It read: "I will never plead or otherwise avail of the bar of infancy against an honest demand. If my client possesses the ability to pay, and has no other legal or moral defense than that it was contracted by him when under the age of twenty-one years, he must seek for other counsel to sustain him in such a defense. And although in this, as well as in that of limitation, the law has given the defense, and contemplates in the one case to induce claimants to a timely prosecution of their rights, and in the other designs to protect a class of persons who by reason of tender age are peculiarly liable to be imposed on, yet in both cases I shall claim to be the sole judge (the pleas not being compulsory) of the occasions proper for their use."
42. Remarks of Justice David Davis in the Federal Circuit Court at Indianapolis, May 19, 1865.
43. It may be of interest to note that these same revolutionary properties, and the same stage-setting of frozen ground flecked with the blood of patriots' unshod feet, had served Patrick Henry, many years before, in the defense of John Venable, Commissary of the Continental Army, sued by John Hook, a Tory, for the value of some steers seized to

feed the hungry troops. But Henry's eloquence had not prevailed as fully as Lincoln's did; for the jury found a verdict, though in a nominal sum, against the great Virginian's client.

44. Herndon, ii, 9–11; see, also, Holland, 127. For brief accounts and comments based on Herndon's and on Holland's narratives the reader is referred to: Hapgood, 108; Browne, 162–63; Hill, 215–16; Coffin, 104–05; Tarbell, i, 250; Pratt, 74–76; Selby, 97–98; McClure's *Stories*, 101.

45. Herndon, i, 328–30.

A brief and less picturesque account of the incident was furnished to the author, about half a century after the event, by the Honorable Shelby M. Cullom, one of the counsel for the defense. He wrote: "During the trial, a question was raised as to the admissibility of certain testimony, which was very important to the defense. The Judge took an hour to come to a conclusion as to what he ought to do; and when he began to decide the question, he seemed to be leaning against the admissibility of the testimony. Lincoln saw that he was inclined that way, and sprang upon his feet, and manifested such intense earnestness that it appeared to change the Judge's disposition, and he decided in favor of the admissibility of the testimony."

Still, Herndon probably did not overstate the case. For the official crier, Captain Thomas W. S. Kidd, referring to that same episode, said: "Mr. Lincoln made a display of anger, the like of which I never saw exhibited by him before or after. He roared in the excess of his denunciation of the action of the Court." (Rochester *Herald*, January 17, 1904. See Kidd, also, in Tarbell, i, 251–52.)

CHAPTER IV

1. Though under very different circumstances, Lincoln's elation seems not unlike that of another famous man whose later life touched his at several points. The first dollar earned by Frederick Douglass, on free soil, in New Bedford, was paid to him, as he tells us, for stowing away a pile of coal for Mrs. Ephraim Peabody, the wife of a Unitarian minister. "I was not long in accomplishing the job," runs his story, "when the dear lady put into my hand two silver half-dollars. To understand the emotion which swelled my heart as I clasped this money, realizing that I had no mas-

ter who could take it from me, — that it was mine, — that my hands were my own, and could earn more of the precious coin, — one must have been in some sense himself a slave." (Douglass, 210.)

2. Lamon, pointing out some inconsistencies in the details of this anecdote as it is generally quoted, expresses doubts concerning its authenticity. He evidently did not know how often Lincoln had told the story to different persons. Their versions, as might be expected, vary somewhat, but they agree in the essential facts. See: Carpenter, 96–98; William D. Kelley, in Rice, 279–80; Leonard Swett, in Rice, 457–58; Holland, 33–34; Brooks, 38; Pratt, 16–18; Morgan, 27–28; Lamon, 72; McClure's *Stories*, 17–18; Hanaford, 156–58; Boyden, 83–84; Irelan, xvi, 62–64; Tarbell, i, 38–39; Browne, 72–73; Banks, 14–16; Ward, 277–78; Thayer, 169–71; Ludlow, 66–68; Curtis's *Lincoln*, 24–25; Whipple, 62–63; Selby, 52–53; Raymond, 754; Onstot, 51–52; Egbert L. Viele, in *Scribner's Magazine*, October, 1878, p. 817; Alban J. Conant, in *McClure's Magazine*, March, 1909, p. 514; interview with Governor Frank Fuller, in the New York *Times*, October 1, 1911, p. 10.
3. Browne's *Lincoln and Men*, i, 259–61, 356; ii, 90–91.
4. Holland, 93.
5. See Lincoln to Speed, June 19, 1841, in *Works*, i, 168–75, and in Lamon, 318–19; also, Gibson W. Harris, in Columbia (Ky.) *Spectator*, January 27, 1905.
6. Oldroyd, 394–95.
7. Onstot, 41–44.
8. Lincoln to Whitney, December 18, 1857, in *Works*, xi, 103.
9. Brockett, 702–03; McClure's *Yarns*, 341–42; Barrett (New), i, 154–55; interview with Mrs. Rose Linder Wilkinson, in Chicago *Times-Herald*, September 11, 1895.
10. The nature of these kindnesses may be inferred from the following despatch: —

EXECUTIVE MANSION, December 26, 1863.

HON. U. F. LINDER,
Chicago, Ill.:

Your son Dan has just left me, with my order to the Secretary of War, to administer to him the oath of allegiance, discharge him, and send him to you.

A. LINCOLN.

(*Works*, ix, 275; see, also, *ibid.*, 272.

11. Boston *Advertiser*, February 12, 1909, p. 7.
12. Stowe, 21; Carpenter, 245; Browne, 229; French, 80; McClure's *Stories*, 89–91; Thayer, 284–85; Gallaher, 39–40.
13. Gibson W. Harris, in Browne, 220.
14. Koerner, ii, 112.
15. Caroline H. Dall, in *Atlantic Monthly*, April, 1867, p. 413.
16. Tarbell, i, 267–68; Curtis's *Lincoln*, 74–75; Thomas Lewis, in *Leslie's Weekly*, February 16, 1899.
17. Browne, 224.
18. G. W. Nance, in Oldroyd, 557.
19. Charles W. Moores, in *American Law Review*, January–February, 1911, p. 92.
20. Henry Rickel, in Cedar Rapids *Gazette*, February 6, 1909, p. 1.
21. Ward, 242–46; Jennings, 93–98.
22. Father Chiniquy reproduces in his book an engraved facsimile of the due-bill, dated May 23, 1856. It is undeniably in Lincoln's handwriting, but no explanation has been offered to reconcile the date with the priest's statement that the paper was written in October, at the time of the second trial. The author based his narrative of this affair upon Chiniquy, 566, 620–67; Whitney, 53–55, 136–37; and a brief of the Circuit Court records at Urbana, Illinois, made for the writer by Judge Joseph O. Cunningham.
23. George P. Floyd, in *McClure's Magazine*, January, 1908, p. 303.
24. Lamon's *Recollections*, 17–19; see, also, Browne's *Lincoln and Men*, i, 348–51. There are a few other examples, in legal history, of high-minded lawyers rejecting what they regarded as excessive fees. One notable English instance is thus related by Lord Brougham concerning Topping: —

    "A general retainer of a thousand guineas was brought to him to cover the Baltic cases then in progress. His answer was, that this indicated either a doubt of his doing his duty on the ordinary terms known in the profession (one guinea particular, and five guineas general retainer) — or an expectation that he should, on being thus retained, do something beyond the line of his duty; and therefore he must decline it. His clerk then accepted of the usual sum of five guineas, and he led on those important cases, for the defendants."

So also Charles O'Conor, leader for many years of the New York bar, subordinated money-making to a sense of professional propriety. His friend, William H. Winters, Librarian of the Law Institute, relates that a client once urged the famous pleader, with some insistence, to accept a very much larger fee than the lawyer had charged. O'Conor, becoming indignant, manifested in his own forcible way how this annoyed him. He denied the right of any one to dictate what his pay for legal services should be, and dismissed the presumptuous client without ceremony.

25. There is a companion tale current among English lawyers concerning another member of the bar, at an earlier period, who was accused by his fellow barristers of having degraded their order by accepting payment for services in copper. Upon being arraigned for this offense at their Common Hall he defended himself, — so the tradition runs, — with the following plea in confession and avoidance: "I fully admit that I took a fee from him in copper, and not one but several, and not only fees in copper but fees in silver. But I pledge my honor, as a Sergeant, that I never took a single fee from him in silver until I had got all his gold, and that I never took a fee from him in copper until I had got all his silver, — and you don't call that a degradation of our order."

26. Whitney, 81.

27. Works, xi, 98–99.

28. E. S. Nadal, in *Scribner's Magazine*, March, 1906, p. 368.

29. Herndon, i, 324–25.

30. That baffling question as to how the value of a lawyer's services should be arrived at was thus stated in Lincoln's trial brief: "Are or not the *amount* of *labor*, the *doubtfulness* and *difficulty* of the *question*, the *degree* of *success* in the *result*, and the *amount* of pecuniary interest *involved*, not merely in the particular case, but covered by the principle decided, and thereby *secured* to the client, all proper elements, by the custom of the profession to consider in determining what is a reasonable fee in a given case?"

For an answer that may serve, in part, at least, the reader is referred to an opinion, which had been delivered some years previously by Chief Justice John B. Gibson, of the Pennsylvania Supreme Court. Discussing the fees earned by an attorney in important litigation, he said: "It is not to be doubted that responsibility, in a confidential employment, is a legitimate subject of compensation, and in proportion to the magnitude of the interests committed to the agents. . . . A lawyer charged with particular preparations for a lawsuit, is not to be made responsible, or paid, as a porter or a shoemaker." (Pennsylvania Reports, vii, 545–46.)

31. Lincoln's attitude in this particular affords another striking contrast to that of David Hoffman, who lays down the rule: "I will charge for my services what my judgment and conscience inform me is my due, and nothing more. If that be withheld, it will be no fit matter for arbitration; for no one but myself can adequately judge of such services, and after they are successfully rendered they are apt to be ungratefully forgotten. I will then receive what the client offers, or the laws of the country may award, but in either case he must never hope to be again my client."

32. The most fruitful references on this topic are: Herndon, ii, 21–22; Whitney's *Life*, i, 184–85; Hill, 250–54, 261, 316–19; Tarbell, i, 258–60; *Works*, ii, 288–89; *Lincoln as Attorney, passim;* Curtis's *Lincoln*, 72; Illinois Reports, xvii, 291–99; Koerner, ii, 111–12.

33. Jesse W. Weik, in *Century Magazine*, June, 1904, pp. 282, 286; Herndon, i, 251.

34. Lincoln to Speed, July 4, 1842, in Lamon, 251; *Works*, i, 219.

35. Browne, 180–82; Coffin, 123; Gallaher, 31; Hapgood, 85; Jesse W. Weik, in *Century Magazine*, June, 1904, p. 280.

36. Four children, in all, were born to Abraham and Mary Todd Lincoln. They were: Robert Todd, August 1, 1843; Edward Baker, March 10, 1846; William Wallace, December 21, 1850; and Thomas, April 4, 1853.

37. Some years after the purchase of this cottage, its modest dimensions were enlarged by the addition of another story to meet the requirements of an increased family.

38. Leonard W. Volk, quoted in the *Outlook*, February 13, 1909, p. 348.

39. Lincoln's straightway habit of waiting on himself had striking illustration while he was in Congress. Calling for some law books at the library of the Supreme Court, as the

librarian relates, he tied them in a huge bandana handkerchief which he took from his pocket, passed a stick, brought for the purpose, through the knotted ends, slung the bundle across his shoulder and carried it thus to his lodgings, whence the volumes were returned later in the same primitive fashion. When a still greater public honor than that of Congressman came to him, one of his neighbors in Springfield exclaimed: "What! Abe Lincoln nominated for President of the United States! Can it be possible? A man that buys a ten-cent beefsteak for his breakfast, and carries it home himself."

40. Herndon, ii, 16.
41. Joseph Gillespie, in Oldroyd, 462. Still another one of the famous cavalcade, Leonard Swett, said: "Beds were always too short, coffee in the morning burned or otherwise bad, food often indifferent, roads simply trails, streams without bridges and often swollen, and had to be swum, sloughs often muddy and almost impassable, and we had to help the horses, when the wagon mired down, with fence-rails for pries, and yet I never heard Lincoln complain of anything."

    In the same vein, Henry C. Whitney wrote: "At the table, he ate what came first, without discrimination or choice. Whatever room at the hotel came handy, or whatever bed he came to first, he took without criticism or inspection."
42. Quoted from manuscript of Ninian W. Edwards by Herndon, i, 186; also: Lamon, 190; French, 60; Coffin, 99; Browne, 138–39; Master, 55–56.
43. Whitney, 32; see, also, Herndon, ii, 15–16.
44. Schurz, ii, 90–91.
45. Chief Justice John Marshall, whom Lincoln resembled in not a few particulars, is said to have made a similarly unfavorable impression upon a prospective client, during his younger days at the Richmond bar. But in the Virginian's case, the critical suitor discovered, even before the trial began, that a poorly dressed lawyer is not necessarily a poor advocate. So Marshall was retained, at the eleventh hour, to assist an immaculately attired colleague, whose ability was found to fall far short of the promise held forth by broadcloth and powdered wig.
46. Master, 224–25, 469.

47. *Works*, iv, 199.
48. Jayne, 11; and Dr. William Jayne to the author, October 2, 1912.
49. Gibson W. Harris, quoted in Columbia (Ky.) *Spectator*, January 27, 1905. The same witness, writing elsewhere (Browne, 219) on the same theme, says: "Mr. Lincoln had a heart that was more a woman's than a man's, — filled to overflowing with sympathy for those in trouble, and ever ready to relieve them by any means in his power."
50. Mrs. Lincoln to Mrs. Keckley, November 15, 1867, in Keckley, 352.
51. John F. Mendonsa to the author, August 31, 1912.
52. Haynie, 7–8.
53. Fellowship, 1908, pp. 12–13; see, also, *Works*, ii, 313–14.
54. Lincoln to Johnston, January 12, 1851, *Works*, ii, 148.
55. *Works*, ii, 96.
56. This deed may be found in Coles County Deed Records, G, p. 5. Of the same date, October 25, 1841, entered in Mortgage Record, i, p. 43, is an instrument whereby Abraham Lincoln binds himself and his heirs to convey the property to John D. Johnston or his heirs, after the death of the parents, upon repayment of the two hundred dollars, without interest and without regard to any increase in the value of the tract.
57. For further light on these matters the reader is referred to the letters from Lincoln to Johnston in *Works*, ii, 135, 144–46, 147–53; and to the deed published in Gridley, 145–46.
58. Lincoln's ownership of this land, in the town named for him, is further evidence of his ready amiability toward friends, where monetary matters were concerned. The lot, situated on the south side of the court-house square, had belonged to James Primm, a well-known court official and public man of Logan County. Finding himself in financial difficulties, he had borrowed four hundred dollars on his promise to pay, which Lincoln obligingly endorsed. But when the time for payment arrived, the maker of the note was unable to meet it, so the endorser had found himself obliged to pay. Lincoln did so, and some time later Primm, by way of reimbursement, had given him a deed of the lot. (See Stringer, i, 221–22.)

59. E. J. Edwards, in New York *Times*, January 24, 1909. For other accounts see: Raymond, 100; Browne, 314–15; Curtis's *Lincoln*, 45; Ward, 281; Thayer, 313–14; *Lincolnics*, 93–94. As having a further bearing on the question of Lincoln's estate in 1860, these references may be serviceable: *Works*, vi, 31; Arnold, 83, 154–55; Whitney, 26; Herndon, i, 91–92; Oldroyd, 32; Lamon, 472; Lamon's *Recollections*, 20; Holland, 127; Hobson, 100–04; Browne, 200–01; Rice, 587; Curtis's *Lincoln*, 74; *McClure's Magazine*, March, 1909, pp. 514–15; New York *Times*, October 1, 1911, p. 10.

CHAPTER V

1. Lamon, 126; *Works*, xi, 97; see, also, the Autobiography, in *Works*, vi, 31.
2. *Works*, vi, 31.
3. Address to the People of Sangamon County, March 9, 1832, in *Works*, i, 8.
4. These scenes, until then happily without parallel in American history, recall the political slaughter with which Charles James Fox had seventy years before signalized a crushing victory in the British House of Commons. To quote his biographer: "The fight was over, and the butchery began. Every one who belonged to the beaten party was sacrificed without mercy, with all his kindred and dependents; and those public officers who were unlucky enough to have no political connections fared as ill as the civil population of a district which is the seat of war between two contending armies. Clerks, messengers, excisemen, coast-guardsmen, and pensioners were ruined by shoals because they had no vote for a member of Parliament, or because they had supported a member who had opposed the peace." (Trevelyan's *Fox*, 28.)
5. Greeley, 20.
6. During Lincoln's first year in the Illinois Legislature he voted steadily with the minority against the adoption of resolutions which the Democratic majority had introduced to uphold President Jackson in his memorable struggle against the United States Bank. But when it came to voting on one resolution which condemned the National

Senate for discourteous treatment of the old hero, and on another which commended the Illinois delegation in Congress for supporting the Administration, Lincoln turned away from his political associates, and had himself recorded, both times, in Jackson's favor. (See Illinois House Journal, 1835, pp. 213–17, 258–63.)

7. *Works*, vi, 31–32.
8. The whole number of citizens who voted at New Salem, on August 6, 1832, amounted to 300; but as 10 of these refrained from expressing their preferences for Representatives, only 13 actually appear on the records as voting against Lincoln. No election-tickets or ballot-boxes were used in Illinois at this time. The *viva-voce* method was employed; and as each voter stated his choice, he saw it recorded opposite his name in the poll-book.
9. It is interesting to add that in this election of 1832, the country at large gave Jackson 219 electoral votes, and Clay 49.
10. Letter from Judge Stephen T. Logan, quoted in Nicolay and Hay, i, 102–03, note; and Master, 47.
11. The practice of carrying documents in his hat became a habit with Lincoln. While at the bar in Springfield, long after the postmastership had become a memory, he explained his failure to answer a communication promptly, by writing: "When I received your letter I put it in my old hat, and buying a new one the next day, the old one was set aside, and so the letter was lost sight of for a time." (See Tarbell, i, 98; and Tarbell's *Early Life*, 179.)
12. Lincoln was appointed Postmaster at New Salem on May 7, 1833. He served until May 30, 1836, by which time the population of the place had fallen off to such an extent that the office was discontinued, and its business transferred to Petersburg.
13. Herndon, i, 111. See, also: Onstot, 249; Tarbell's *Early Life*, 181; Tarbell, i, 99; Coffin, 81. Some currency having been given to an exaggerated and obviously erroneous report of the incident, Mr. Carpenter (110–12) repeated that version one day in the White House to Mr. Lincoln. The President thought they had "stretched the facts somewhat"; but his denial, such as it was, leaves the original story told by Simmons to Herndon, practically unimpeached.

14. For a comprehensive note in which the local election returns of 1834 are collated, the reader is referred to Master, § 22, pp. 445–46.
15. In a referendum of the question submitted to the people at the election of 1834, 7514 voters expressed a preference for Alton, 7148 for Vandalia, 7044 for Springfield, 744 for Illiopolis the geographical center, 486 for Peoria, and 272 for Jacksonville. When the final balloting took place in the General Assembly, twenty-nine places were voted upon. (See Parrish's *Illinois*, 313.)
16. Whitney, i, 139; Nicolay and Hay, i, 139.
17. Details of these encounters are related in Master, 60–62.
18. Lamon, 195; Herndon, i, 166.
19. General T. H. Henderson, in Tarbell, i, 139.
20. Whitney's *Life*, i, 146.
21. Statement of Coleman Smoot, in Lamon, 157. As Lincoln was thus supplied with sufficient means to defray his traveling expenses, the oft-repeated story, which depicts him as trudging, pack on back, over the road to Vandalia, may perhaps, with propriety, be assigned to a place among those pleasing traditions of history that are found, upon close scrutiny, to be more picturesque than plausible.
22. Nicolay and Hay, i, 158; Pratt, 52–53; Coffin, 125–27; Nicolay's *Boy's Life*, 59. Lincoln's experience, it should be noted, in canvassing his district with a nominal outlay of money, was not uncommon. Gustav Koerner, running for the Illinois Legislature on the Democratic ticket, a few years later, did so under similar circumstances. "There were hardly," he tells us, "any election expenses. We always stayed with friends when traveling through the county. We had our horses anyway. My entire electioneering expenses amounted to four dollars, and that for the printing of tickets. One Democratic Frenchman from the Bottom afterwards sent me a bill of $6.65 for which he said he had gratuitously treated for me. As he was a good fellow, I paid him, although I had not given him the slightest authority to do so." (Koerner, i, 468–69.)
23. See letter of Lincoln to Stuart, February 14, 1839, in *Works*, xi, 98.
24. *Works*, i, 6–7.

25. This is exclusive of what was appropriated for the Illinois and Michigan Canal, then already in process of construction. That enterprise, the other improvement projects, and a few smaller public outlays carried the State debt, by the close of 1842, above $15,000,000.
26. *Works*, i, 146.
27. An Act to establish and maintain a General System of Internal Improvements. Approved February 27, 1837. Section 22, Illinois Session Laws, 1836–37.
28. *Works*, i, 154–55; Lamon, 213–15.
29. Gillespie, 24–25; Lamon, 216–17; Nicolay and Hay, i, 161–62; Davidson, 422–27; Herndon, i, 217; Morse, i, 60; Hapgood, 72–73. It may be of interest to note that Lincoln and his two colleagues were not the only acrobatic legislators revealed by our early local histories. General Lew Wallace, in his *Autobiography* (i, 251), tells, with contrition, how he bolted from the Indiana Senate to prevent an election of United States Senator; and Thaddeus Stevens, during his turbulent days in the Pennsylvania House of Representatives, jumped from a window after a scene of violence, in which, by a singular coincidence, he too had acted as the Whig leader.
30. Lamon, 324; Browne, 237.
31. *Works*, i, 27.
32. *Works*, i, 135–37.
33. Joshua F. Speed in Herndon, i, 161–63; Speed, 17–18; Speed, in Oldroyd, 143–45; Master, 50–52, 446.
34. Holland, 97–98.
35. Eulogy on Henry Clay, in *Works*, ii, 165.
36. In the ballot for Speaker of the Illinois House of Representatives on December 3, 1838, William Lee D. Ewing received 43 votes, and Abraham Lincoln 38 votes. In a similar contest on November 24, 1840, Ewing received 46 votes, and Lincoln 36 votes.
37. Browne's *Lincoln and Men*, 185.
38. White, 19–20.
39. Joseph D. Roper, in Springfield (Ill.) *Journal*, January 30, 1909.
40. Gibson W. Harris, in *Woman's Home Companion*, December, 1903, p. 15.
41. Herndon, ii, 45.

42. *Works*, i, 142–45.
43. During Lincoln's last term in the Illinois House of Representatives he offered the following resolution: —

"RESOLVED, that so much of the Governor's message as relates to fraudulent voting, and other fraudulent practices at elections, be referred to the Committee on Elections, with instructions to said committee to prepare and report to the House a bill for such an act as may, in their judgment, afford the greatest possible protection of the elective franchise against all frauds of all sorts whatsoever."

This failed of adoption, and in its stead was passed a substitute offered by John A. McClernand, one of the Democratic leaders. (See Illinois House Journals, 1840–41, p. 34; and *Works*, i, 152–53.)
44. Horace White, in Herndon, i, xxii.
45. Lincoln to Herndon, June 22, 1848, *Works*, ii, 50. See, also: Herndon, i, 270–72; Lamon, 295.
46. Phillips's *Men Who Knew*, 160–62.
47. Whitney, 117.
48. Schurz, ii, 91.
49. The sequel to this little adventure, as Mr. Nelson tells it, should not be omitted. "I had many opportunities after the stage ride," he relates, "to cultivate Mr. Lincoln's acquaintance, and was a zealous advocate of his nomination and election to the Presidency. Before leaving his home for Washington, Mr. Lincoln caused John P. Usher and myself to be invited to accompany him. We agreed to join him in Indianapolis. On reaching that city the Presidential party had already arrived, and upon inquiry we were informed that the President-elect was in the dining-room of the hotel, at supper. Passing through, we saw that every seat at the numerous tables was occupied, but failed to find Mr. Lincoln. As we were nearing the door to the office of the hotel, a long arm reached to my shoulder and a shrill voice exclaimed, 'Hello, Nelson! Do you think, after all, the world is going to follow the darned thing off?' It was Mr. Lincoln." (Herndon, i, 303–06. See, also: Coffin, 132; Selby, 89–90; Williams, 136–37; McClure's *Yarns*, 410.)
50. Herndon, i, 253.

51. The affair with James Shields. See Master, 65–77.
52. Lincoln to Martin M. Morris, March 26, 1843, *Works*, i, 262.
53. A. Y. Ellis, in Lamon, 143; and in Herndon, i, 255.
54. For an amusing account of how Lincoln exposed one of these demagogues to public ridicule, on the stump, see Master, 54–56.
55. *Works*, v, 238–39.
56. "He took his friend James Matheney out into the woods with him one day and, calling up the bitter features of the canvass, protested 'vehemently and with great emphasis' that he was anything but aristocratic and proud. 'Why, Jim,' he said, 'I am now and always shall be the same Abe Lincoln I was when you first saw me.'" (Herndon, i, 256; Lamon, 273.)
57. Lincoln's second son, born a few years later, on March 10, 1846, was named for Baker.
58. Lincoln to Speed, March 24, 1843, *Works*, i, 261.
59. Lincoln to Morris, March 26, 1843, *Works*, i, 262–65. See, also, the letter to Morris of April 14, 1843, *Works*, i, 265–66.
60. General J. M. Ruggles, quoted in Tarbell, i, 195–96; Curtis's *Lincoln*, 138.
61. Lincoln to Speed, May 18, 1843, *Works*, i, 268. This letter was written after the convention. To accord with that fact, the obvious printer's error in punctuation has been corrected.
62. Lincoln to Hardin, May 11, 1843, *Works*, i, 266–67.
63. Lincoln's Autobiography, in *Works*, vi, 36–37; Scripps, 18, the authorized campaign biography of which Lincoln critically read the advance sheets. See, also: Nicolay, 73–74, 90; Newton, 19; Dr. Robert Boal, in Peoria (Ill.) *Herald*, February 14, 1899; Gibson W. Harris, in *Woman's Home Companion*, December, 1903, p. 15. But to the contrary see: Lamon, 275–77; Herndon, i, 257; Nicolay and Hay, i, 242–43; Morse, i, 72.
64. Baker resigned from Congress to engage in the Mexican War, a few months before the end of his term. The short period that remained was of no interest to the leading Whigs, so a local politician named John Henry secured the office for the unexpired time.

65. Lincoln to Hardin, January 19, 1845, *Works*, i, 271–74. This letter is also printed in the Lapsley Edition of the *Works*, ii, 5–8, as of 1845. But the date evidently should be 1846. See also Lincoln to B. F. James, January 16, 1846, *Works*, i, 285–86.
66. *Woman's Home Companion*, December, 1903, p. 15; Browne, 222.
67. Lamon, 277–78; Nicolay and Hay, i, 248–49.
68. Browne's *Lincoln and Men*, i, 300.
69. Lincoln to Speed, October 22, 1846, in *Works*, i, 298

INDEX

INDEX

The Riverside Press
CAMBRIDGE · MASSACHUSETTS
PRINTED IN THE U.S.A.